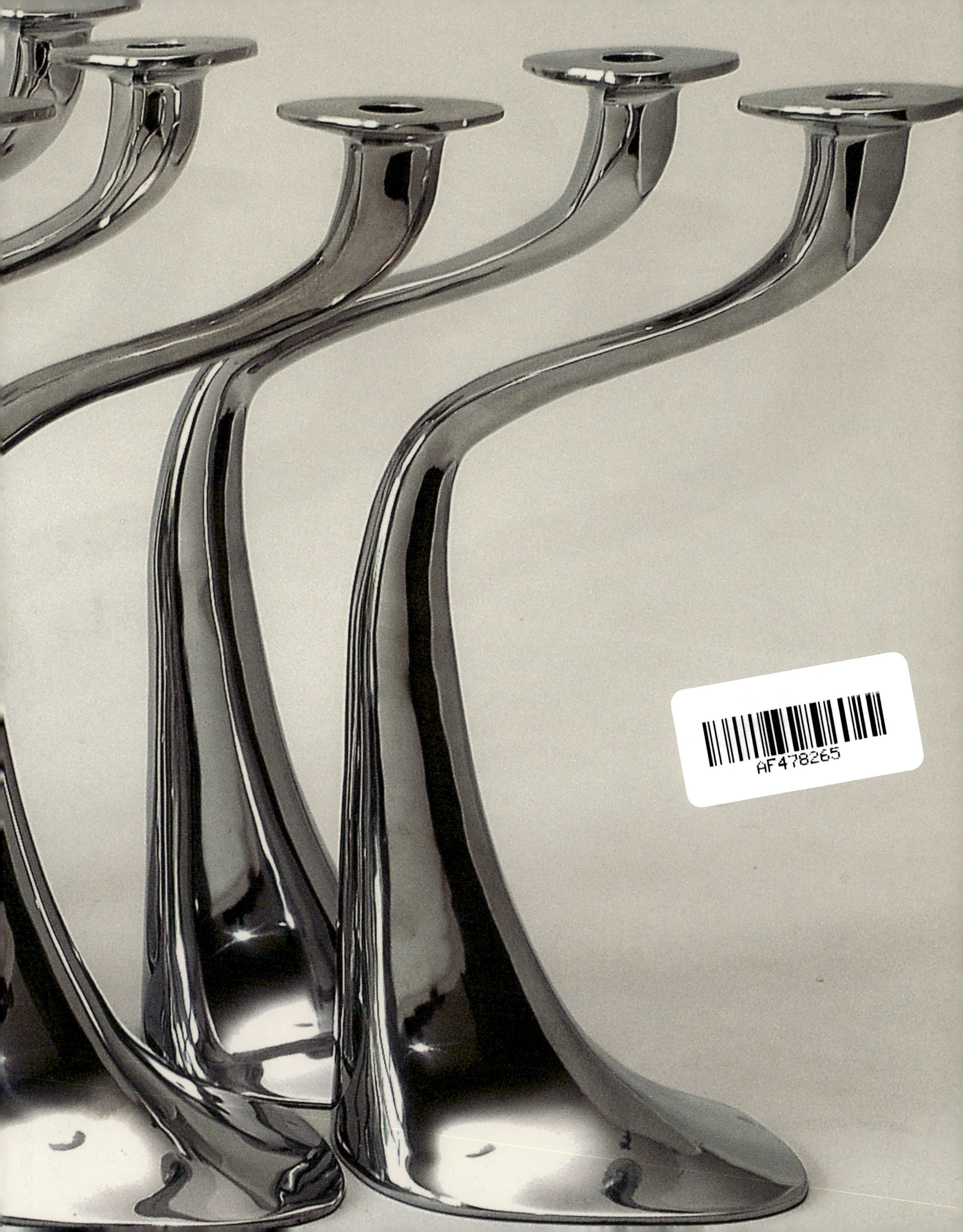
AF478265

xavier lust

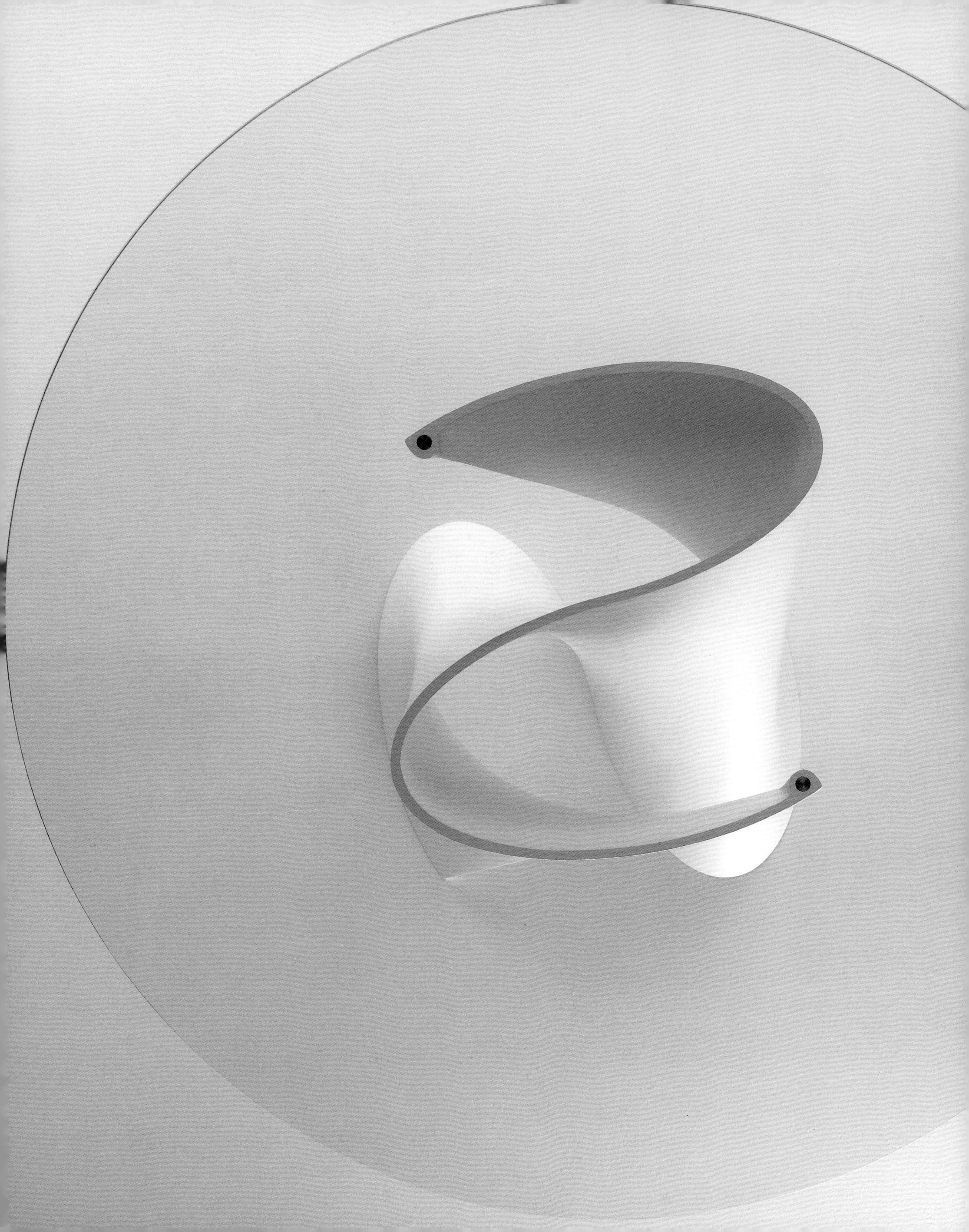

xavier lust
(de)formations

stichting
kunstboek

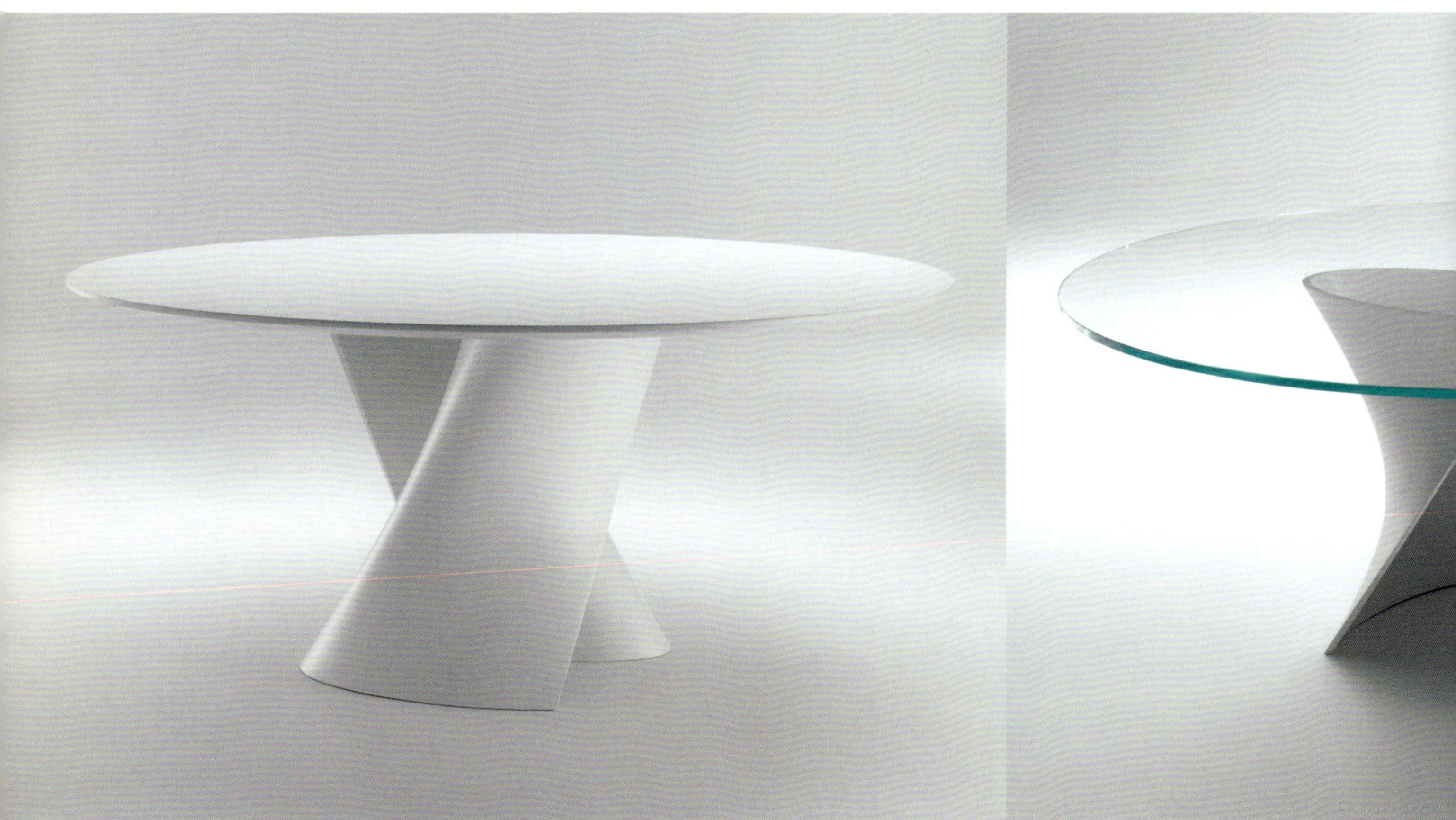

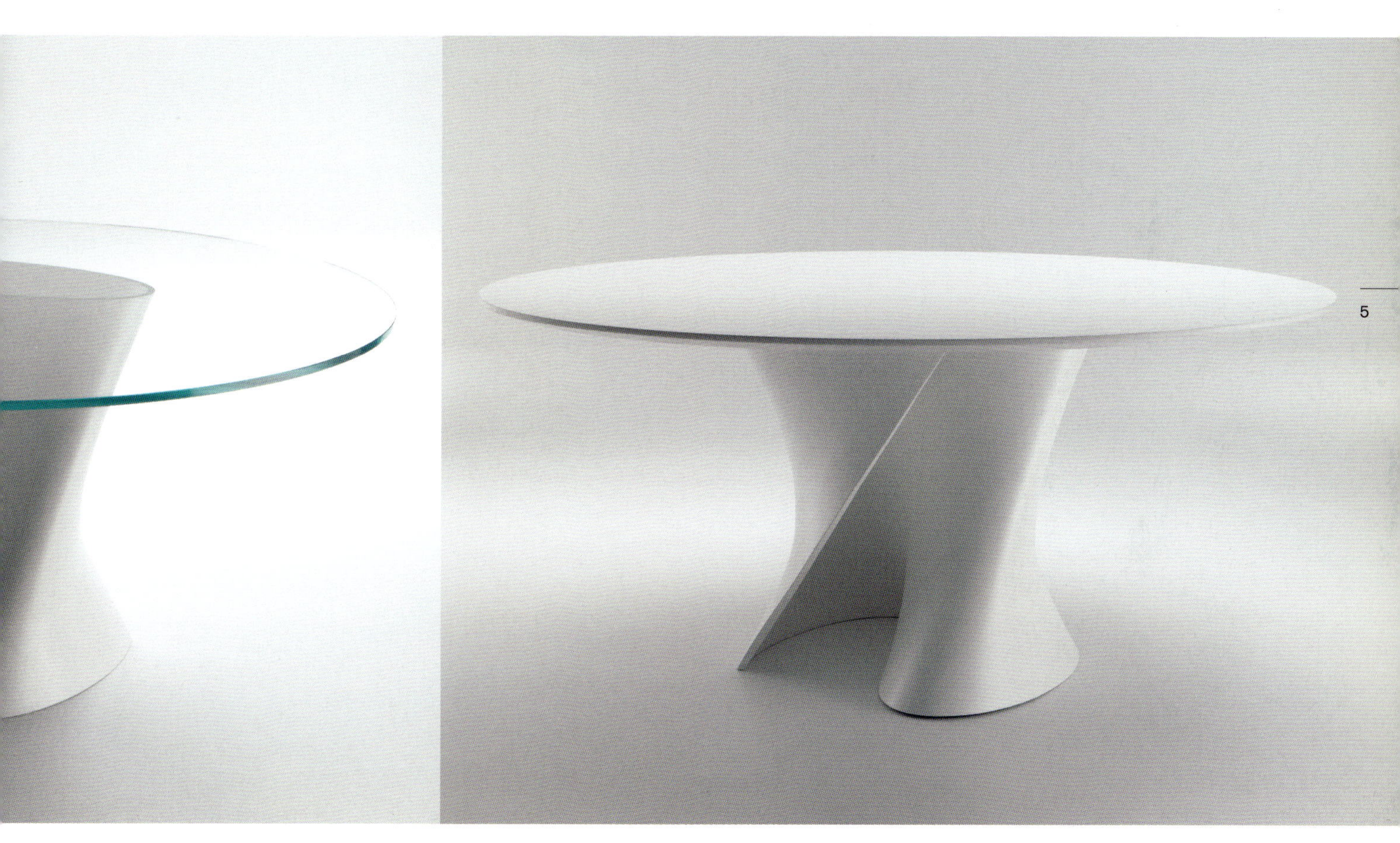

When I first met Xavier in Brussels back in 1999, my first impression was that here was true talent, and an astounding capacity for synthesis. Xavier was the first designer, after myself, to create for the MDF collection.

The first product chosen was 'Le Banc', an article where material, design, technique and form blend into a surprising oneness. After that, and to mark the company's tenth anniversary, I asked Xavier to design a table. This was another surprise. Xavier produced a 440 cm long piece that used an entire 6 m aluminum sheet. Working with the production people, he showed great willingness to help overcome any manufacturing difficulties, coming up with mature, knowledgeable proposals in a creative process of give-and-take that ended in success.

In 2002, two years after the bench, 'La Grande Table', in its largest version, was presented at the Milan International Furniture Show. It certainly did not go unnoticed, and the following year received the 'ADI INDEX 2003' award, and subsequently a special mention at the 20th edition of the Compasso d'Oro award of 2004.

Lust's creations do not seem to date. They have each been knowingly pared to the essential so that no further reduction is possible. They cannot be any less than what they are. Yet what they are has a striking impact.

Xavier recently created the 'S-table', a round table with an incredible base. We are sure it will be a resounding success. Xavier seeks out new forms of figurative expression. Each of his creations has a unique allure, an aesthetic that is nonetheless functional, fully compliant with technical and production requirements. Presented at the 2007 Milan *Salone Internazionale del Mobile*, Xavier's project was a focal point of the week and admired by all.

Bruno Fattorini, MDF Italia

Quando nel lontano 1999, per la prima volta, incontrai Xavier a Bruxelles la mia prima impressione fu di trovarmi di fronte ad un talento grande per la capacità di esprimere segni di impressionante sintesi. Xavier è stato il primo designer a disegnare per la collezione MDF Italia dopo di me.

Il primo prodotto scelto fu 'Le Banc' ove materiale, disegno, tecnica e forma manifestano una unicità sorprendente. Fatto 'Le Banc', per celebrare i 10 anni dell'attività aziendale, gli chiesi di progettare un tavolo, una sorpresa perché lo volle lungo 440 cm per utilizzare interamente i grandi fogli di alluminio che misurano fino a 6 m. Al lavoro con la produzione fu forte della volontà di riuscire aggirando le difficoltà con nuove proposte, competenti e mature e alla fine il processo dialettico creativo trovò compimento.

A due anni dalla presentazione della panca, nel 2002 presentammo 'La Grande Table'. Il prodotto, presentato al Salone Internazionale del Mobile nella sua massima dimensione, non passò inosservato, tanto che l'anno successivo ottenne il riconoscimento 'ADI INDEX 2003' e la menzione speciale del XXe premio Compasso d'Oro nel 2004.

I suoi pezzi sembrano non soffrire il tempo, non possono essere ridotti, il processo di riduzione è così maturo che non appare. In un certo senso non possono essere meno di come sono ma appaiono con grande evidenza.

Recentemente ci ha proposto 'S-table', un tavolo rotondo con un incredibile basamento che, siamo certi, sarà un successo enorme. Cerca nuove forme di espressione figurativa conferendo al prodotto fascino e personalità estetica nel rispetto della funzionalità consapevole di tutti i dati tecnici compresi quelli imposti dai processi di fabbricazione. Il progetto è stato presentato al Salone Internazionale del Mobile 2007 ed stato al centro dell'attenzione e dell'ammirazione di tutti.

Bruno Fattorini, MDF Italia

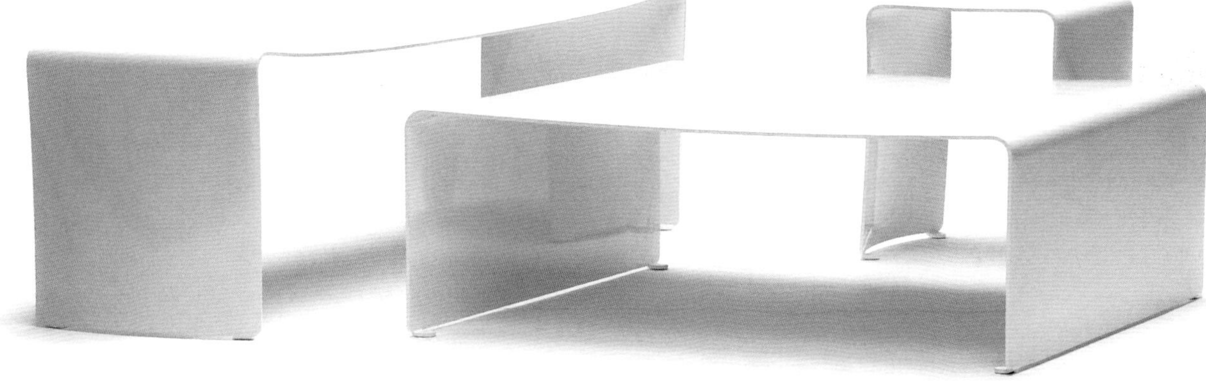

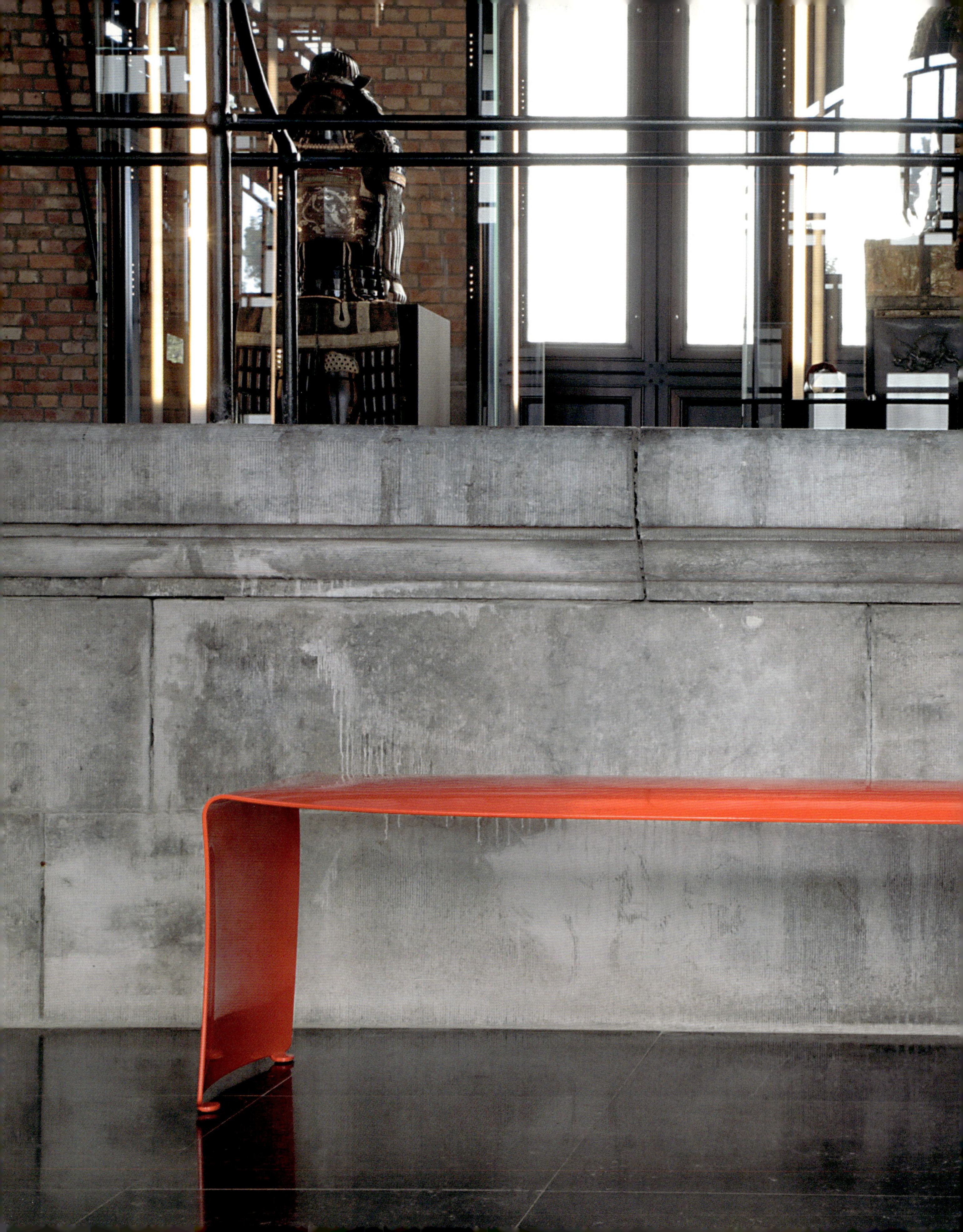

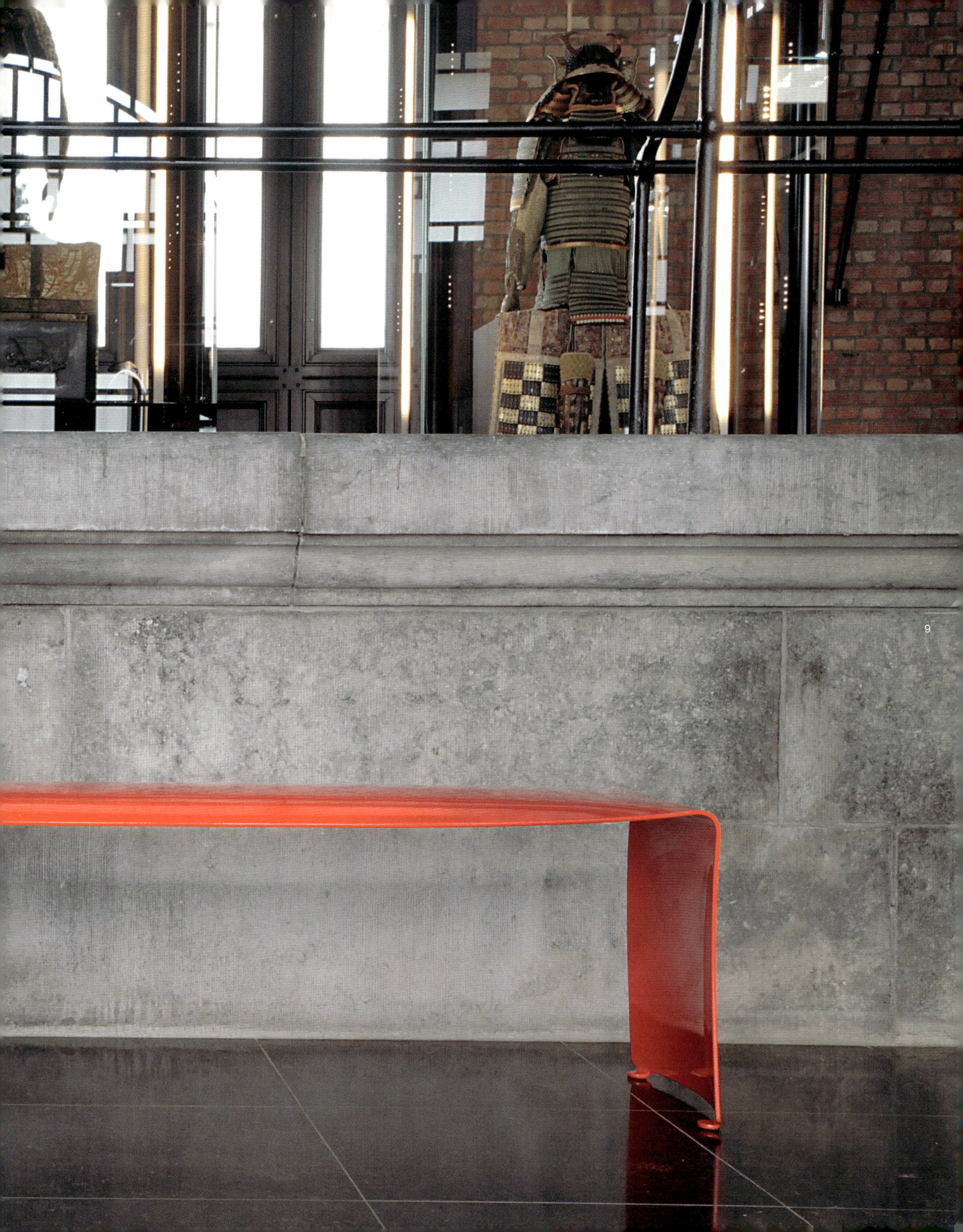

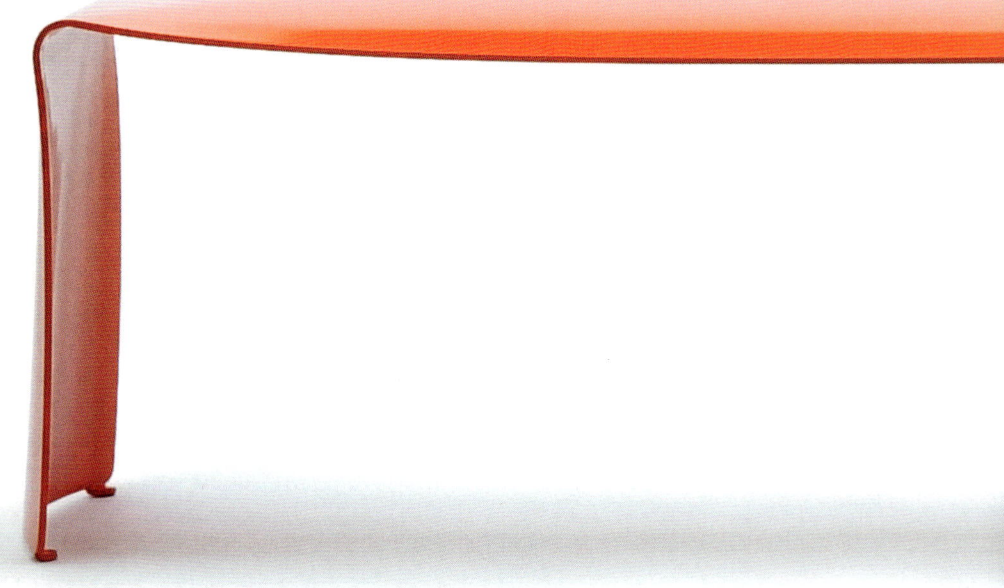

Le Banc 170 cm, MDF Italia 2001

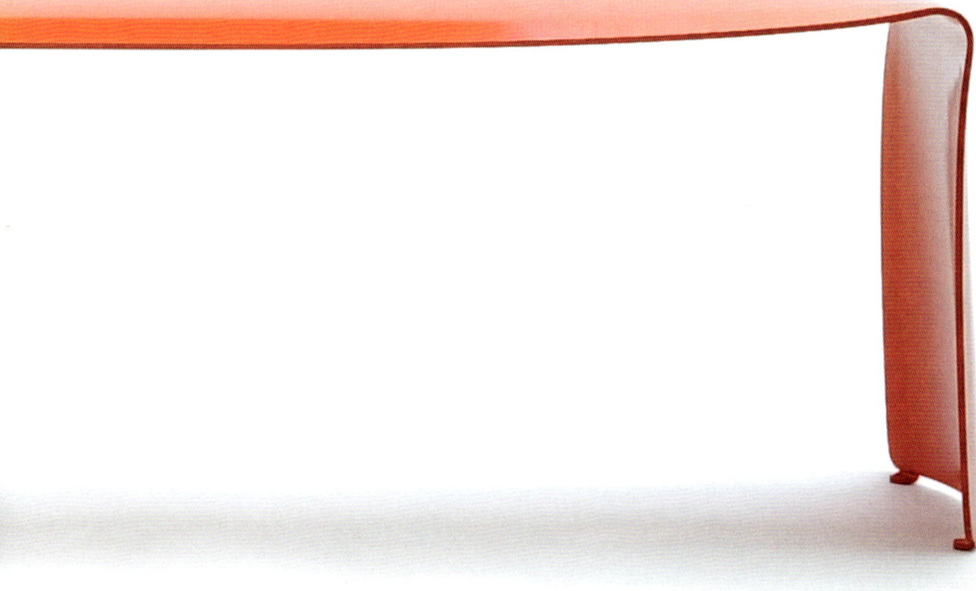

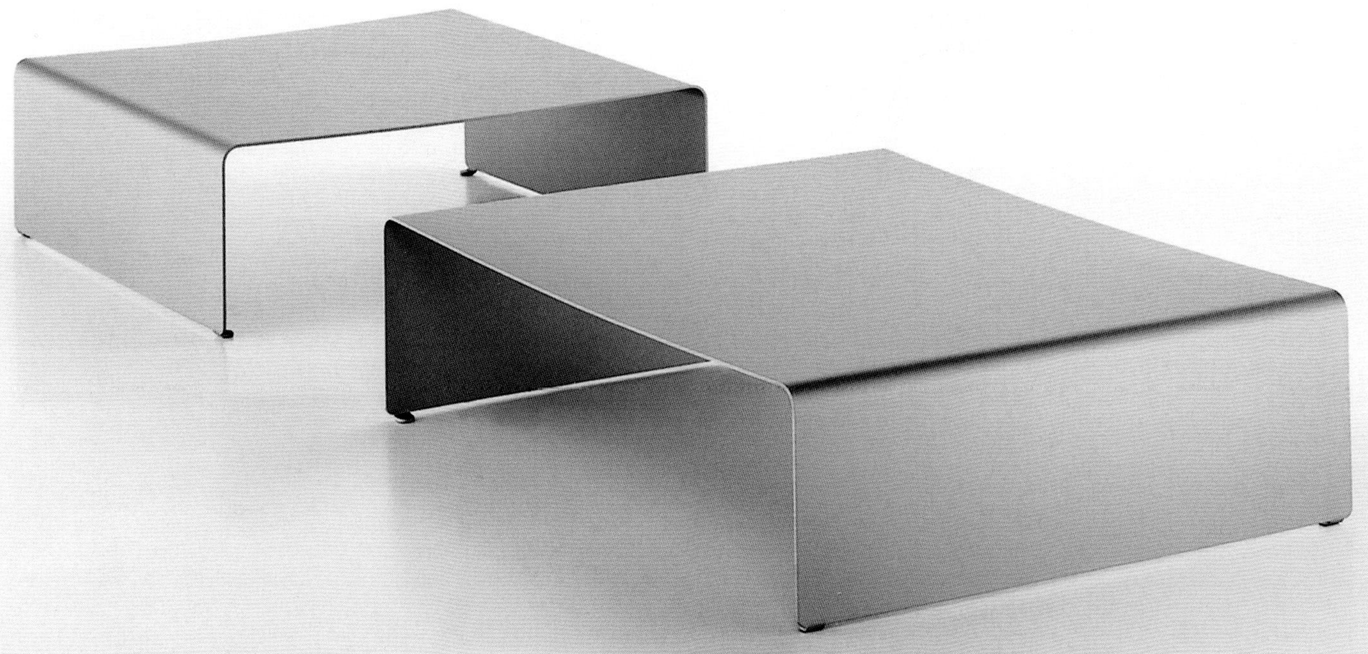

La Chaise MDF Italia 2002

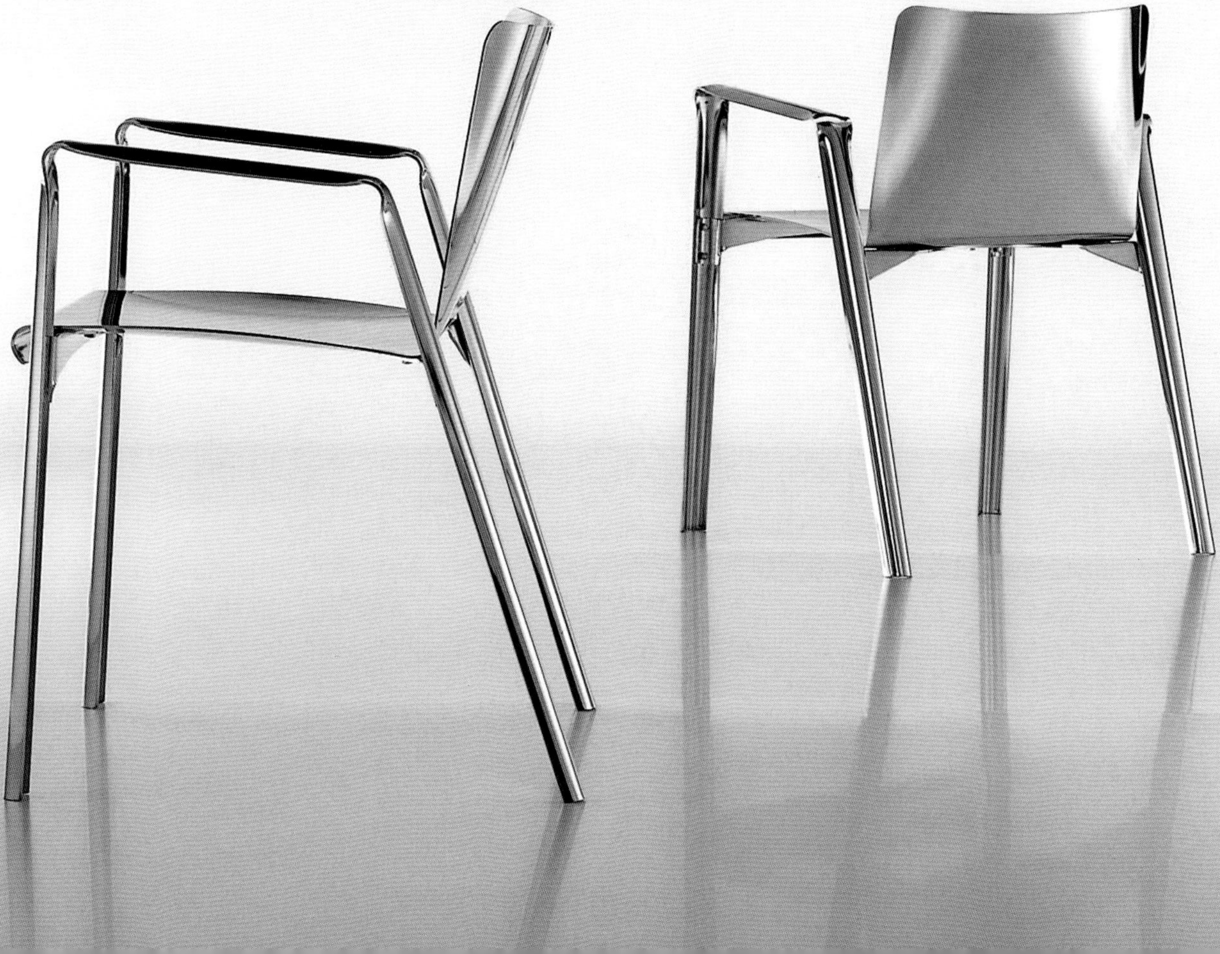

Beauty is nature with its curved lines

Cristina Morozzi

Wandering through the novelties at the 2002 Milan *Salone*, I was pulled up sharp by a sofa. It was presented by MDF. This was the first surprise: that MDF should be presenting a red sofa called 'Lounge'. Those of us for whom design is a way of life, out of love or necessity, can get set in our ways. Years of sifting through company catalogues and pouring over designer repertories create expectations – or perhaps prejudices – about what we are likely to find. Just as we form a mental picture of the yet-to-meet wife or husband of someone we know in the conviction that 'like goes with like' and that people always seek out their own kind, so too with designers and manufacturers. Once you know a company's market approach, you think you have a pretty shrewd idea of what their signed-up designers will produce for the next collection. You know you can expect surprises from some companies while others will stick to a well-honed system. In my eyes, MDF belonged – by deliberate choice – to the second category: a high-end manufacturer of exquisitely made, specialist items. So that red sofa burst into my preconceptions like a falling star lighting up the sky as it streaked past its immobile sisters. It was nothing like anything the company had ever produced. Coming up with a new kind of upholstered divan is no mean feat. Precious few differ from the model of modernity set by Le Corbusier's LC2 in 1928: a frame with padded seat and back cushions. Lounge has no cushions. It looks like a lap. Or a kneeling figure. Even compared to Xavier Lust's other work, the S-shaped silhouette of 'Lounge' stood out for its poetic originality. 'Beauty lies in nature and her curves', says Xavier Lust, accompanying his words with a sinuous movement of the hands almost as if caressing a female figure. Hearing someone talk about beauty is almost a shock. It's a very uncool word, to be avoided for fear of being thought guilty of clinging to an obsolete idea of design. The surprise is even greater if the B-word is pronounced by a designer of the new, 30-something generation! Eccentricity seems the hallmark of the contemporary aesthetic. Even, says the theorist of aesthetics, Mario Perniola, to the point of in-your-face provocation and delight in arousing 'disgust' (*Disgusti.* Costa&Nolan, Genoa, 1998). It's a way of getting yourself heard above the clamor of myriad new designers jostling to place their wares on the market. Unlike so many of his soapbox colleagues who declaim their message with theatrical gesture or in creations overladen with meaning, Xavier Lust is self-effacing. Words are used sparingly, as if inadequate to describe work that is essentially a

La bellezza è la natura con le sue curve

Cristina Morozzi

Passando in rassegna le novità del Salone del 2002 rimasi colpita da un divano. Lo presentava MDF. La prima ragione del mio stupore era che quel sofà rosso, nominato 'Lounge', fosse proposto proprio da MDF. Chi milita nel drappello di coloro che si occupano di design, per passione o professione, nutre delle aspettative, basandosi su convinzioni, che magari sono pregiudizi, maturate attraverso la conoscenza dei cataloghi aziendali e la frequentazione con i repertori dei designer. Come nelle coppie, sulla falsa riga del diffuso proverbio, 'chi si somiglia si piglia', conosciuto il marito s'immagina la moglie e viceversa, anche nel rapporto azienda-designer, nota la filosofia aziendale, si tende a prefigurare i prodotti. Da alcune imprese si attendono sorprese, da altre conferme e sicurezze. Ho sempre pensato che MDF appartenesse, per scelta consapevole, alla seconda categoria; che preferisse all'espressività uno standard di alta qualità, affinato nei dettagli e nelle finiture, dotato di prestazioni specializzate. Quel sofà mi parve un bagliore, simile a quello di una stella cadente che illumina con il suo lampo un cielo di stelle fisse. Era diverso, anche tipologicamente, dagli altri. Produrre un imbottito diverso non è cosa da poco. Si contano sulle dita quelli che differiscono dal modello della modernità, originato dall' LC2 (1928) di Le Corbusier: scocca e cuscini di seduta e schienale. Lounge non ha cuscini. Assomiglia ad un grembo. Pare una figura in ginocchio. La sua silhouette piegata ad esse, considerata alla luce di altri progetti del suo designer è da considerarsi il preciso segnale di un'originale poetica. 'La bellezza è la natura con le sue curve', afferma Xavier Lust, e accompagna la sua convinzione con eloquenti gesti delle mani, quasi carezzasse un fondo schiena femminile. Sentire parlare di bellezza, una parola dalla quale oggi pare convenga prendere le distanze, quasi sia legata ad un'idea sorpassata di design, stupisce. A maggior ragione se a pronunciarla è un designer della nuova generazione, non ancora quarantenne. Sembra che l'eccentricità e, persino, per dirla con il teorico dell'estetica Mario Perniola, 'il disgusto', strumento di sfida e provocazione (Mario Perniola, *Disgusti*, Costa&Nolan, Genova, 1998), siano le categorie dell'estetica contemporanea. Quelle in grado di garantire quel clamore che molti nuovi designer inseguono per farsi intendere nel rumore diffuso prodotto dall' affollamento di merci. A differenza di molti suoi colleghi affabulatori che affidano il loro messaggio alla propria teatralità o all'eccesso semantico dei loro prodotti, Xavier Lust si pone sullo sfondo. E'parco di parole, quasi non ve ne siano di adeguate per descrivere un lavoro che deve molto della sua unicità nell'essere modellato a mano. Racconta che la sua fortuna è

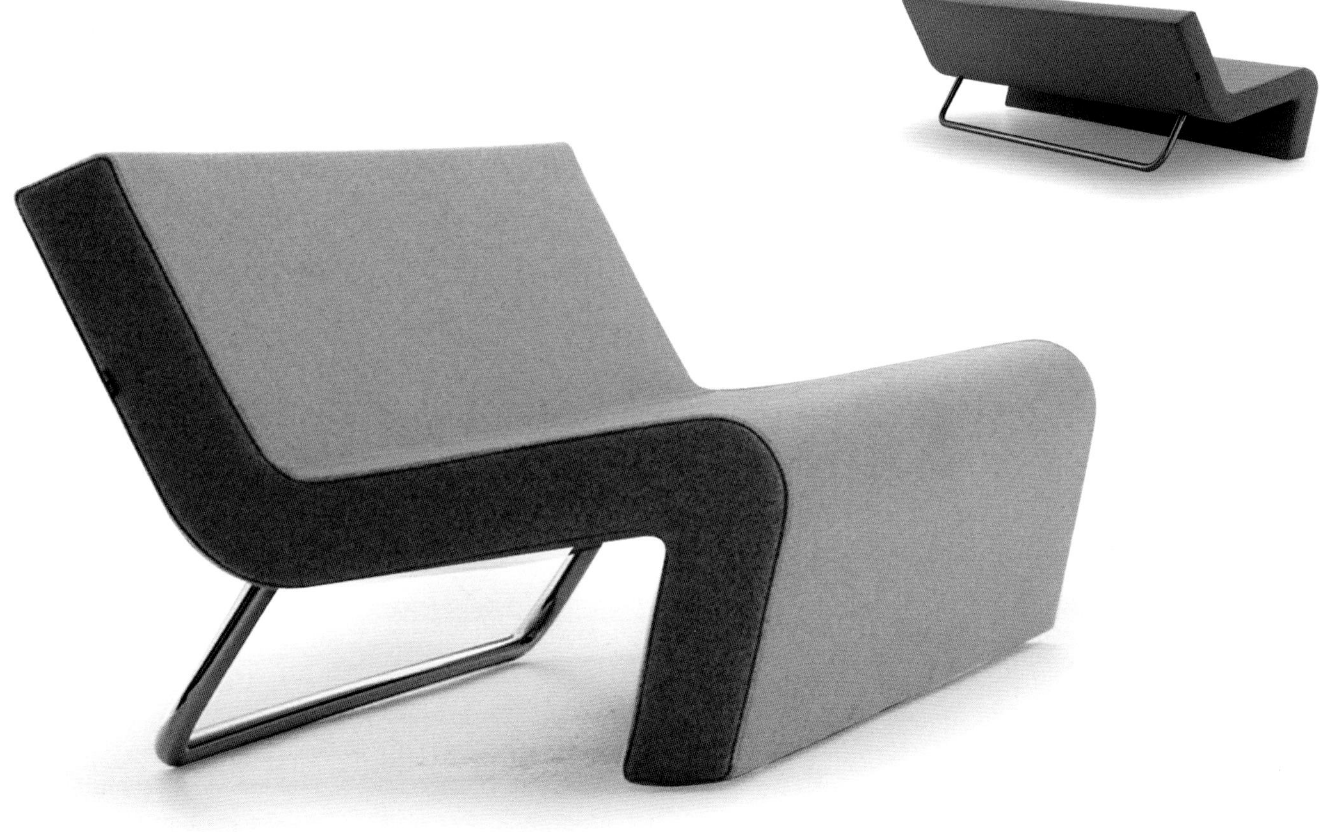

series of single, handmade pieces. He speaks of his good luck at finding an extraordinary metalworking craftsman in Liege. Shapes are equally minimal. Even when using aluminum – the material that first brought him to public notice – he avoids virtuosity. Xavier Lust is a counterpoint to the flourish of Ron Arad and his daring volumes. Lust works on the flat, like a bespoke tailor following a paper pattern. The aluminum bench, 'Le Banc', presented at the Milan Satellite Salon in 2000 that put him on the map, is fashioned from a single sheet of aluminum. Included in MDF's 2001 catalogue, it is still, as then, made in Liege at the original workshop. Its gentle curve seems molded by the lightest of touch; the bench looks suspended in the air, almost weightless. Xavier is concerned not so much with volumes as with planes. His work has to do with surfaces that stand out in space. They are shaped, planed and rounded into alluring forms. The play of light on metal surfaces turns them into a kaleidoscope of changing patterns and viewpoints like a *trompe l'oeil*. Again, he is concerned not so much with volume as with the flow of line. His lines resemble gently rolling landscapes whose folds have been formed by the interminable erosion of coasts and mountains and the inexorable creep of geological structures, to paraphrase Joan Didion in *The Year of Magical Thinking*. The front panels of Lust's 'Crédence' (De Padova, 2003) swell naturally like a pregnant womb, lending a delicate rotundity to the whole sideboard. Everything speaks of fullness and plenitude. Its exquisite production and complex construction – that includes a double chamber concealing hinges and a total absence of handles – focus attention on the smooth shiny surfaces.

Xavier is fully aware that design must seduce. Like Raymond Loewy, the father of streamlined design, he knows that customers must not be inundated with facts, but seduced. For him, this dictate is mediated by a total faith in industrial design. And here lies a paradox that is key to Lust's originality. Although an orthodox industrial designer, his working methods are those of the artisan. His craftsman's tools are not used to produce virtuoso value-added – in the form of arresting decoration or special effects – but to pare down, smooth out and restrain. They are not used to complicate but to simplify; to give fluidity, curves and roundness, now possible with modern die-casting technology. It is paradoxical that Lust works with his hands – and those of his trusted artisan – to arrive at the 'machine-made' perfection of mass-produced articles.

Xavier Lust is retiring in an unassuming way. There's a noble quality to

stata trovare un artigiano straordinario a Liegi che lavora con passione il metallo. Ed è parco pure nelle forme. Anche quando utilizza l'alluminio, il materiale che l'ha imposto all'attenzione, non è un virtuoso, come Ron Arad che scolpisce volumi arditi. Lavora a piatto, come i sarti, seguendo un cartamodello. La panca in alluminio, 'Le Banc', con cui si presentò nel 2000 al Salone Satellite di Milano, divenuta una sorta di suo biglietto da visita, proposta dal 2001 nel catalogo della MDF, che la fa tuttora costruire nella fabbrica artigiana di Liegi, è un solo foglio d'alluminio.
E' un unico nastro che delicatamente s'incurva, quasi fosse agitato da un polso esile e che levita nell'aria, come fosse privo di peso. Lavora, non sui volumi, ma sui piani, esaltando le loro superfici che offre piene e distese alla luce. Li modela per renderli sensuali, levigandoli e smussandone gli angoli. Fa apparire caleidoscopici quelli metallici con i giochi di riflessioni, moltiplicando, come nei *trompe l'oeil*, i punti di vista. Le sue superfici non sono volumetrie, ma planimetrie. Hanno la dolce materialità di un paesaggio collinare; le ondulazioni di un terreno plasmato 'dall'interminabile erosione delle coste e delle montagne, dall'inesorabile scorrimento delle strutture geologiche' (Joan Didion, *L'anno del pensiero magico*, Il Saggiatore, Milano, 2006). Le ante della sua 'Crédence' (De Padova 2003) si gonfiano con naturalezza, come un ventre pregno, regalando una delicata rotondità alla sua sagoma. La raffinatezza dell'esecuzione, la complessa costruzione a doppia camera che permette di nascondere le cerniere, l'assenza di maniglie, espone i piani nella loro interezza alla luce che ne esalta il turgore.
Sa bene che il design deve sedurre, come già sosteneva Raymond Loewy, il padre della *stream line*, che amava ripetere: 'i clienti non li si può inondare di fatti in una sala riunioni, bisogna sedurli' (Bruce Sterling, *La forma del futuro*, Apogeo, Milano, 2006). Ma ricorre ad una seduzione filtrata da una fede purissima nel design industriale. E' nel paradosso che sta la sua singolarità. Xavier Lust è un designer industriale ortodosso, ma lavora da artigiano: non tanto per dare ai suoi pezzi il valore aggiunto dell'esecuzione virtuosa, della decorazione, degli effetti speciali; quanto per sottrarre, smussare, lisciare. Non per complicare, ma per semplificare; per dare alle sue forme la fluidità, le curve e le rotondità, che la tecnologia a stampo ha reso possibili. E' paradossale che ricorra al fare con le mani, che modelli con un suo artigiano di fiducia per produrre un risultato che pare 'fatto a macchina'; per raggiungere una perfezione che aspira alla serialità, più che all'unicità.

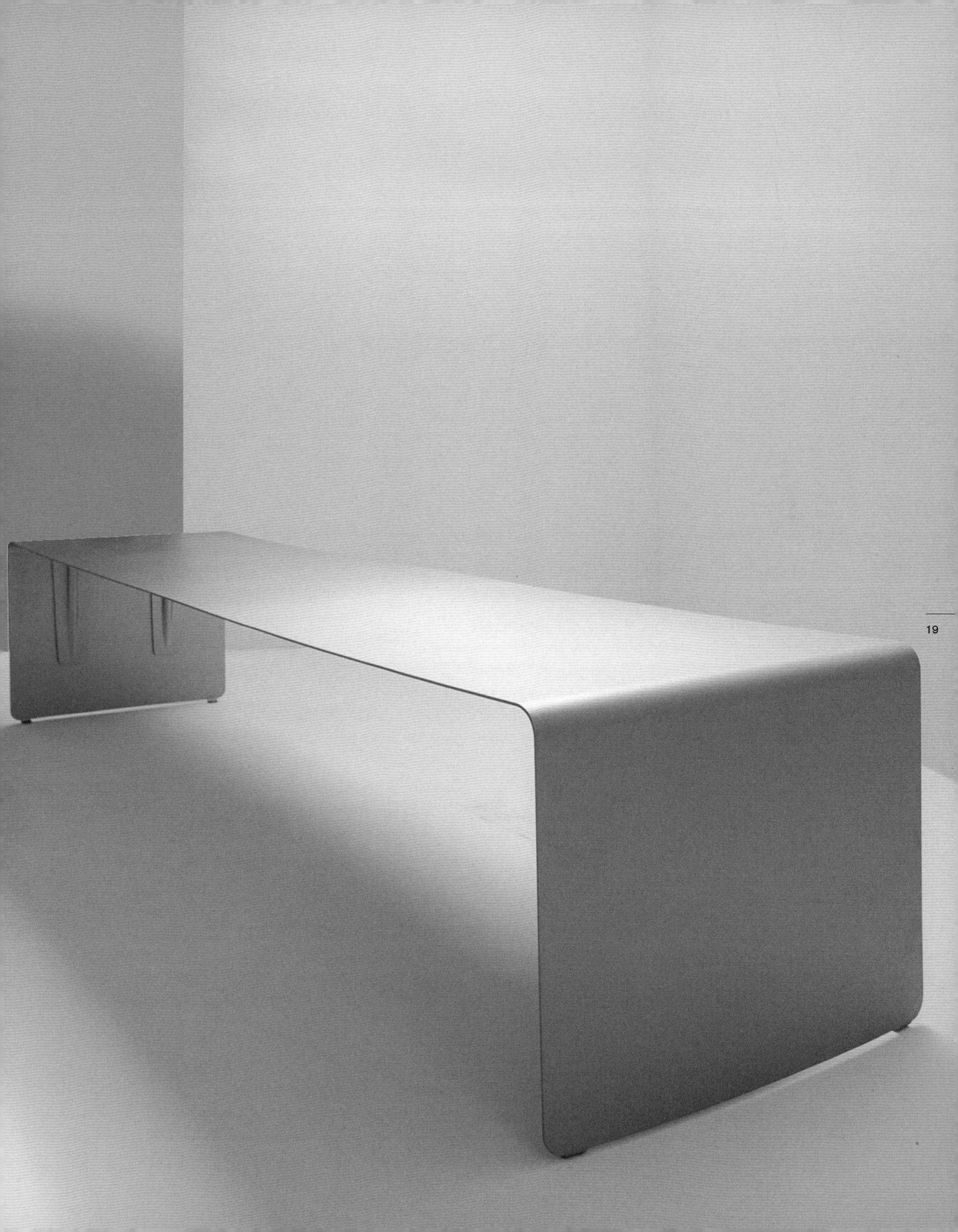

his reticence that is enhanced by his tall stature. He eschews theatrical flourish, unlike many of his generation, firm in his belief in industrial design. Yet he caused a furor even with 'Crédence' (2003), sending ripples through the design world. This was doubtlessly magnified by the partnership with De Padova and the surprise effect of such a cutting-edge creation among the comfortable refinement of one of Italy's top-drawer furniture brands. In his interchange with producer companies, Lust listens carefully to the production and marketing side, willing to be part of the give and take that goes into making a good industrial project. Because he is both industrial designer and artisan, he has succeeded in shaking up the catalogues of manufacturers more inclined to reassure than to startle.

When Lust leaves metal for wood he changes artistic register. Instead of lightness he goes for substantiality, using solid, at times untreated, wood. Fluidity gives way to squared, earthy volumes, almost as if the very weight of the material dictates the design approach. You have to study closely, even touch, the furniture to realize that although rudimentary, it is very special. Xavier has a gift for softening volumes. His gentle profiles and rounded corners seem molded by loving hands. It's as if his large workman hands hold the strength and warmth of a healer as he models inert material. His most successful creations have an almost feminine elegance.

On the subject of silhouettes, Lust's creations elicit irresistible parallels with the world of haute couture. This is true whether it be the 'Turner' chandelier produced by Driade Kosmo in 2004, or his latest – an aluminum chair not unlike a stately, straight-backed figure advancing gracefully in a wide flared skirt. I don't know if Lust is a fashion fan. His mention of paper dress patterns would suggest a certain familiarity with the fashion world, or at least an absence of hostility or fear of the sector. However, unlike other designers of his generation who have dipped into fashion, diligently applying themselves to embroidery and sewing, stealing superficial effects to give their designs handmade kudos, Xavier seems more concerned with the cutting and construction side of haute couture.

Cristobal Balenciaga springs to mind. The Basque's generous volumes, broad sleeves and full backs reinvented the female figure, lending a poise that seemed almost suspended in the air, buoyed up by the ample shapes. Perhaps this parallel with haute couture – now also a regular feature among many ardent champions of ready-to-wear –

Si pone sullo sfondo con nobiltà, dall'alto della sua statura. Non ha scelto la teatralità, come molti altri della sua generazione, per via di questa sua fede nel design industriale. Eppure anche con 'Crédence' (2003) è riuscito a far clamore. Nel mondo del design il pezzo ha provocato un'eco cui, senza dubbio, ha contribuito l'abbinamento con De Padova: non tanto per il riverbero dell'aura della 'Signora del design', quanto, ancora una volta, per la sorpresa suscitata dall'inserimento di quel progetto nel tranquillo corso del marchio. Nel dialogo con le imprese, che cerca e sollecita, disponibile a porsi all'ascolto delle ragioni del produrre e del vendere; sensibile alla dialettica che sempre è all'origine d'ogni buon progetto industriale, è riuscito, per questa sua volontà di essere designer, a dispetto del suo essere anche artigiano, a scompaginare il meditato catalogo di aziende abituate, più che a stupire, a rassicurare.

Quando abbandona il metallo per utilizzare il legno, la sua poetica cambia registro. Al posto della leggerezza sceglie la consistenza, utilizzando il massello, talvolta al naturale. In quei volumi squadrati pare si perda la sua fluidità, quasi che il peso del materiale condizioni il suo disegno. Bisogna guardarli, magari toccarli, quei mobili, per rendersi conto che, anche se elementari, sono speciali. Xavier possiede il segreto per ammorbidire i volumi. I profili dolci e gli angoli smussati pare siano plasmati da mani carezzevoli. E vien da pensare che le sue grandi mani abbiano la forza e il calore di quelle di un pranoterapeuta per modellare la materia inerte, regalandole, nei pezzi più riusciti, un'eleganza quasi femminile.

Considerando certe sue silhouette, come quella del candeliere 'Turner', (Driade Kosmo, 2004) oppure quella del prototipo di una sedia in alluminio cui sta lavorando, che pare inceda a busto eretto, regale nella sua ampia gonna a corolla, diventa irresistibile azzardare un parallelo con la couture. Non so se guardi alla moda. Il suo alludere al cartamodello fa supporre che quel linguaggio non gli sia estraneo, o che, perlomeno, non lo avversi o lo tema. Ma, a differenza di altri designer della sua generazione che hanno imparato a frequentarla per rubarle gli effetti di superficie e che si applicano con dedizione al ricamo e al cucito, regalando ai loro pezzi una patina di artigianalità e di fatto a mano, Xavier non prende spunto dalla confezione, ma dal taglio e dalla costruzione dell'abito. Per questo viene voglia di avvicinarlo a Cristobal Balenciaga, il sarto basco che lavorava sui volumi, gonfiando le maniche e il dorso, per reinventare la figura femminile, donando-

helps throw light on Xavier's recent interest in working with art galleries, which in turn are showing increasing interest in design. Indeed, art dealers seem to have replaced manufacturing companies as today's talent scouts, and are highly skilled at promoting their discoveries. Crossing the threshold into artistic design, while not abandoning industrial design, has given Xavier fame and verve. And here is another paradox: Xavier's ability to straddle art and design yet keep separate the distinctive features of both.

This ambiguity is emblematic of design's new place in the world. Among furniture manufacturers, genuine, Castiglioni-type industrial design is increasingly rare. What most companies do today can be classed as 'stylism': they are in the business of offering lifestyle proposals. The consummate professionals they engage lend impeccable quality to glossy domestic landscapes in line with the 'supposed' trends. Very few are willing to risk the production of landmark items that say more about the designer than their brand image. Many have opted for a solid catalogue, built up over the years, recognizable but safe. Which brings me back to my opening and the jolt I received on coming across Xavier's sofa. A laudable example but an exception. Few companies are willing or able to be conductors of a chorus, harmonizing the different parts of a complicated score whose rich melodic vein has nonetheless a recognizable rhythm. As a result designers are progressively turning into 'artists', aided by a market willing to go to enormous lengths to secure one-off or limited-edition designer pieces. Xavier Lust's dogged determination in seeking out manufacturing companies is a welcome signal. Producing one-off items for art galleries is a shortcut to his real agenda — and a way of paying the bills! It is a fast track to getting projects off the ground. It assuages his creative drive, the compelling urgency to do that sits so uncomfortably with the ponderous decision-making process of the manufacturing company. But even if Xavier is wooed by certain art galleries, nothing gives him the same buzz as seeing his creations, complete in each exacting detail, in the catalogues of furniture makers. In a certain sense, each item is unique: the product of the craftsman, only replicated.

I believe that industrial design able to deliver mass-produced products that are innovative and original, deserves to survive.

That's why I think Xavier Lust and his unswerving faith in industrial design is a good thing for the contemporary design scene.

le un incedere sospeso, come se quelle ampiezze levitate la ponessero a mezz'aria. Forse, il parallelo con la couture, una tentazione che sta contagiano molti degli stilisti strenui paladini del prêt-à-porter, aiuta a comprendere la recente voglia di Xavier di lavorare con le gallerie d'arte, sempre più interessate al design; il suo corteggiare i mercanti che hanno sostituito le aziende nel fiutare i talenti e che li sanno far valere. Il suo mettersi in viaggio sul binario del design artistico, senza peraltro abbandonare quello del design industriale, che gli ha dato notorietà e slancio, sottolinea la sua dimensione paradossale: lo stare in equilibrio sul crinale tra l'arte e il design, mantenendo di ciascuna disciplina la purezza. Questa sua ambiguità rappresenta in modo emblematico la nuova condizione del design. Nell'arredo il vero design industriale, quello, tanto per intendersi, alla Castiglioni è sempre più raro. La maggior parte delle aziende fa stilismo. Cioè produce e orchestra stili di vita, utilizzando la competenza di professionisti consumati, capaci di dare qualità impeccabile a paesaggi domestici patinati in linea con le 'supposte' tendenze. Poche sono quelle che osano mettere in cantiere pezzi segnale; che accettano di dare voce al linguaggio dei designer e non solo al proprio. Molte preferiscono costruire nel tempo un catalogo coerente, senza dissonanze. Si torna così all'inizio delle mie riflessioni e a quel salutare stupore, da intendersi come nota di merito anche per i produttori. Da questa difficoltà a trovare imprenditori/direttori d'orchestra, in grado cioè di armonizzare le diverse voci in una canzone dotata di un ritmo riconoscibile, ma melodicamente ricca e varia, ha origine la progressiva conversione dei designer in 'artisti', complice un mercato che pare disposto a fare follie per pezzi unici o in serie limitata di design. L'accanimento con cui Xavier Lust contatta le aziende induce a ben sperare. La deriva verso il pezzi unico che fa subito cassa è nel suo caso una scorciatoia. E' un modo rapido di fare esistere i progetti; colma l'ansia di fare e l'urgenza d'esprimersi che mal s'adattano ai tempi decantati dell'industria. Ma anche se è corteggiato da qualche galleria, niente lo appaga tanto, quanto vedere i suoi pezzi costruiti alla perfezione nei cataloghi delle aziende: unici, in un certo senso, per quel loro nascere dal fare artigiano, ma replicabili.

Credo che il design industriale in grado di concepire pezzi di serie innovativi, dotati di un' originale espressività, meriti di sopravvivere.

Per questo penso che Xavier Lust con la sua pura fede sia importante nel panorama del design contemporaneo.

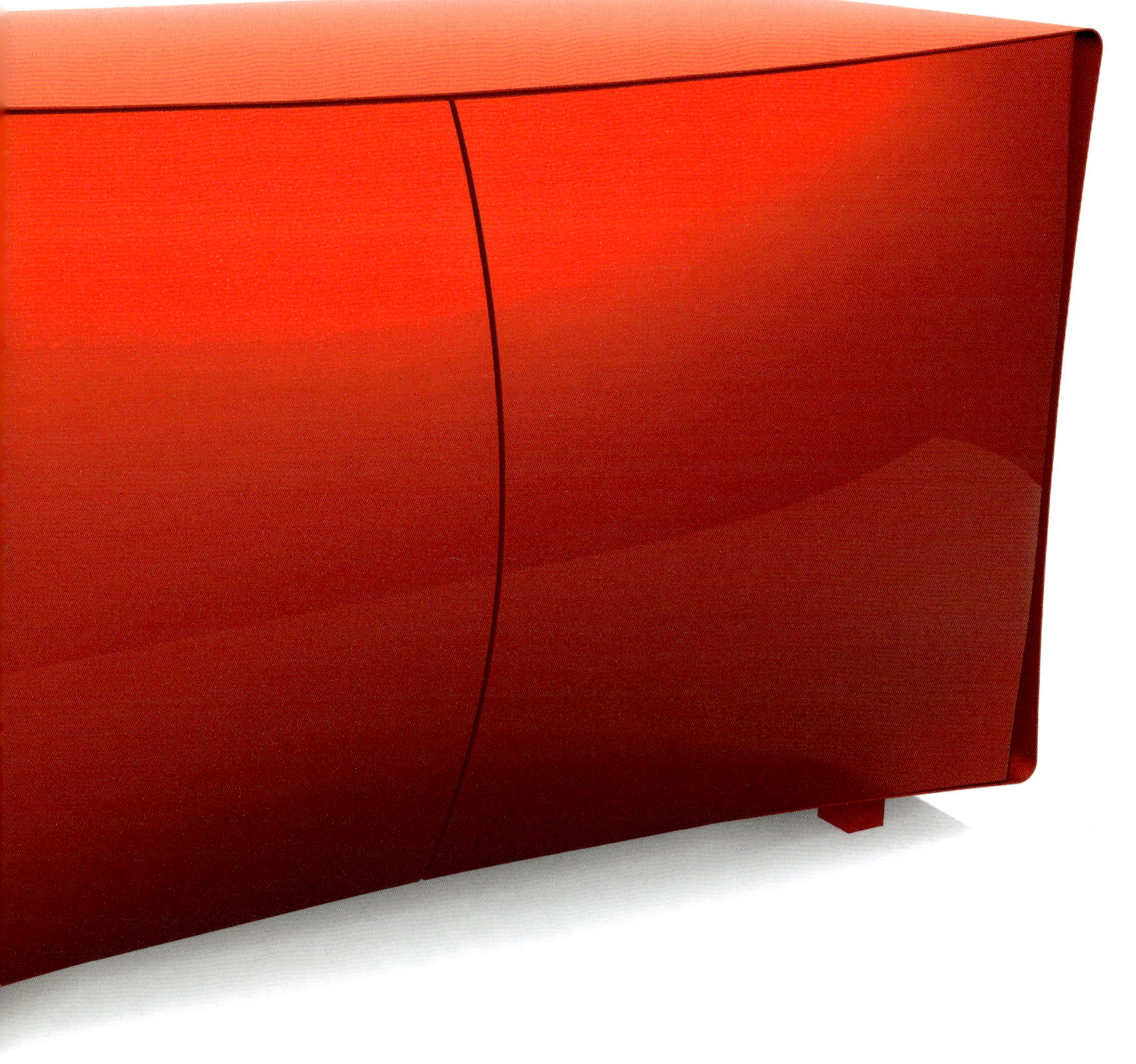

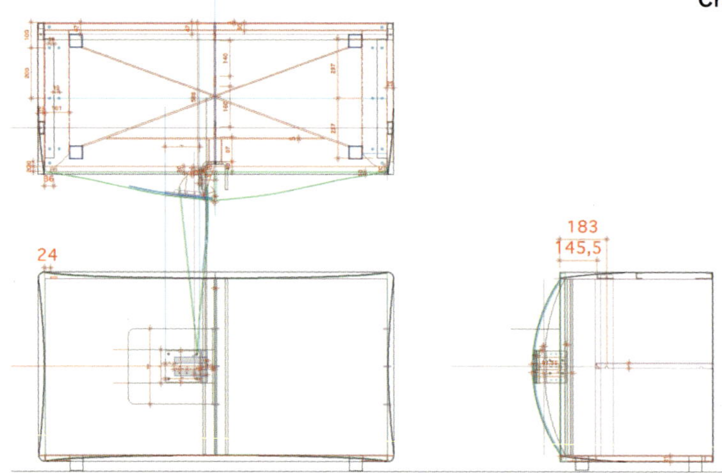

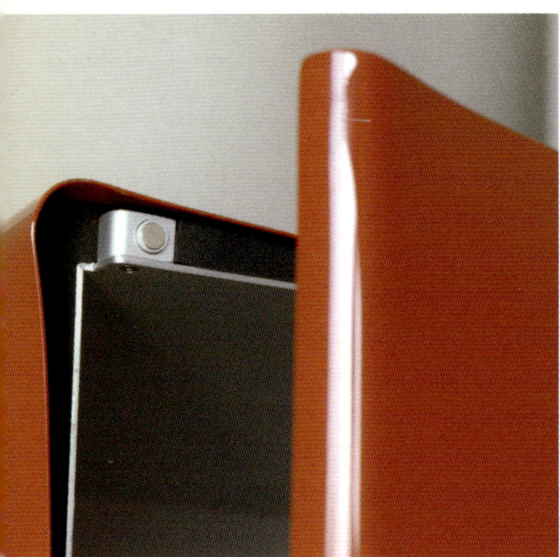

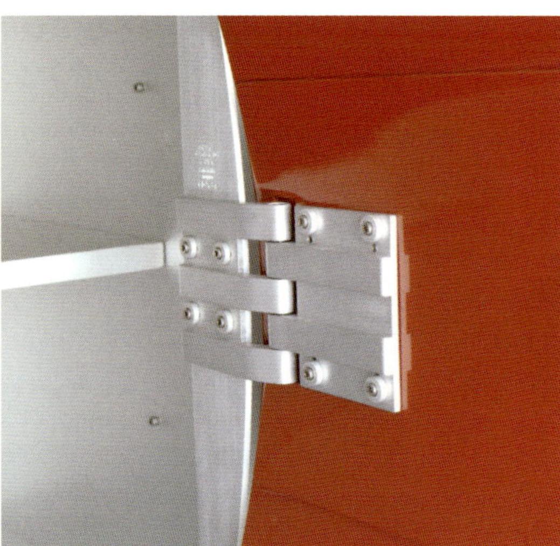

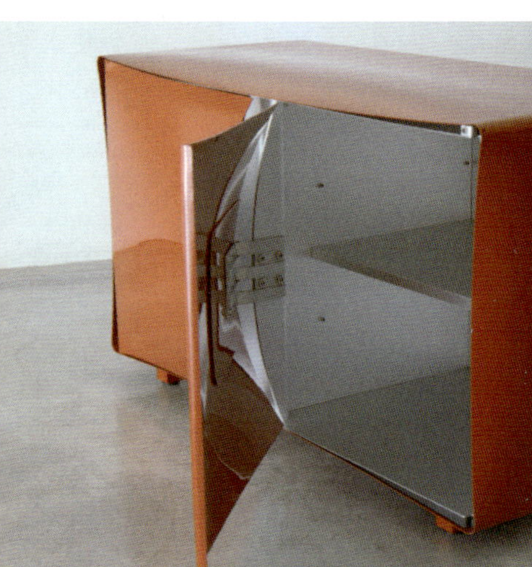

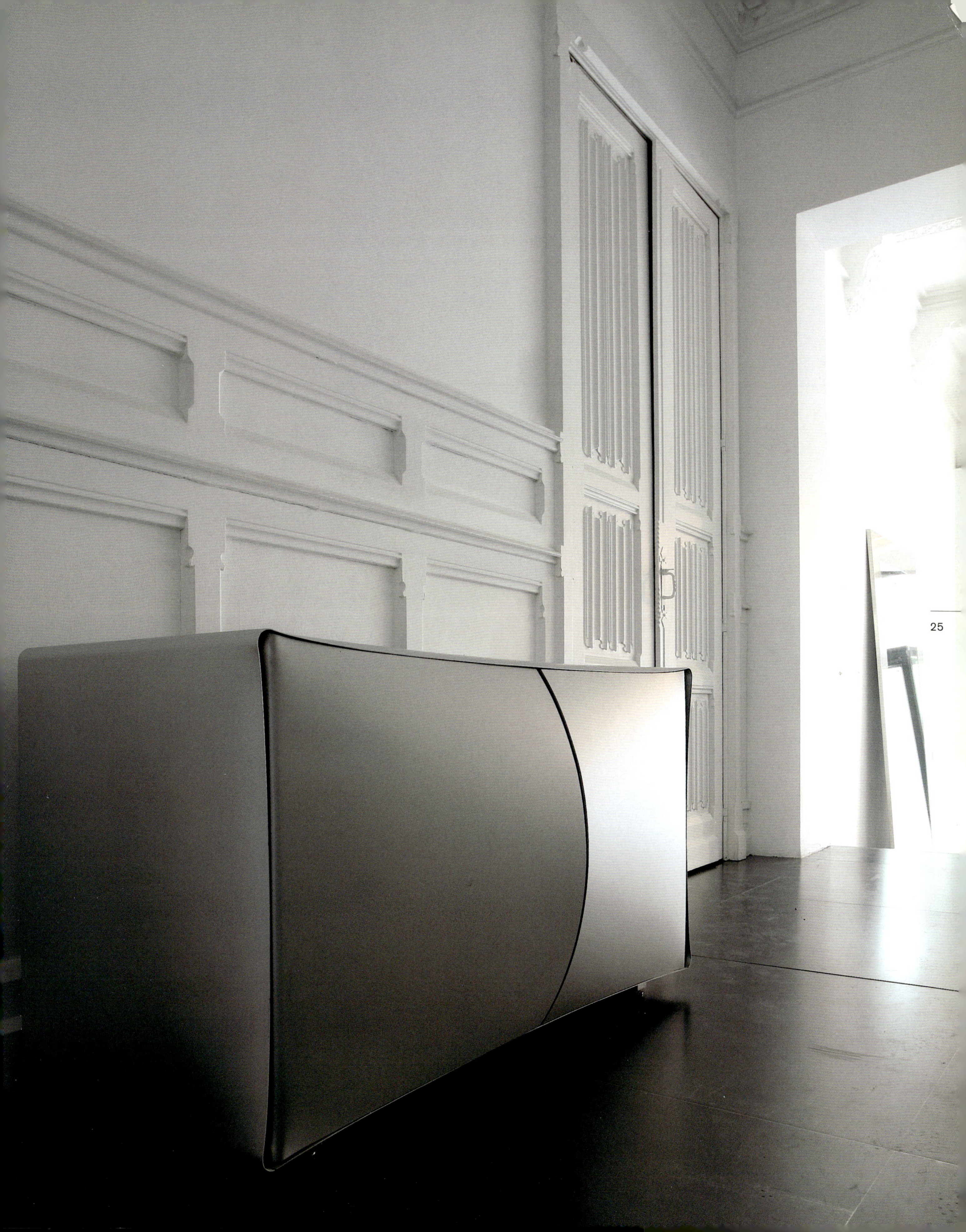

Lusting for 'Crédence'
Nick Vinson

There is one piece of work by Xavier Lust that I lust after more than any other. Yes, I would be more than happy to wait for the bus at one of his 'Abri-Voyageurs' bus shelters and wish my apartment building had a few of his 'Abri-Vélo' bike racks downstairs (a good home for my Kronan). A 'PicNik' table and chairs combo from Extremis would sit very well in the garden and had I the space (I don't as it's 4.4 m or 14.4 ft long) his 'La Grande Table' from MDF Italia would be top of the list for big family dinners (or re-enactments of the last supper). But what I really lust after is his 'Crédence' from De Padova.

Refined, elegant and masculine, I come across a lot of products and this one really stands out. Like most of Xavier Lust's work it's made of his signature (de)formed metal sheet construction, but unlike the others it has been lacquered in a rich thick gloss. The first time I saw it was in the window of De Padova during *Salone di Mobile* when it was launched in 2003, in a rich Chinese red. When the Rover green came out a year or so later I loved it even more (I have a problem with owning anything in red) and now with the Prussian blue (it lies somewhere between blue and black). I know which one is on the top of my wish list as the new color is as refined and precious as the piece itself.

The shape is inspired by a Regency bombe-fronted commode something Xavier confirmed to me although he refers to it as pot bellied. I think it's this delightful bombe-front as well as the gentle curve of the top and sides that seem to envelope the piece combined with the high gloss that makes it so exceptional and gives it that rare elegance. Completely contemporary with a nod to the past (1715 to 1723 to be precise, a brief period preceding Louis XV) its construction, material and finish ensure it has an eye on the future. Its neoclassical beginnings mean the proportions are very pleasing to the eye and will stand the test of time.

Once you examine it further you will discover its other joys. Each door hangs on just one high tech hinge in the centre rather than on the outside, which means the doors open from the outside in. Opening like this, it reminds me of an old Citroën car (Xavier says Rover hence the name of the Green) that in a way makes it very masculine. This also means that strangers won't manage to fathom how to open it at all giving an air of secrecy to the contents. I have an original Florence Knoll Crédence, originally designed for office use, a discreet lock meant only the Chairman was able to get to his whiskey. With Xavier's 'Crédence' the lock would not be necessary, only those in the know would have access.

I would have no problem deciding what to put on top; an Angelo Mangiarotti sculpture in marble or bronze, definitely something very rococo from Porzellan Manufaktur Nymphenburg and probably my Baccarat crystal rock by Arik Levy. On the wall above I would hang either the 'Green Mirror' from Pierre Charpin or one of Tomas Maier's new Bottega Veneta mirrors with woven leather frames. Inside? That would have to be my secret.

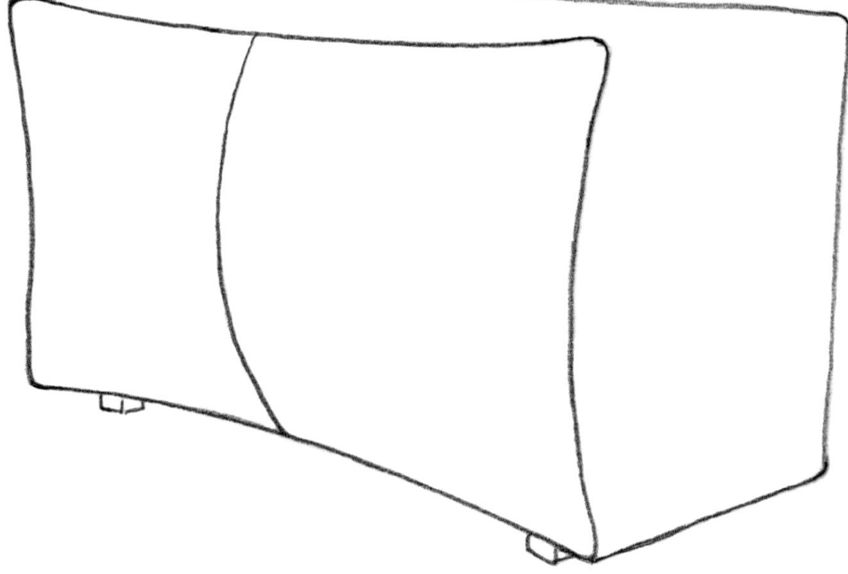

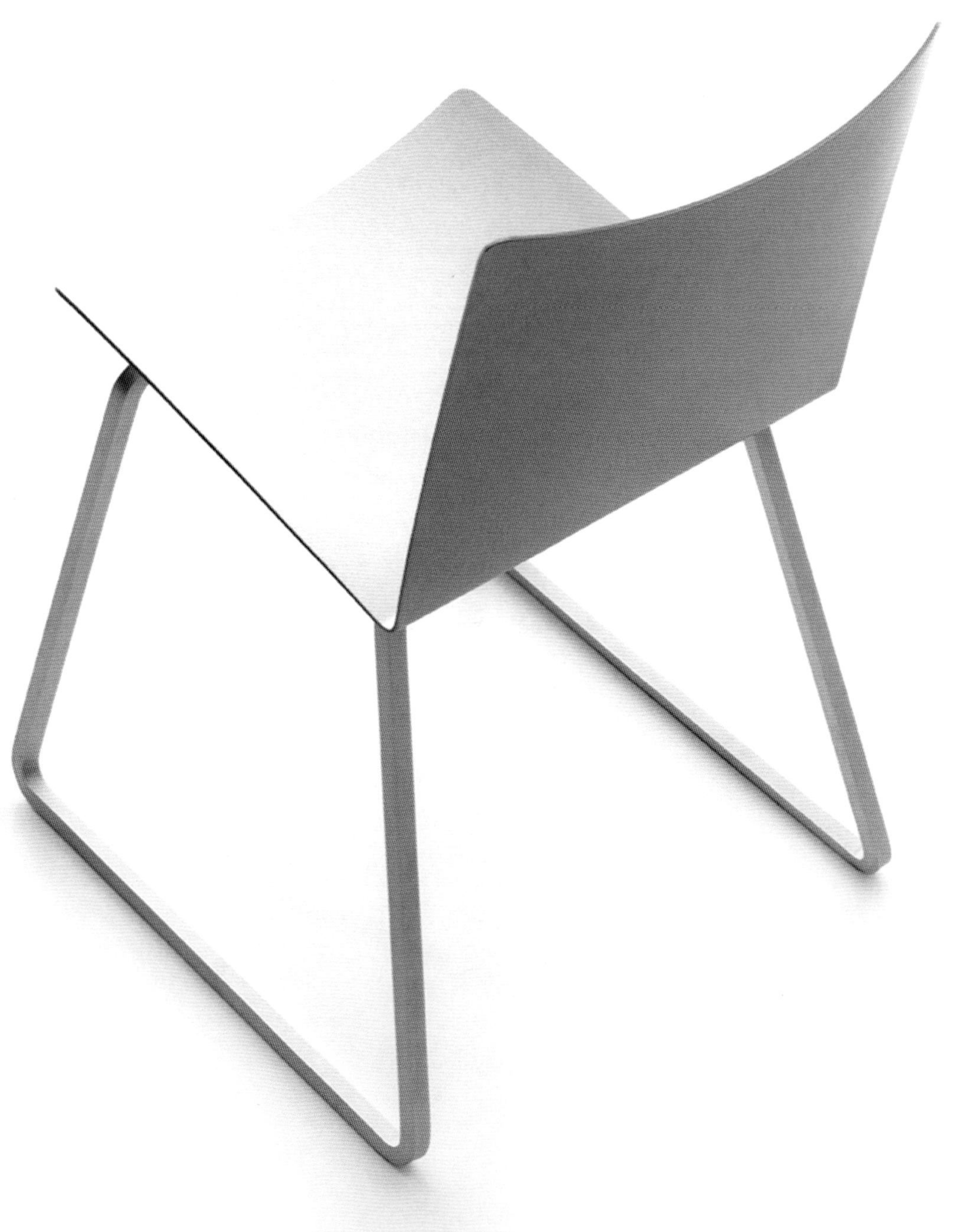

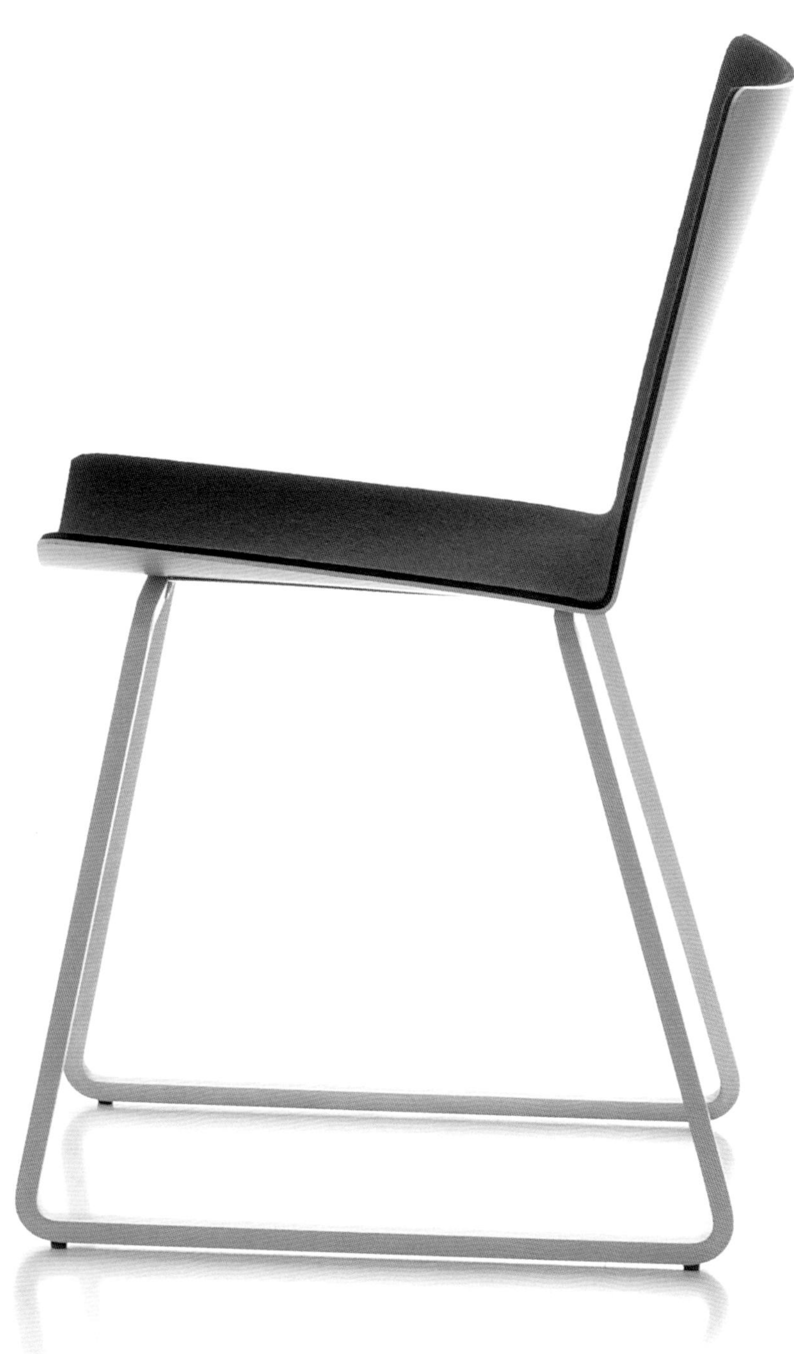

Public library of Watermael-Boitsfort, Brussels, Belgium

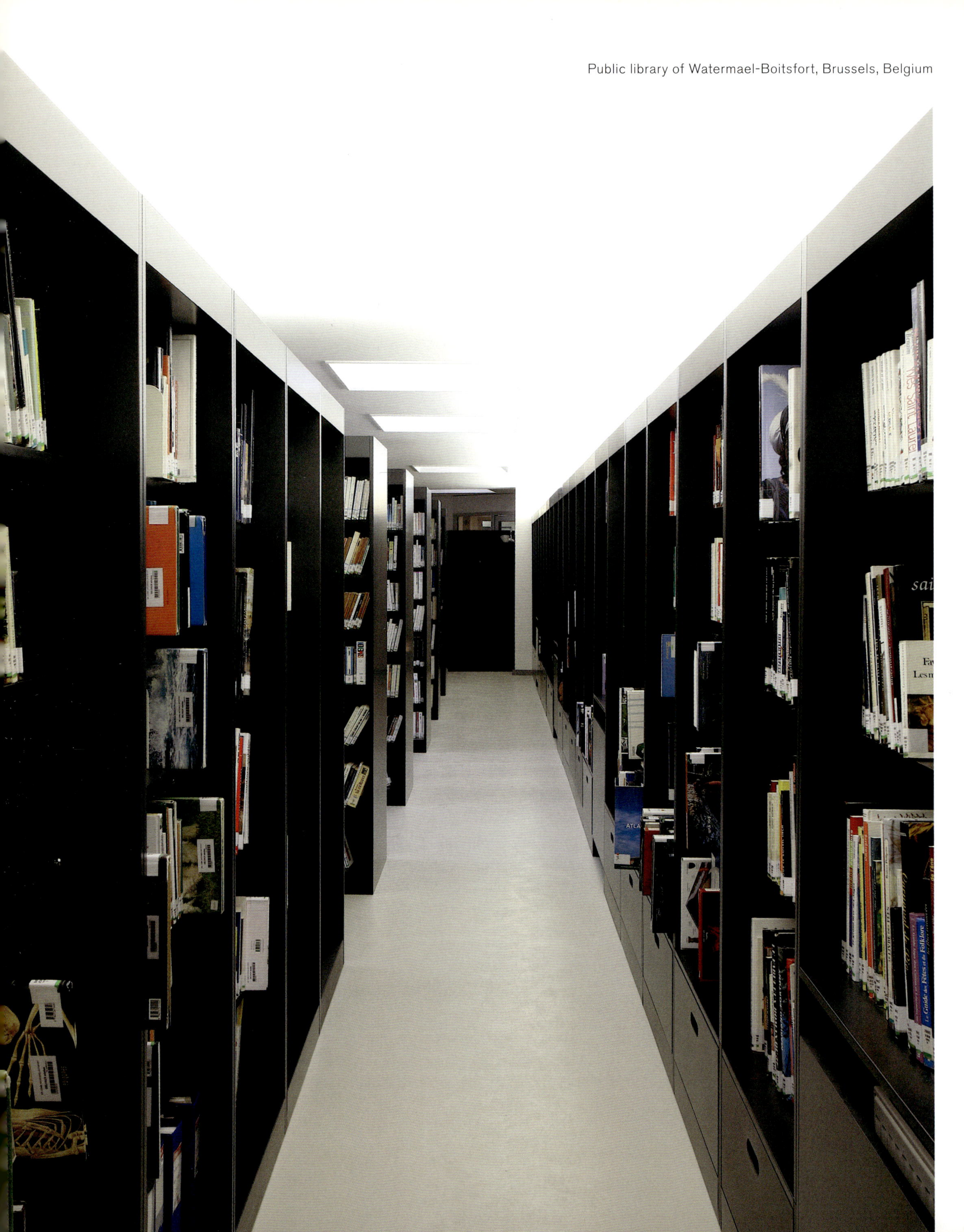

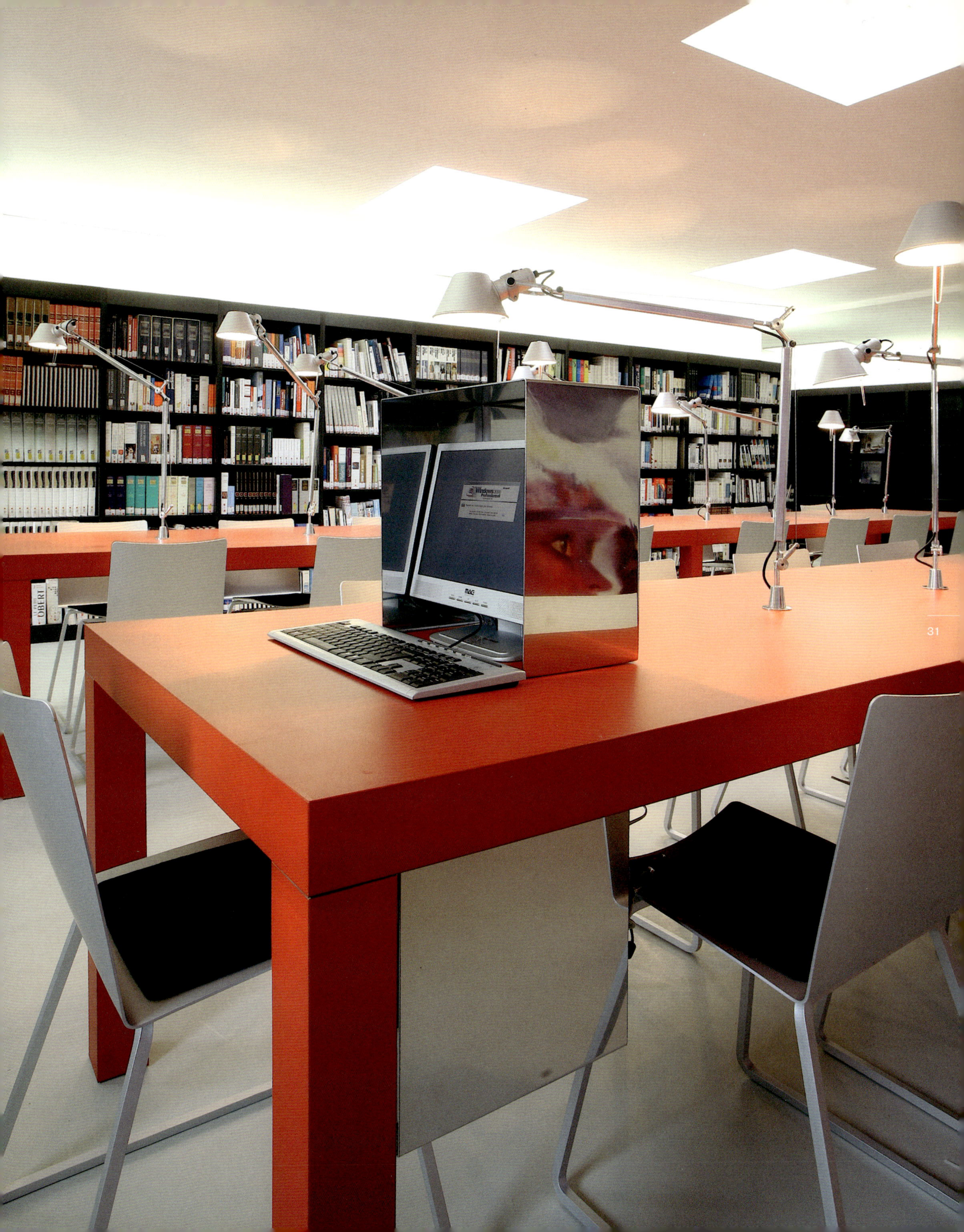

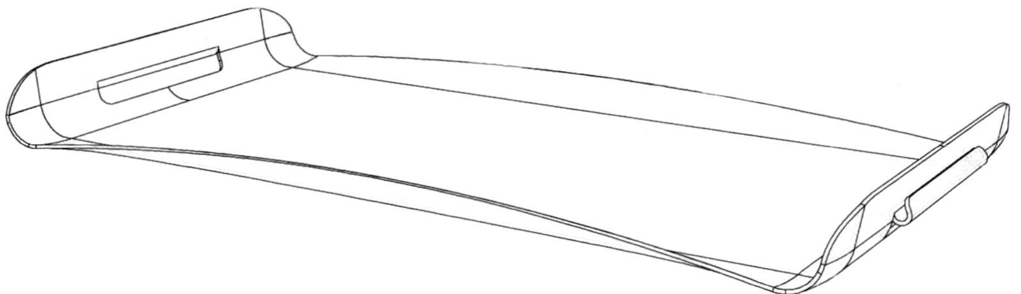

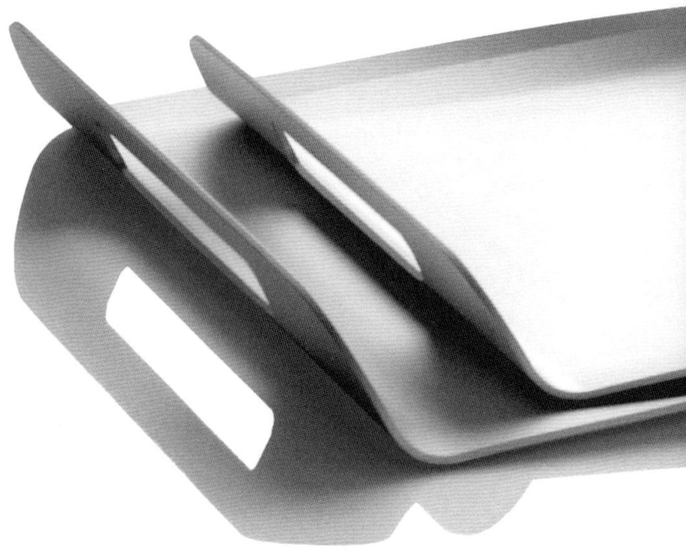

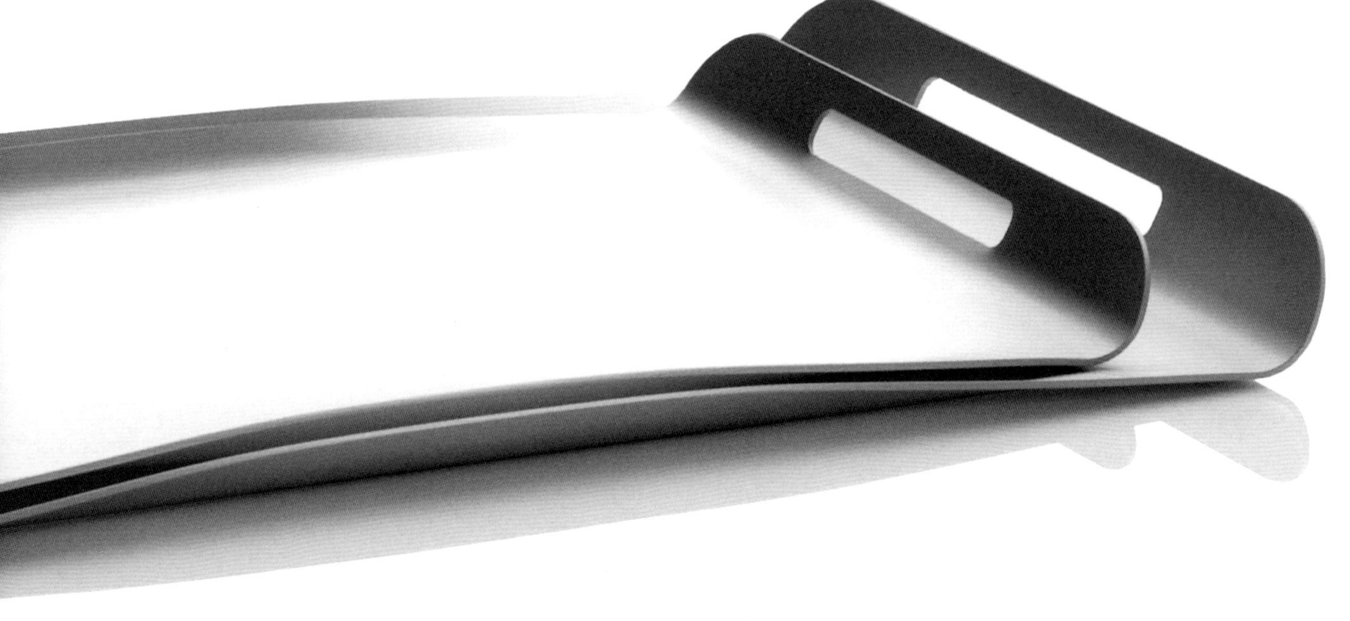

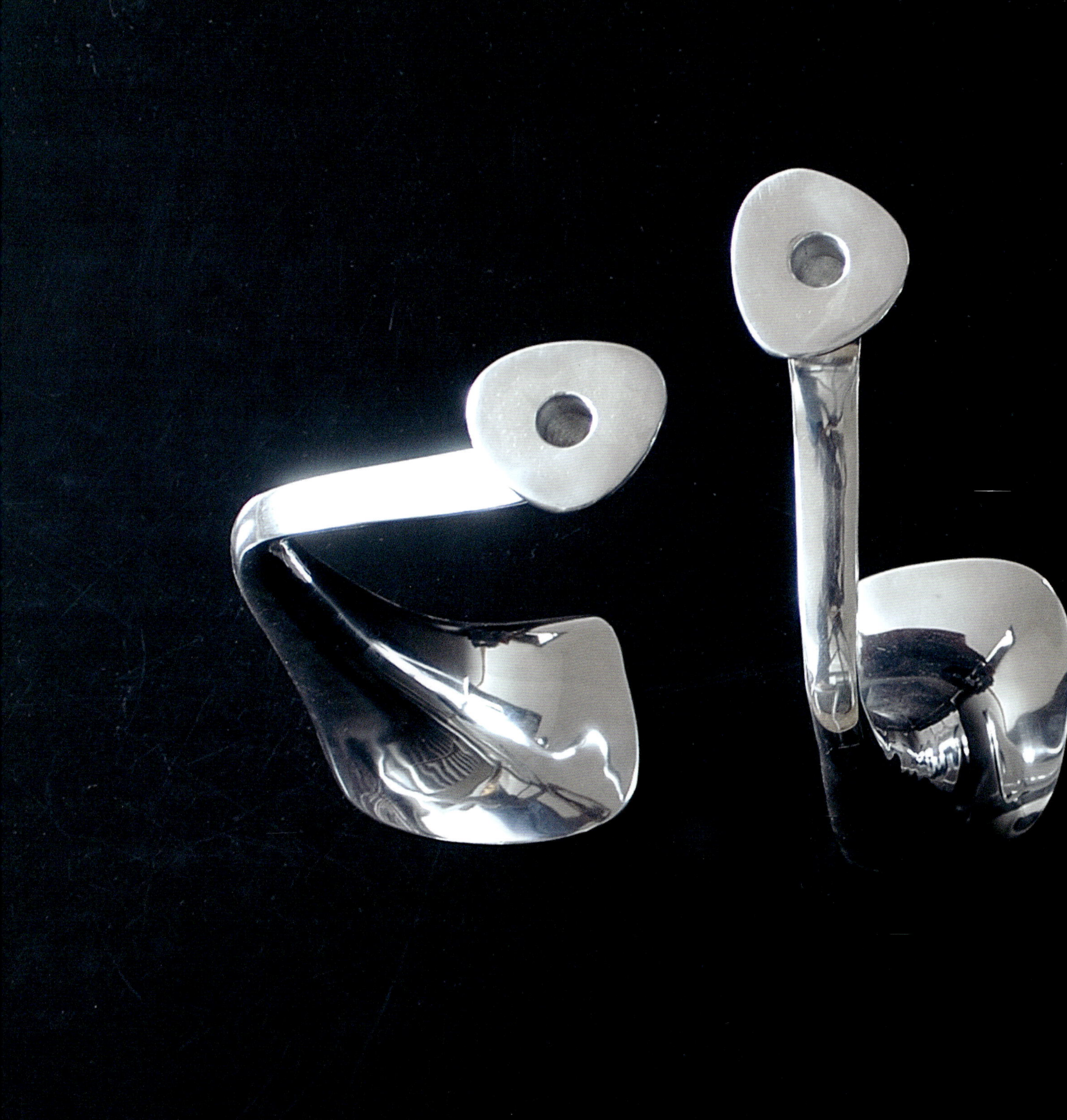

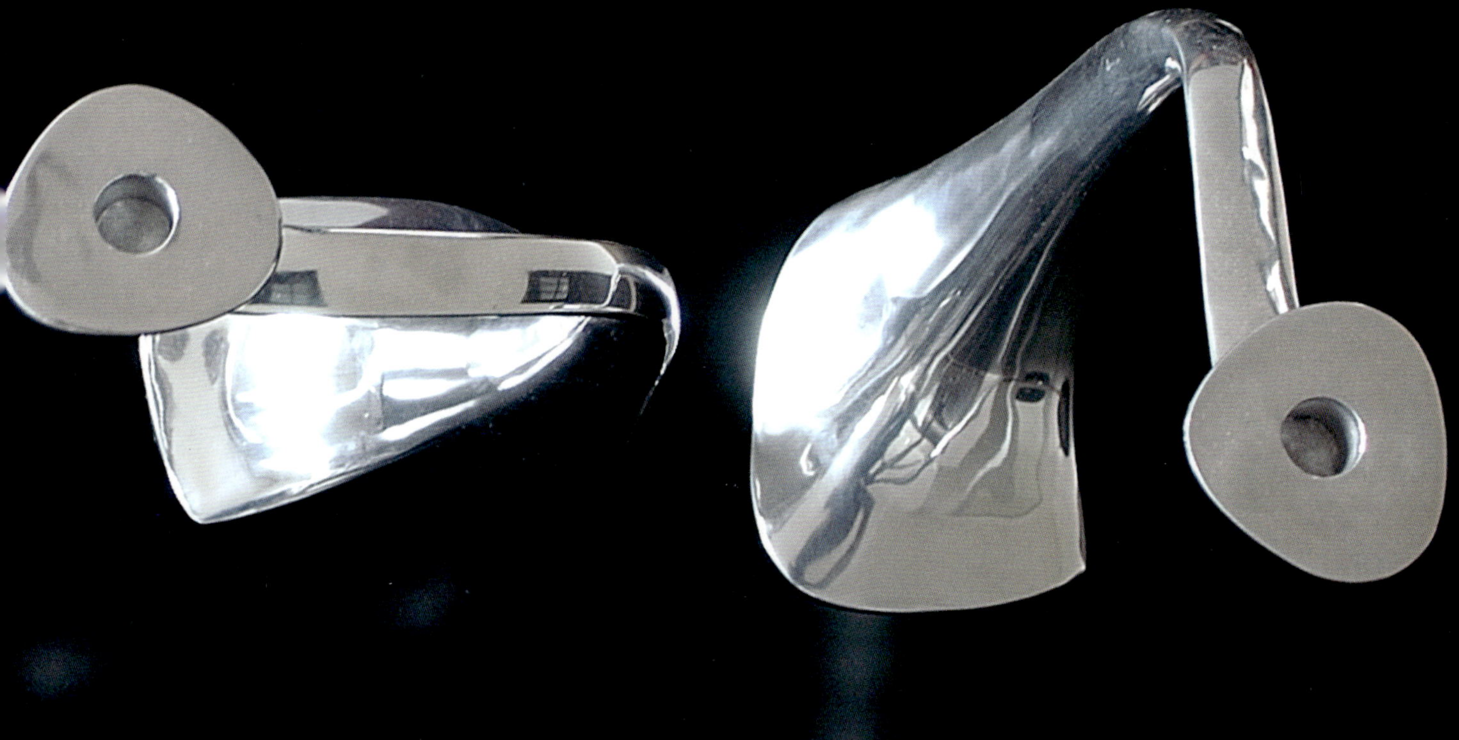

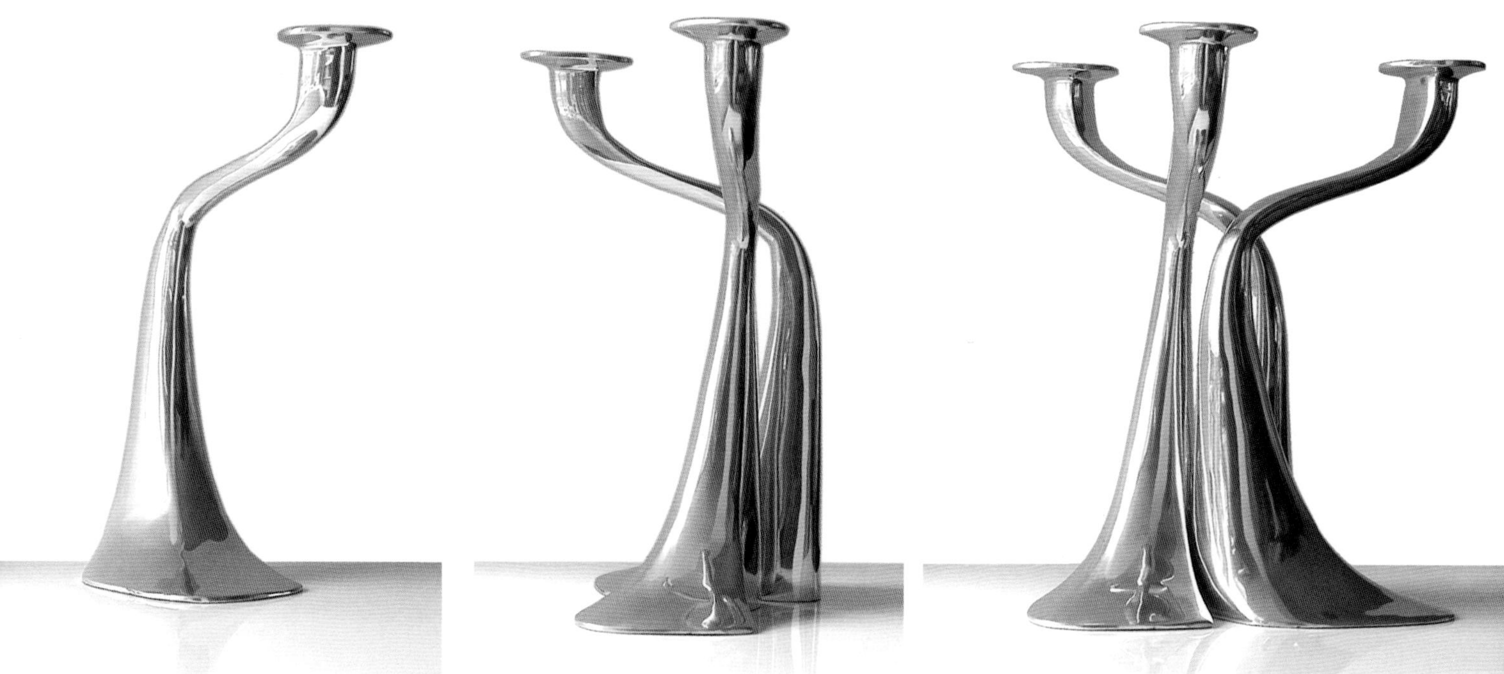

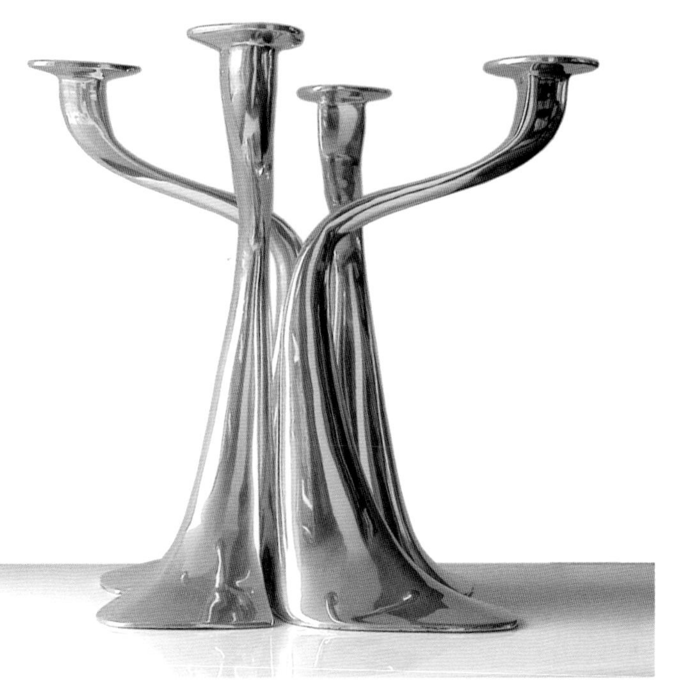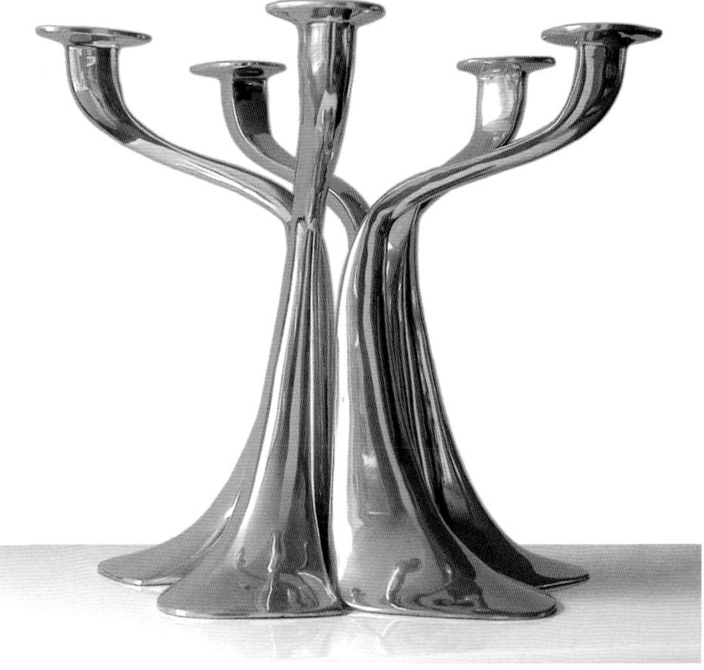

Xavier Lust is a sculptor, an artist who molds and bends sheets of metal into 'moving' shapes and objects.

We started working with Xavier in 2004, presenting a 'sculpture': the umbrella-stand 'Paso Doble', a parallelepiped whose lines gradually bend to produce different cross-sections top and bottom.

Our collaboration continued with the 'Tetra' table, an anthracite grey or amaranth red folded steel frame supporting a crystal glass top painted in the same color as the structure; the 'Extra Chair', in polypropylene, where the gentle twist given to the legs turns their square floor section into a triangular top section; the 'Turner' candlestick, in polished cast aluminum recalling the exquisite silver creations of art nouveau or Jugendstil artists; trays 'T42' and 'T43' made from a single sheet of anodized aluminum, cut and shaped by special tools developed by Lust in his continuing investigation into materials and how they can be creatively shaped.

Bending and twisting has been the key theme developed up to now with Lust. Working with him is always interesting, always refreshing. He is an artist who draws inspiration for innovative designs from the very materials he uses.

Elisa Astori, Driade

Xavier Lust è uno scultore, un artista che plasma e torce la lamiera realizzando forme ed oggetti 'in movimento'.

Abbiamo cominciato a lavorare con Xavier nel 2004 presentando un oggetto 'scultura', un parallelepipede che, attraverso la torsione delle linee, cambia sezione tra la base e l'altezza. E' il portaombrelli 'Paso Doble'.

La collaborazione è continuata con il tavolo 'Tetra', con struttura in lamiera piegata di colore grigio antracite o rosso amaranto e piano in cristallo verniciato dello stesso colore della struttura; la sedia 'Extra Chair' in polipropilene, dal disegno variabile delle gambe, simile a una torsione, che le porta da una sezione quadrata a terra a una sezione triangolare; il candelabro 'Turner' in fusione di alluminio lucidato che rimanda alla ricchezza formale ed espressiva degli argenti Art Nouveau o Jugendstil; i vassoi 'T42' e 'T43' ricavati da un unico foglio di alluminio anodizzato, tagliato e deformato tramite apposite attrezzature che continuano il suo processo di ricerca tecnico-creativo di rimodellazione di forme e materiali.

La torsione è stato il tema che abbiamo sviluppato sino ad oggi con Lust. Lavorare con Xavier è interessante e sempre nuovo, come il lavoro di un artisa che trova nella libertà del segno e della materia, l'ispirazione per continuarela sua ricerca.

Elisa Astori, Driade

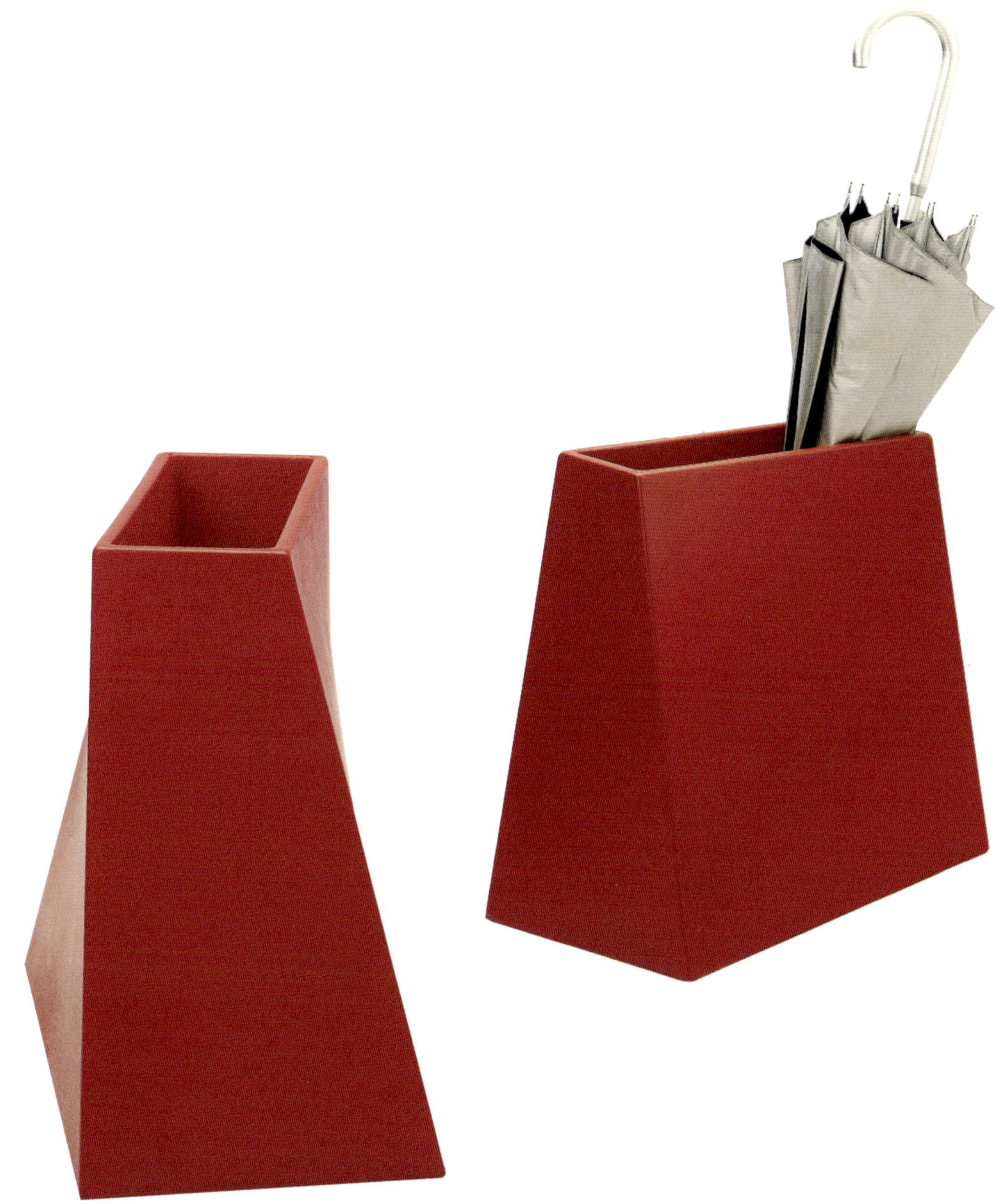

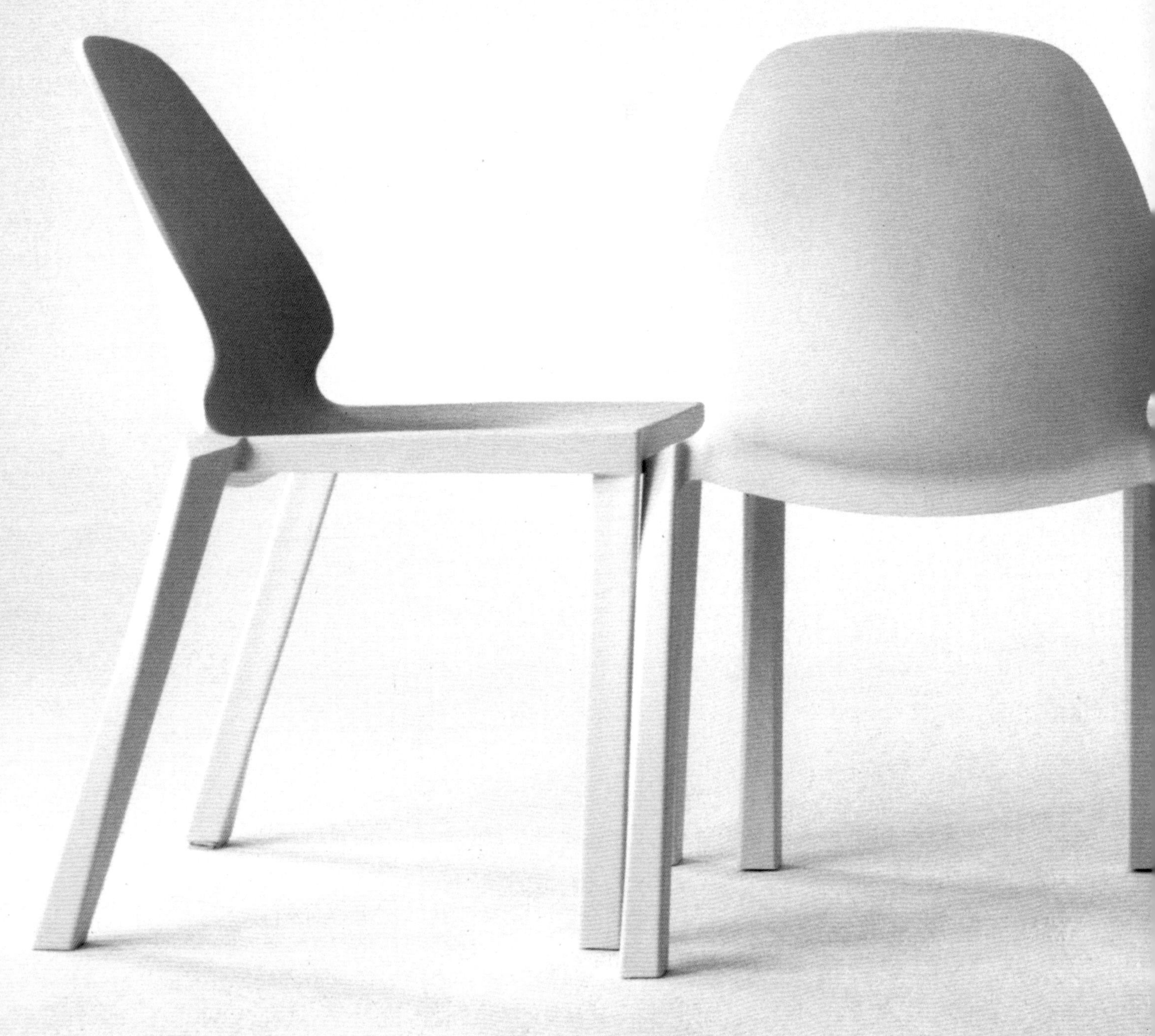

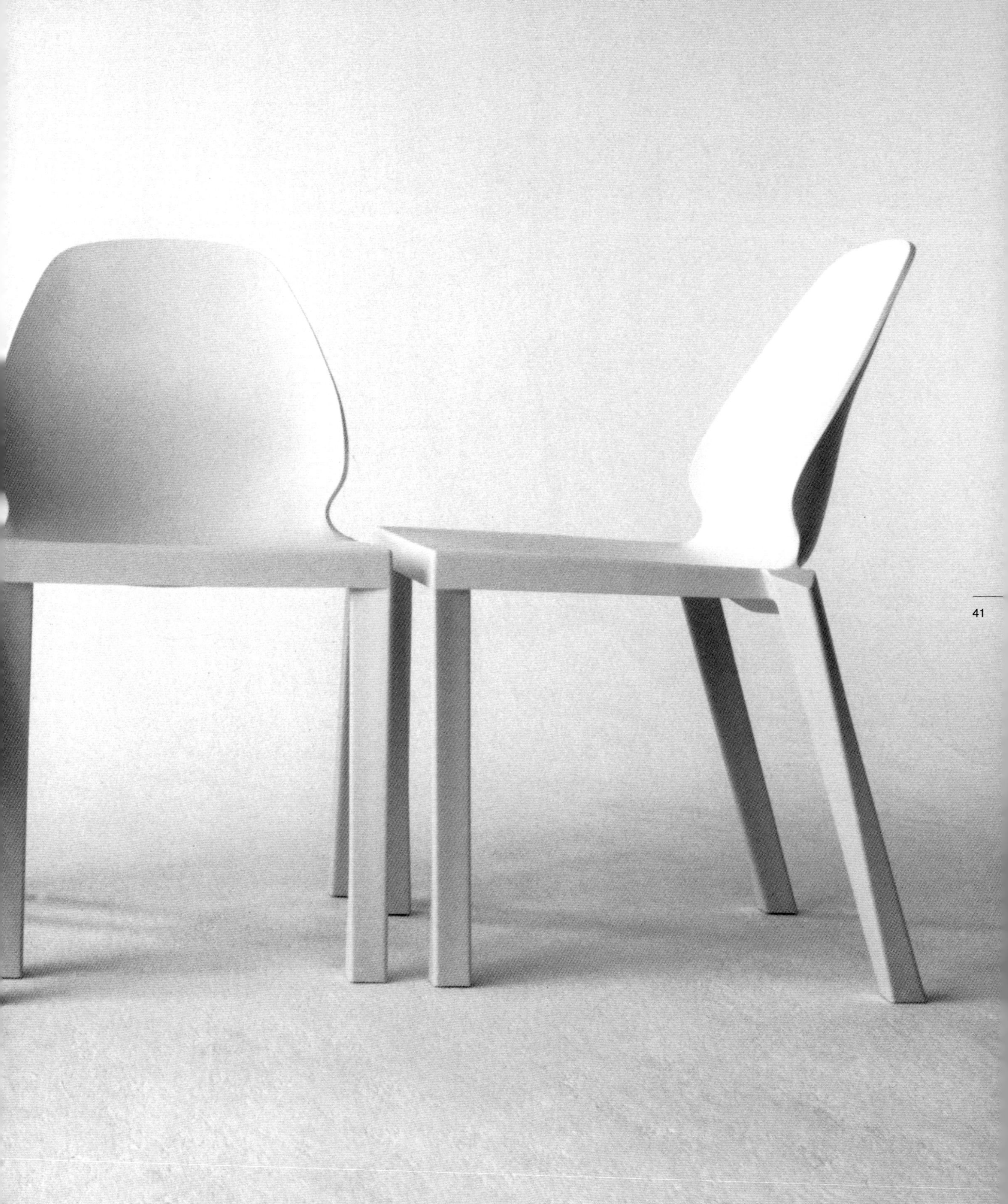

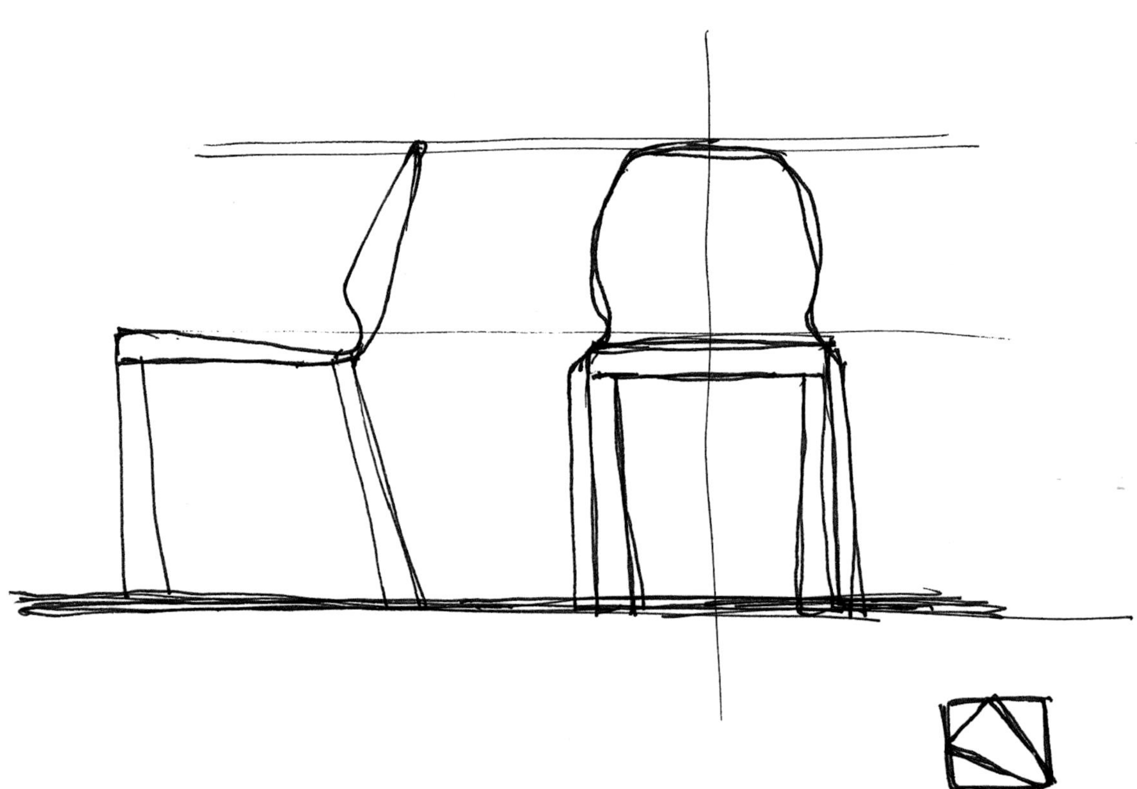

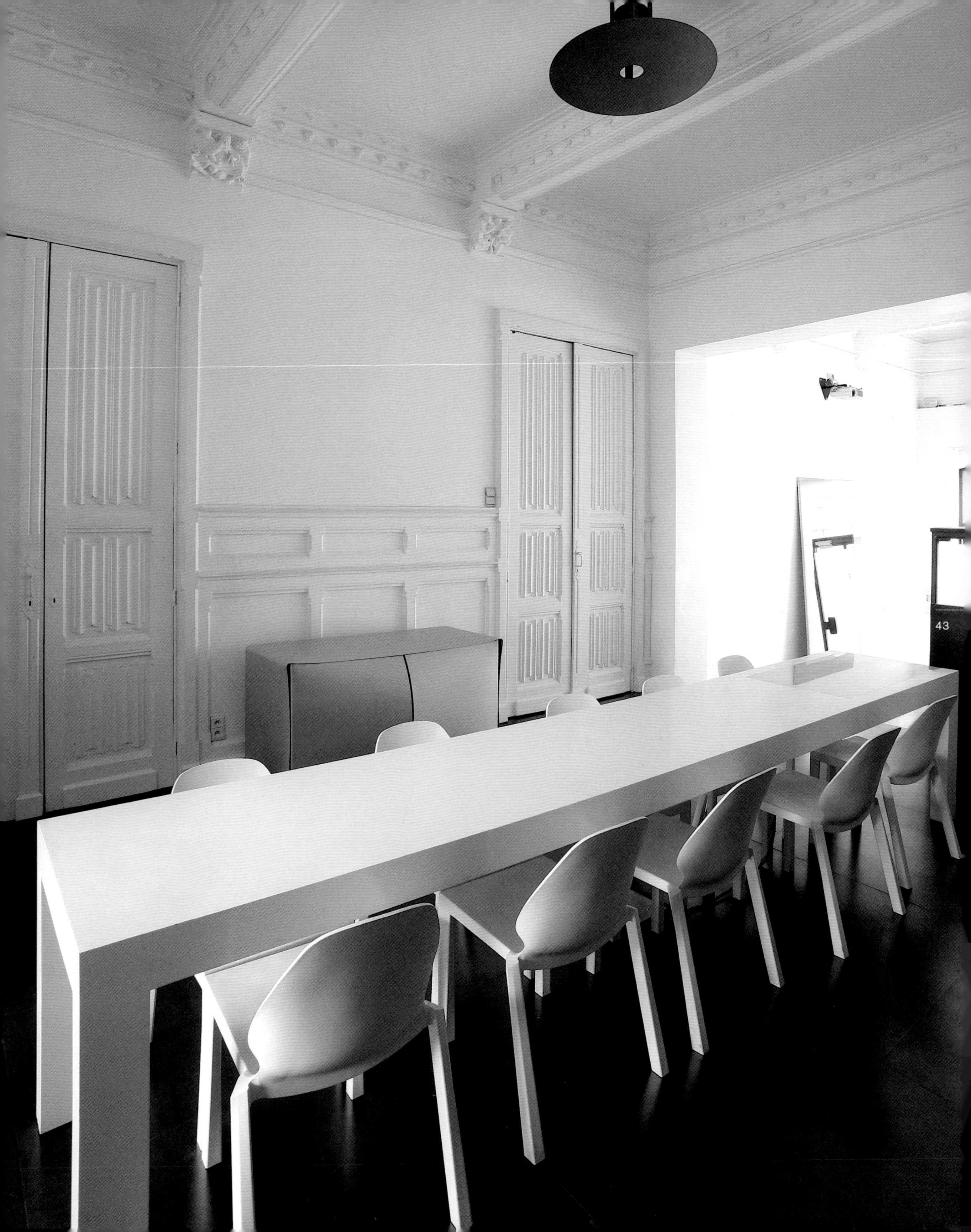

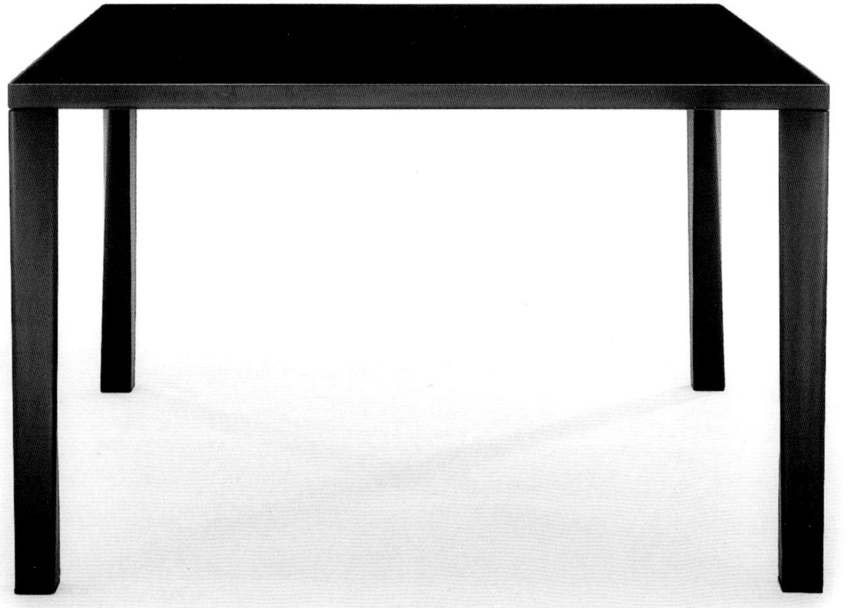

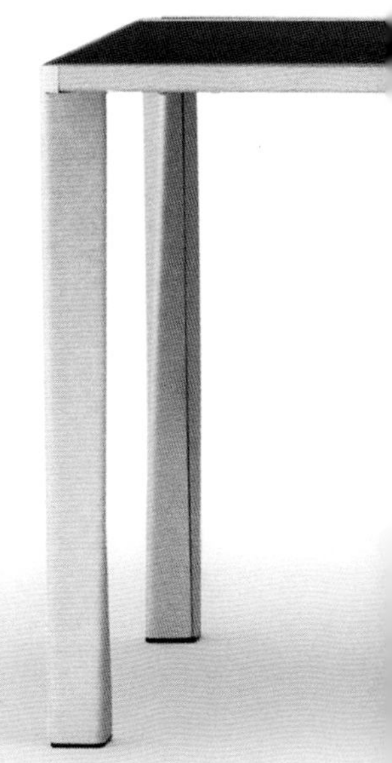

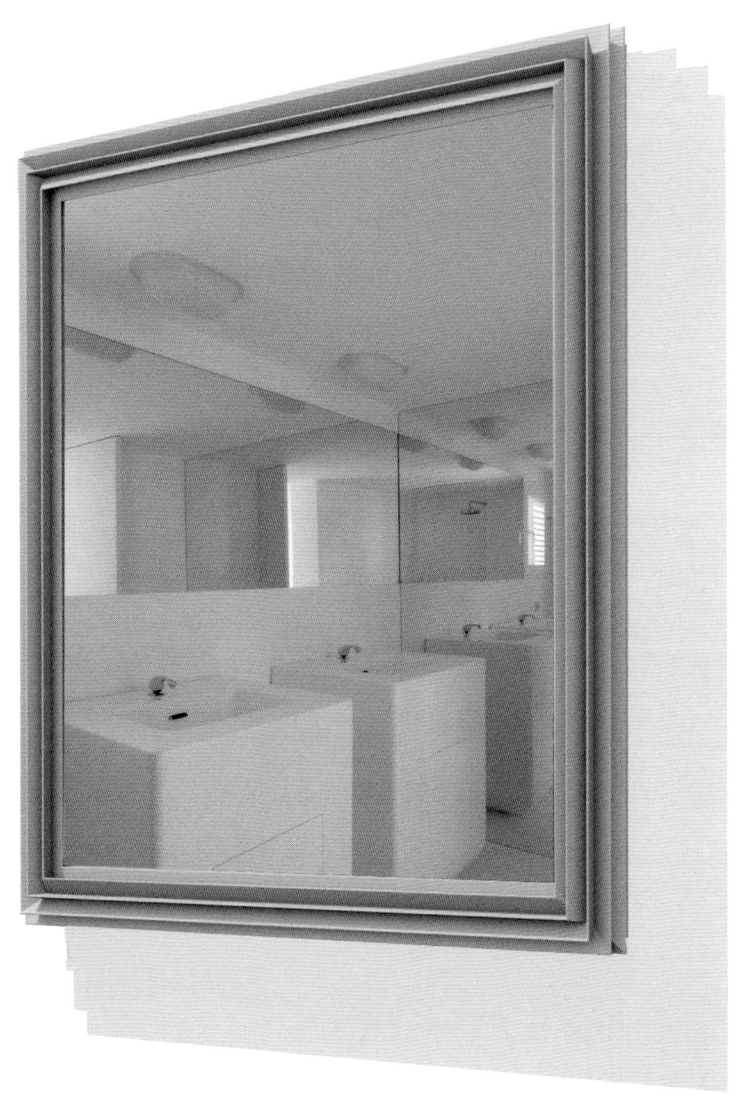

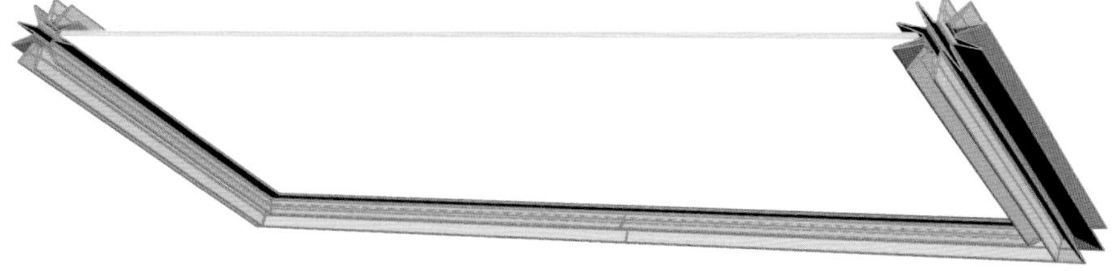

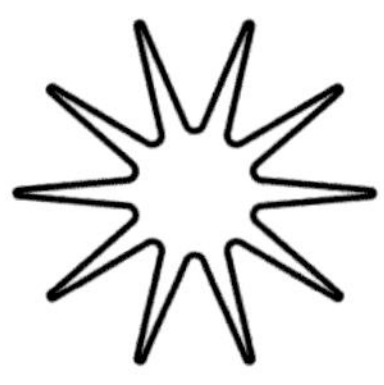

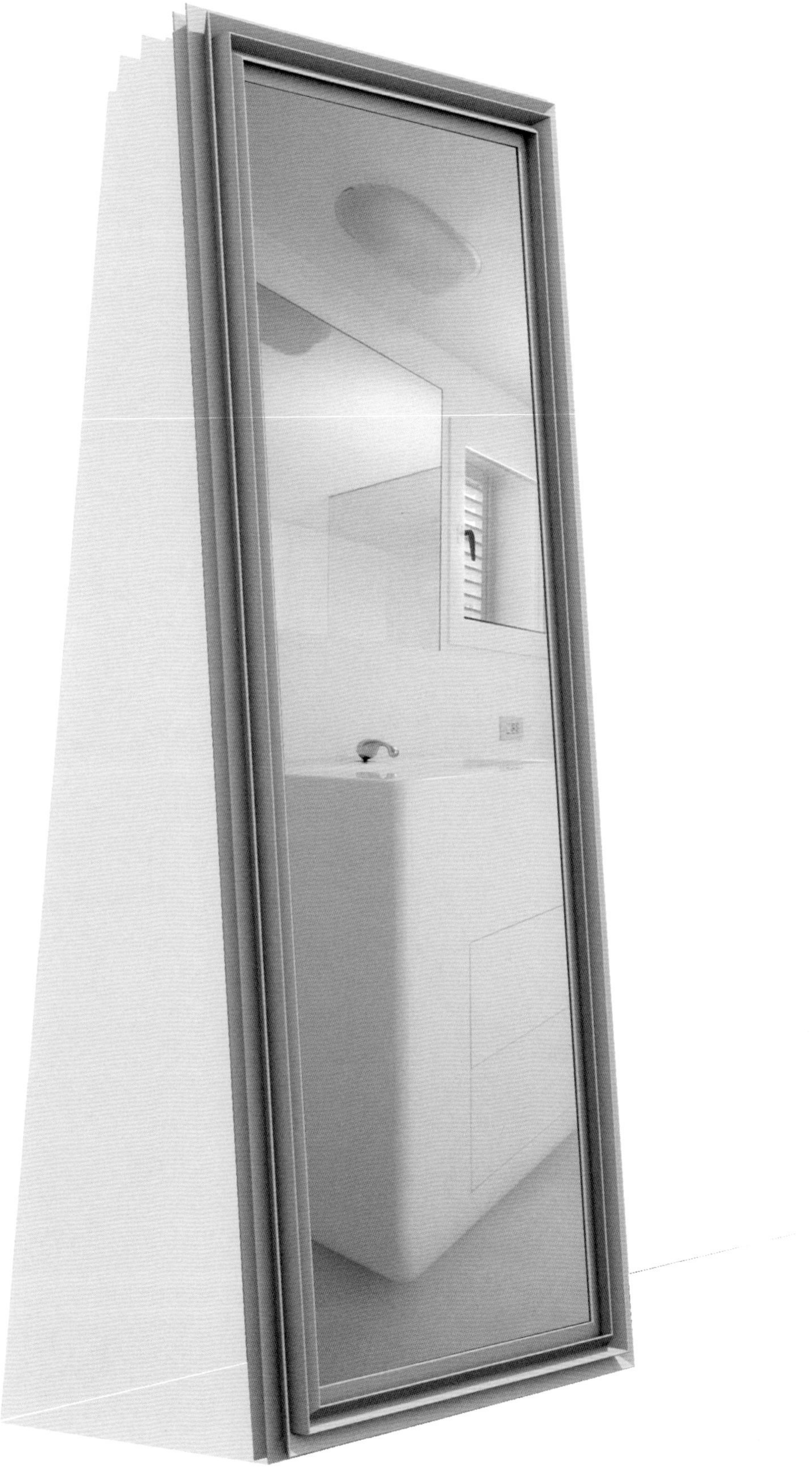

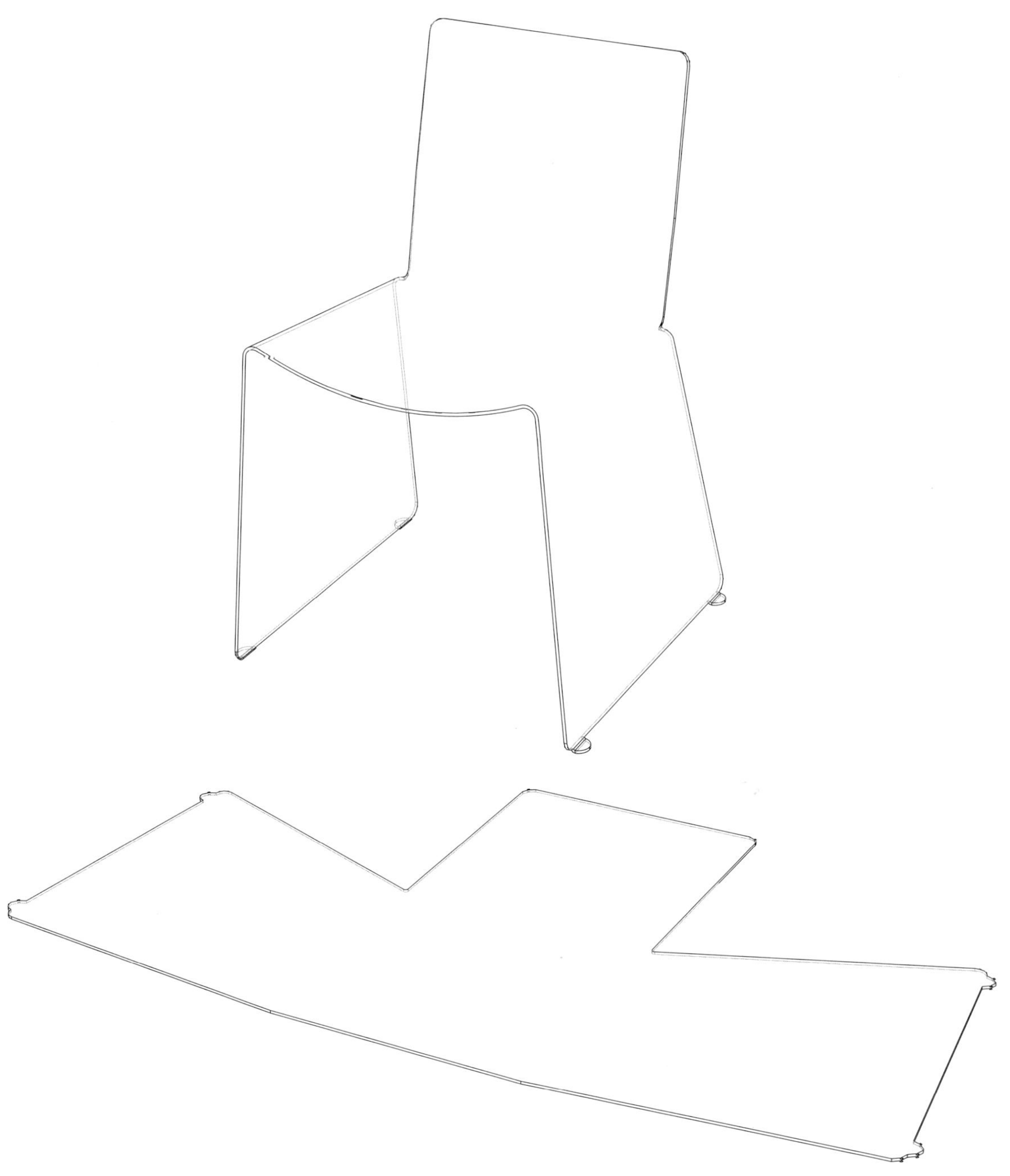

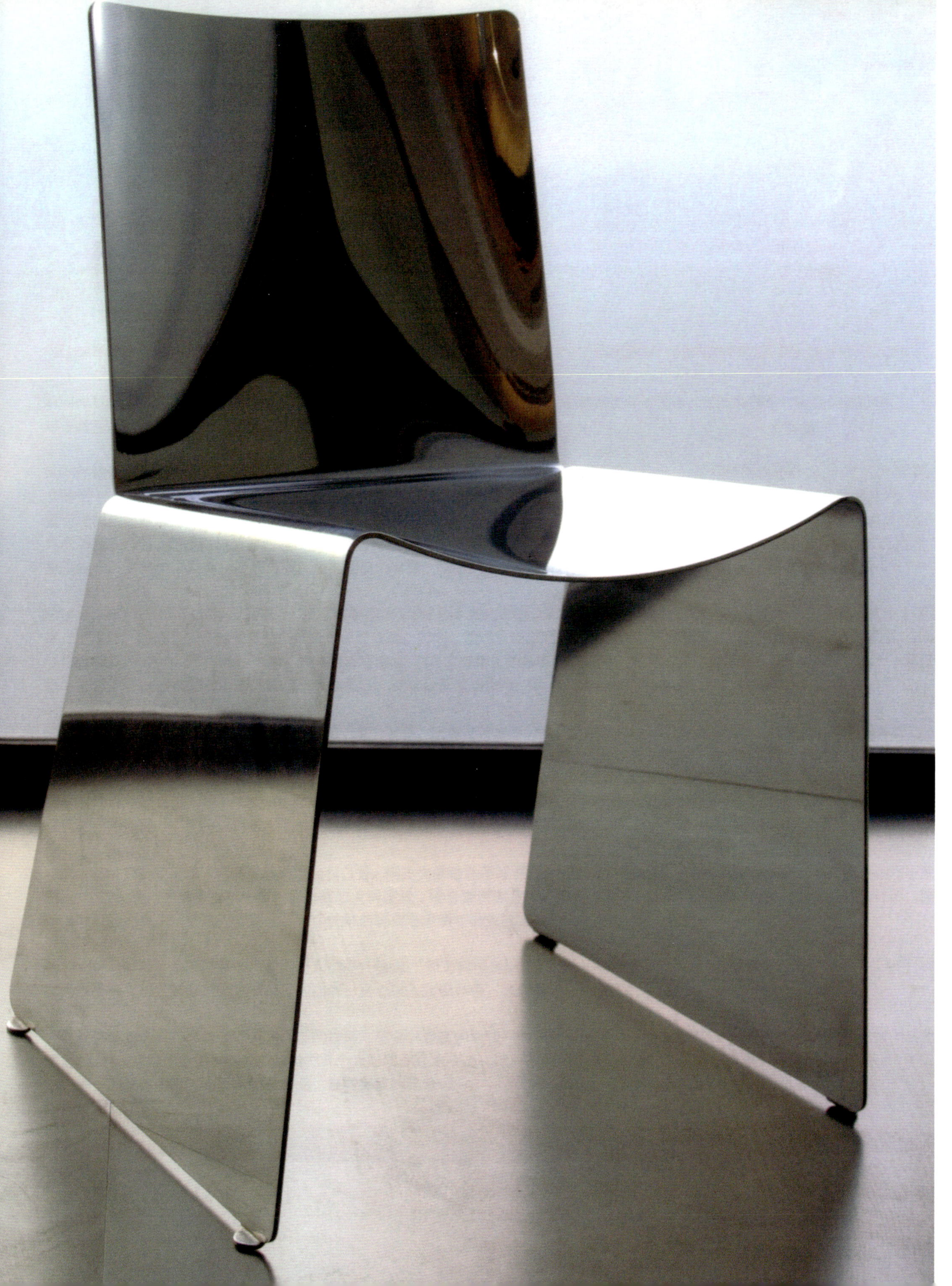

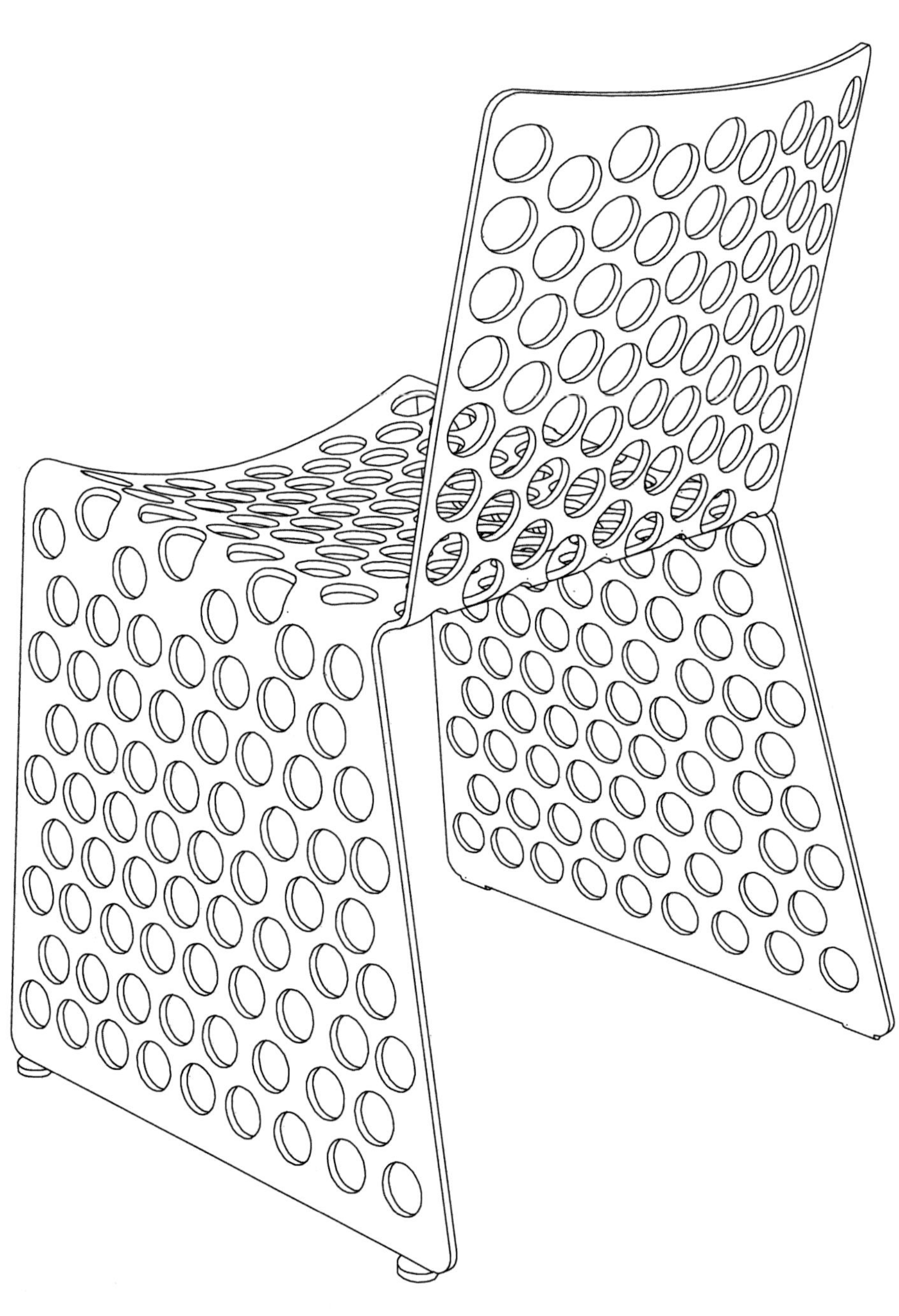

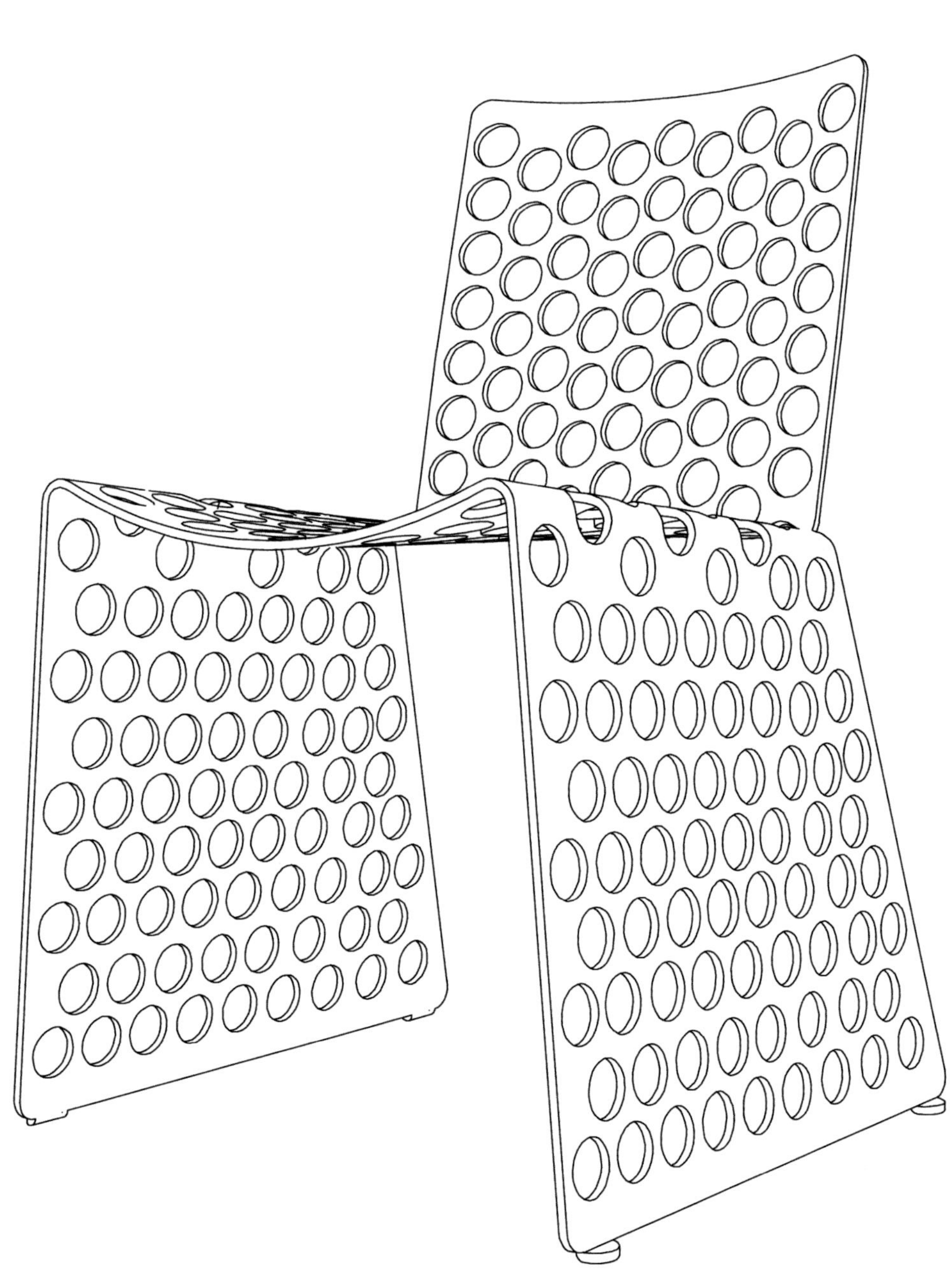

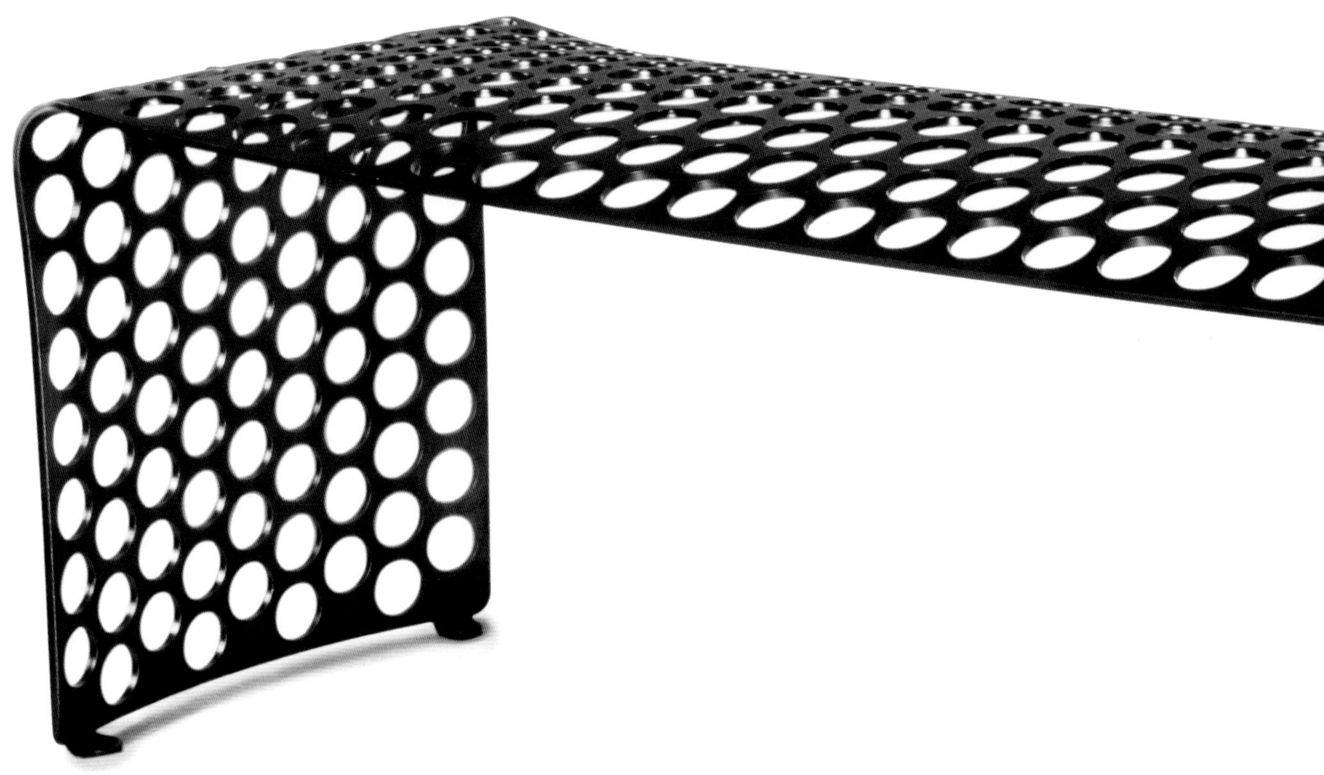

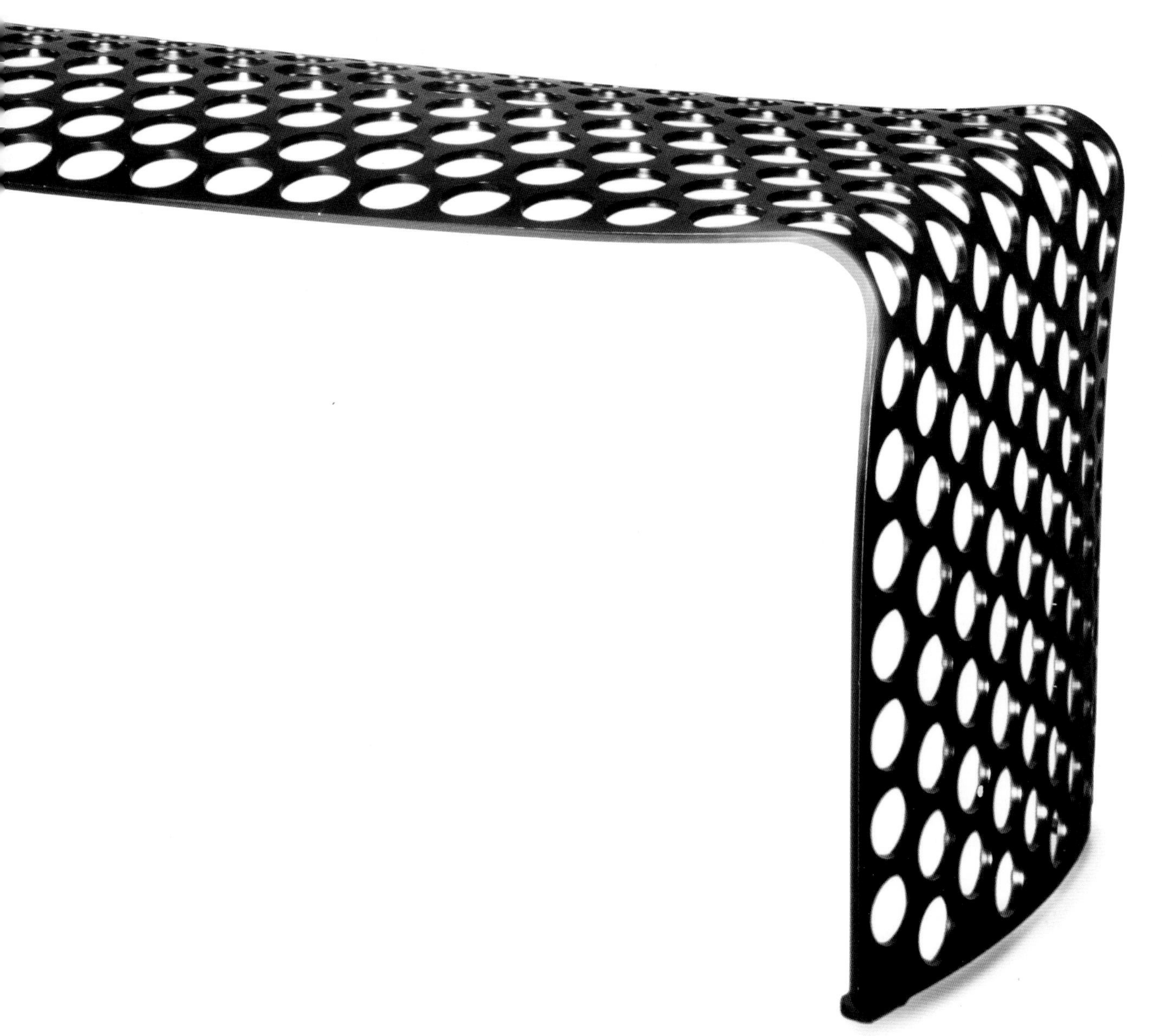

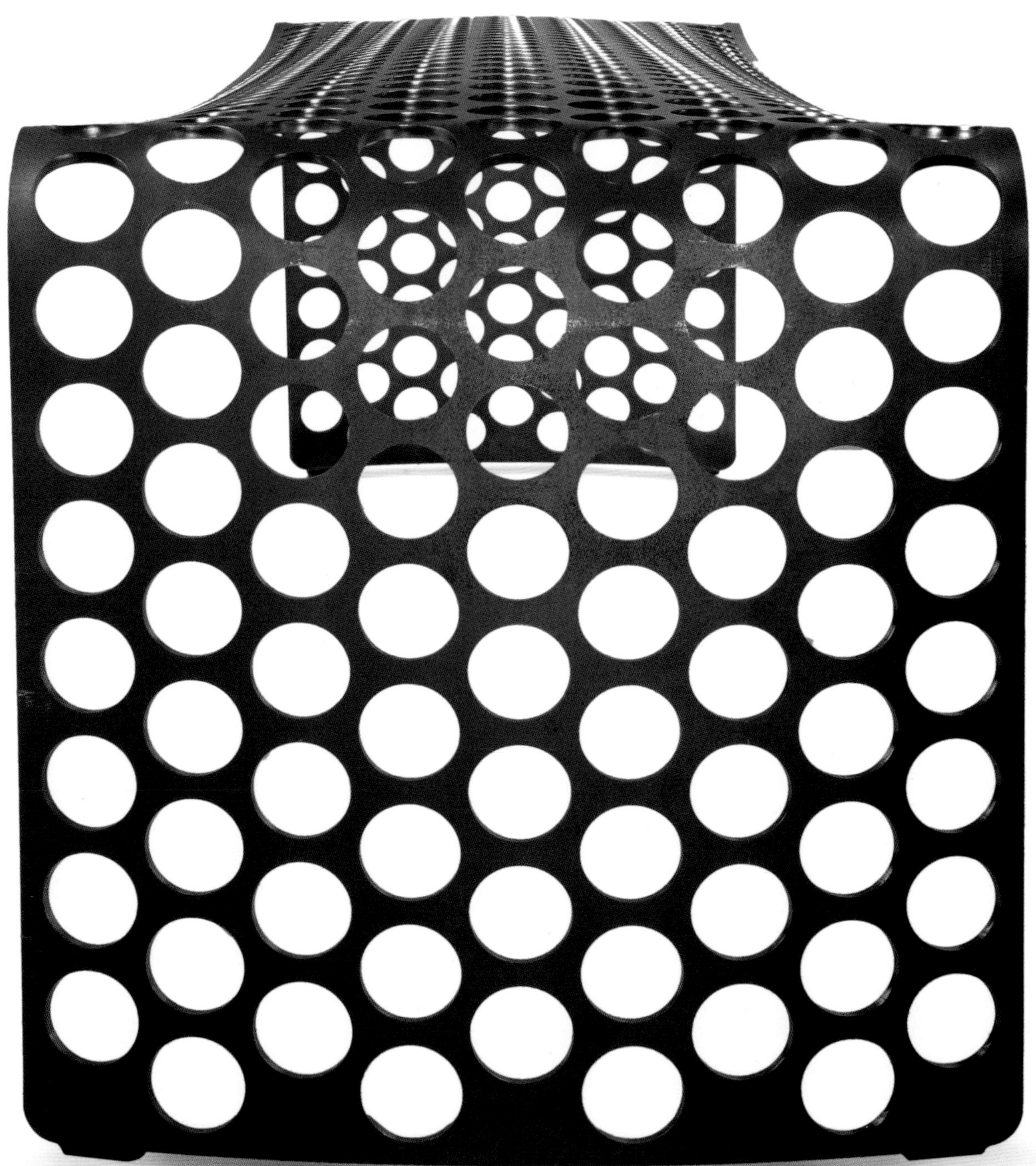

Art gallery Isy Gabriel Brachot
Brussels, Belgium

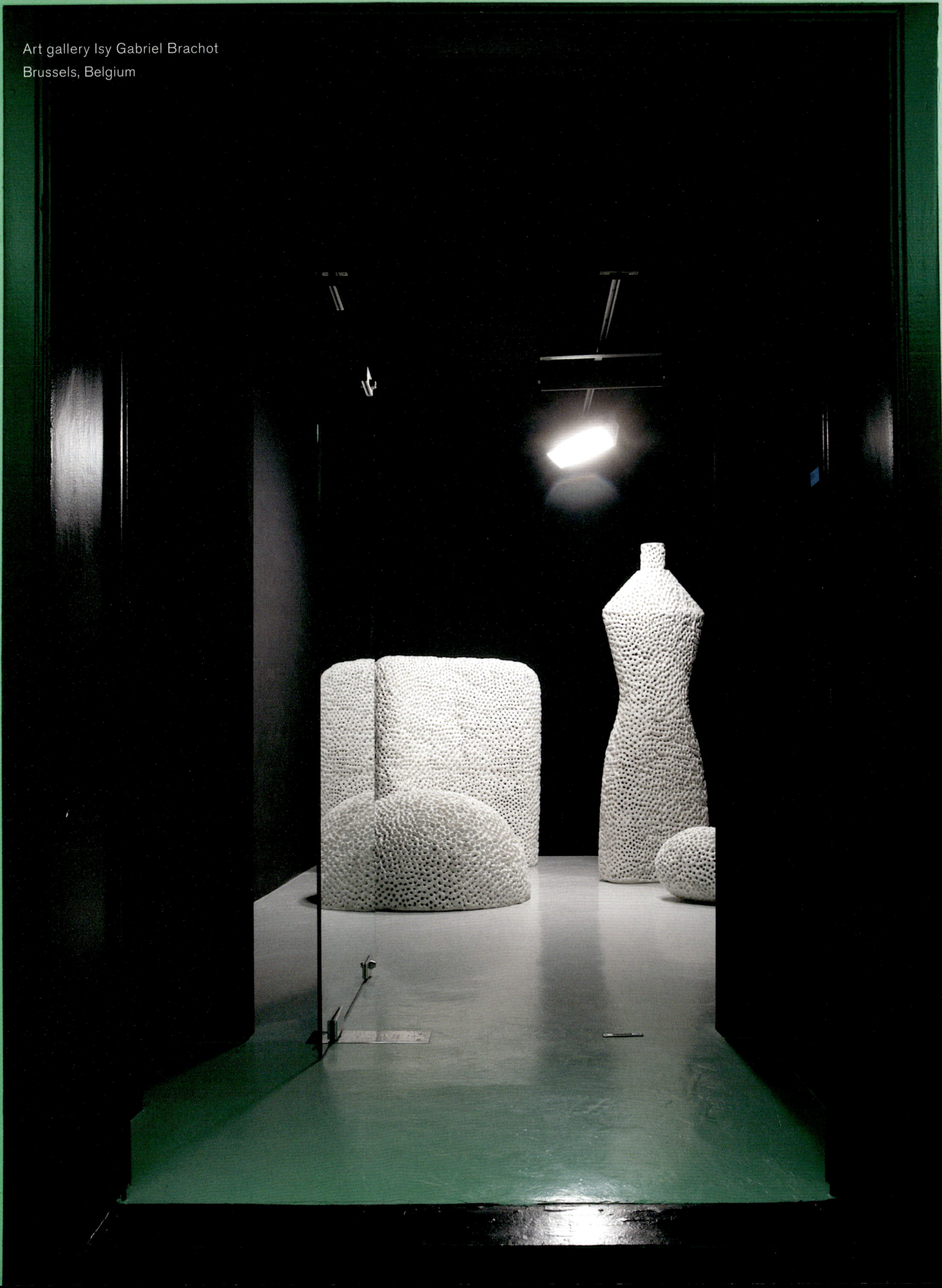

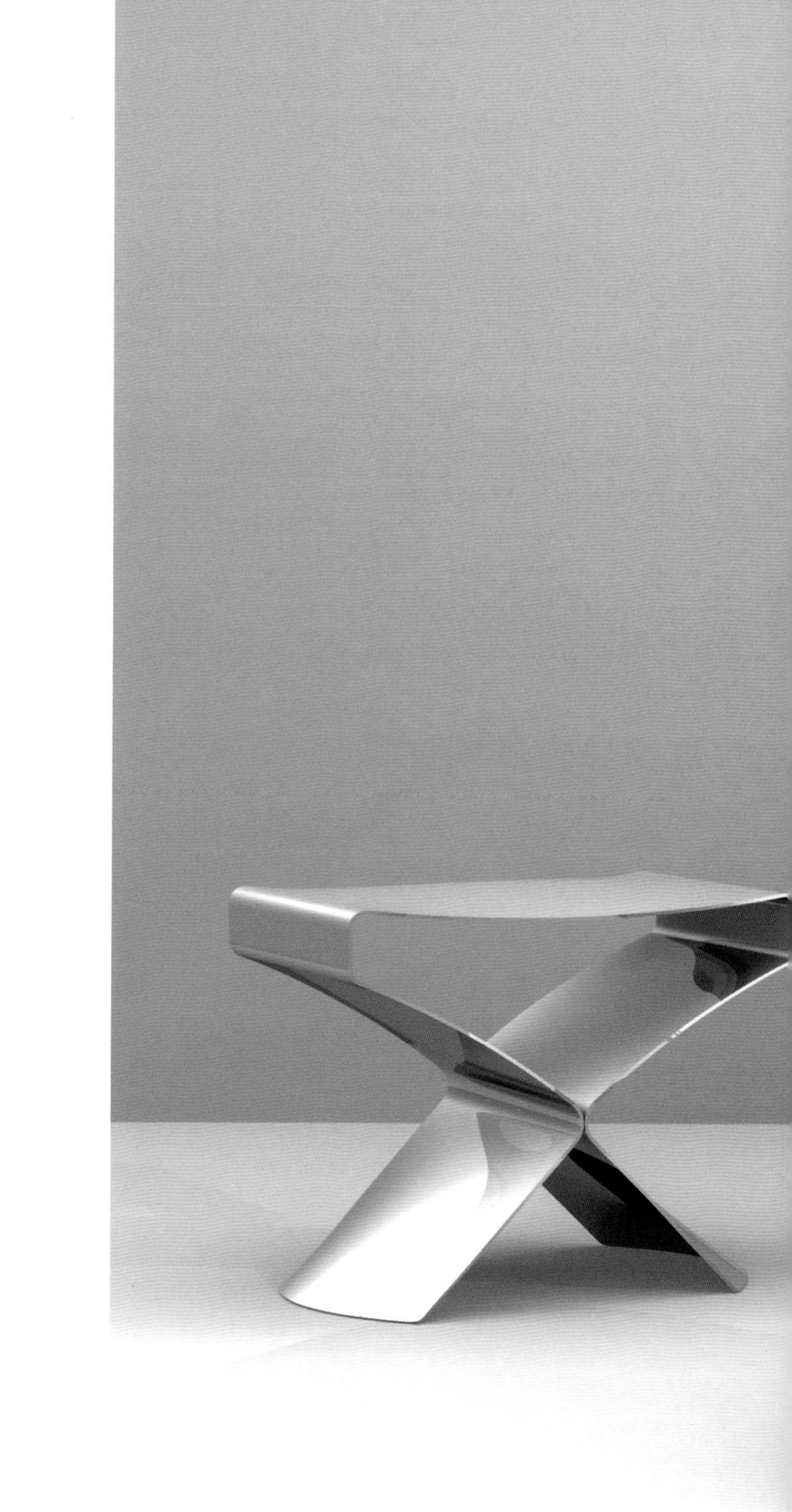

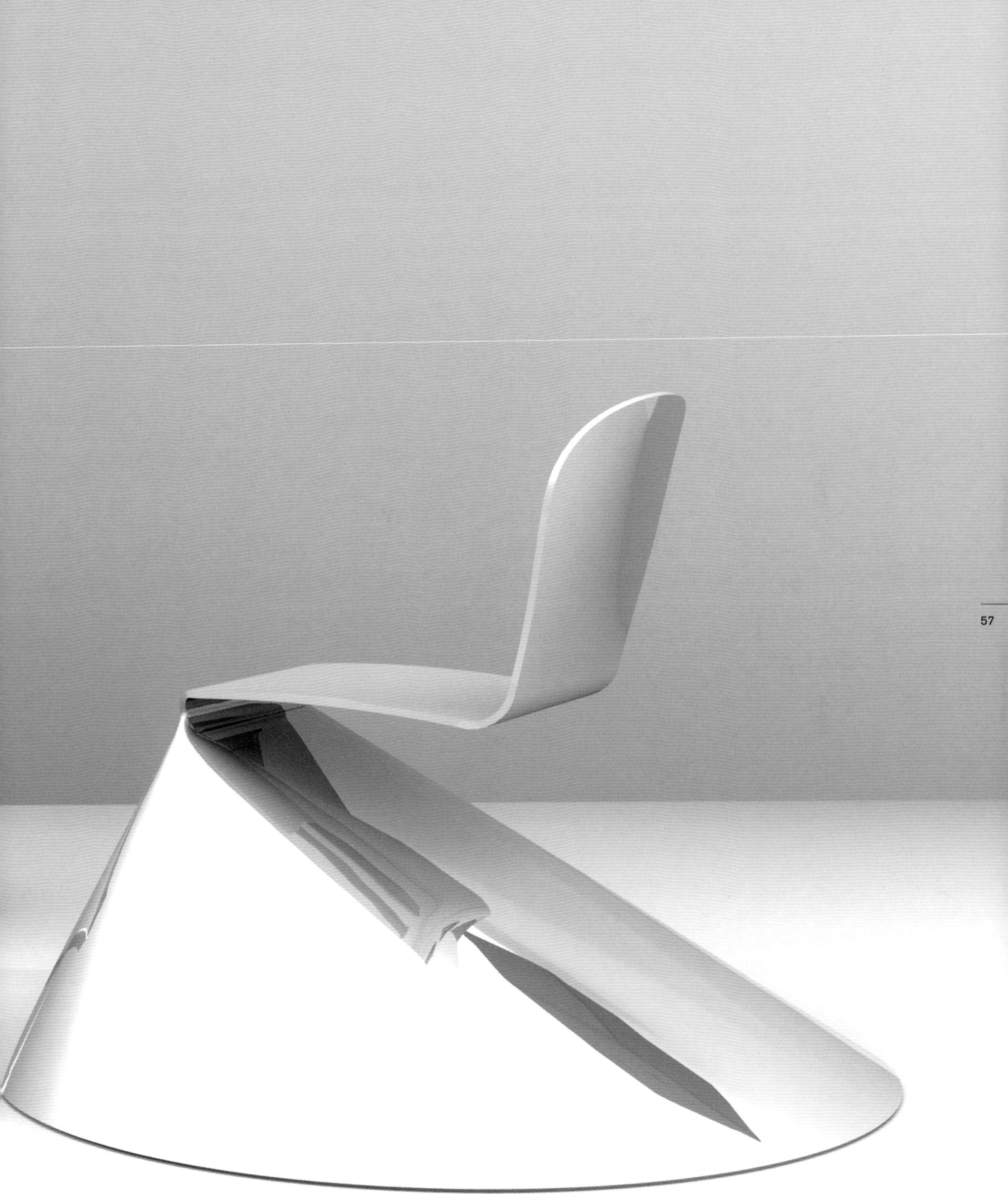

Archiduchaise Limited edition

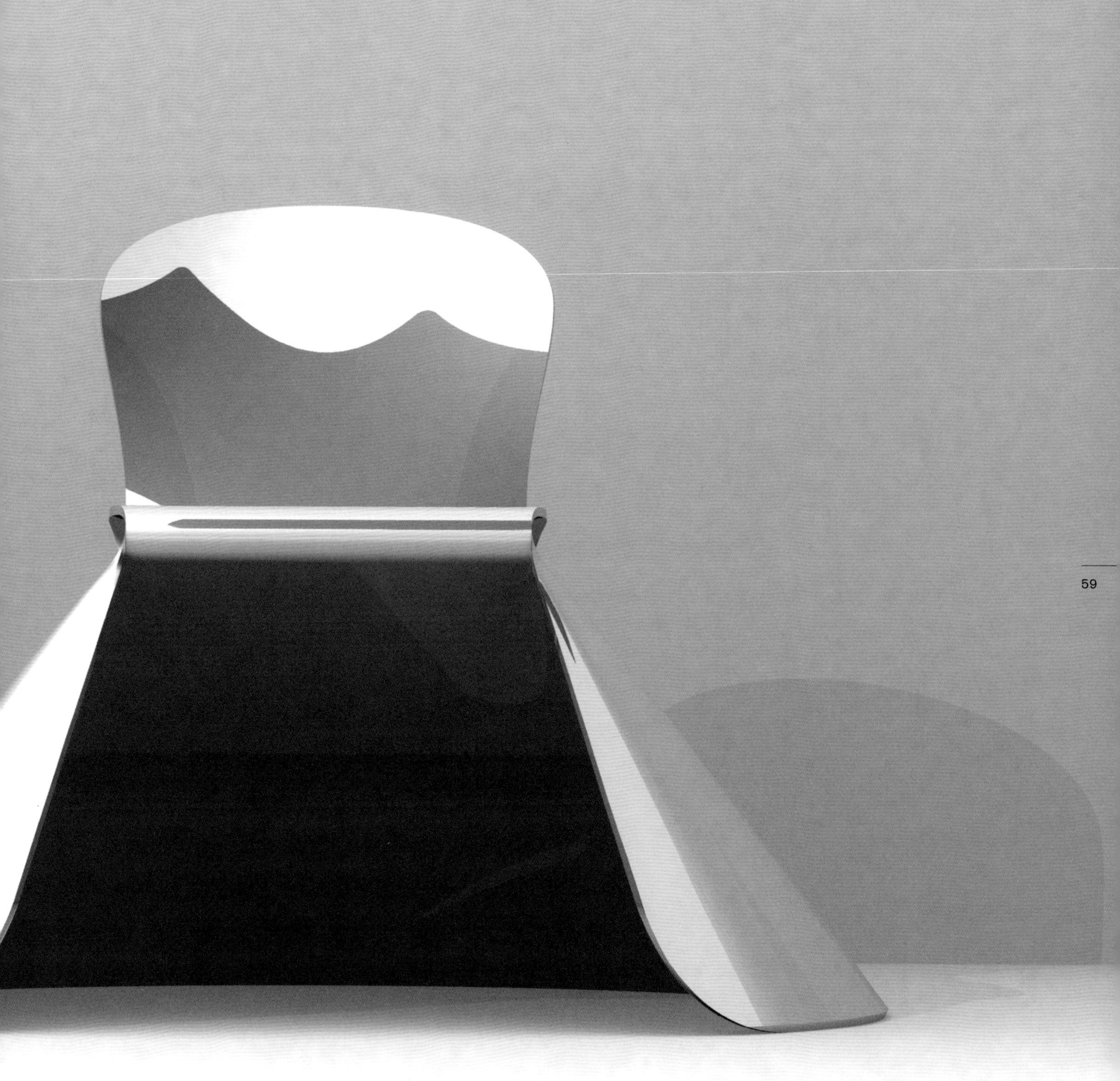

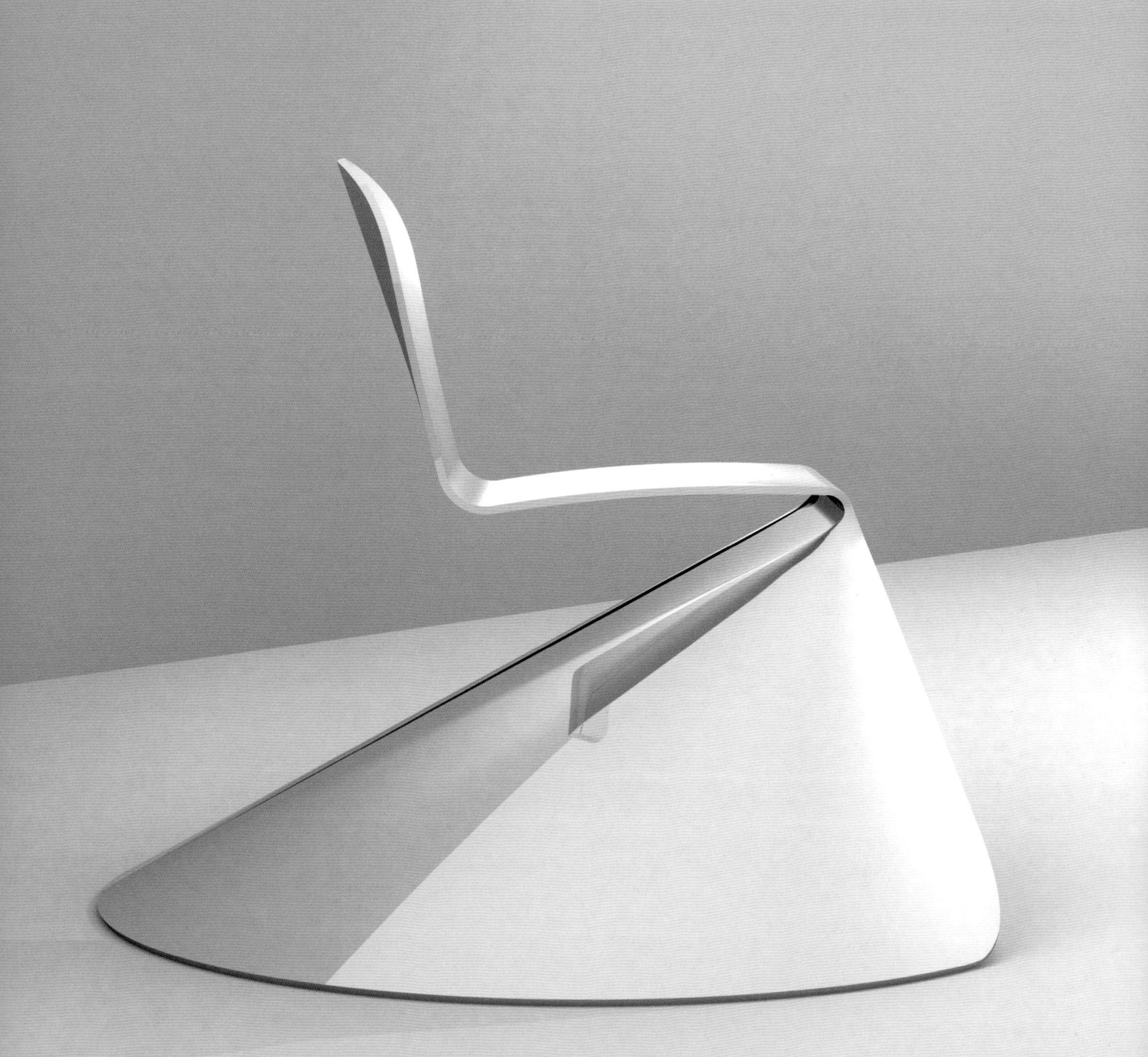

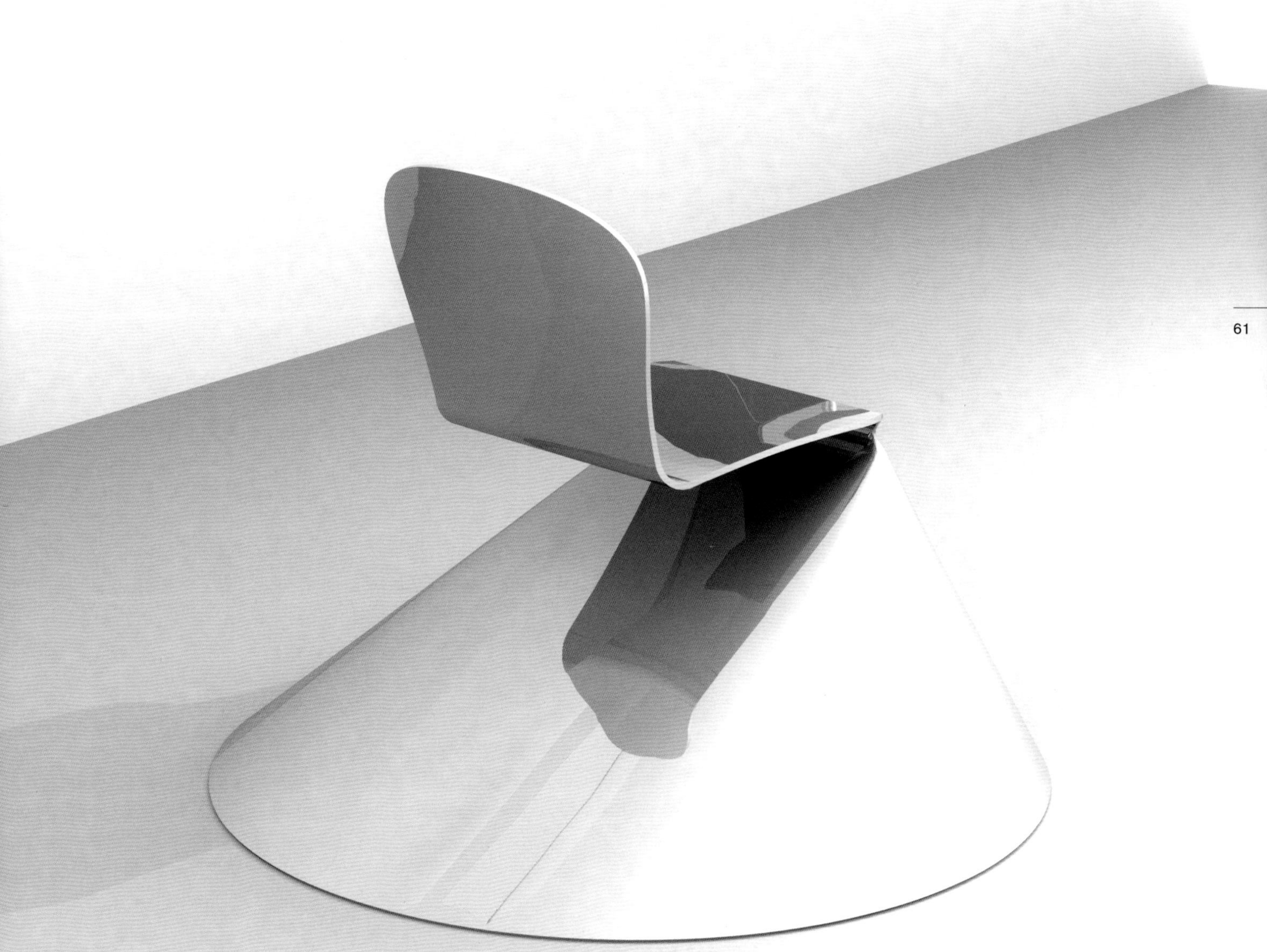

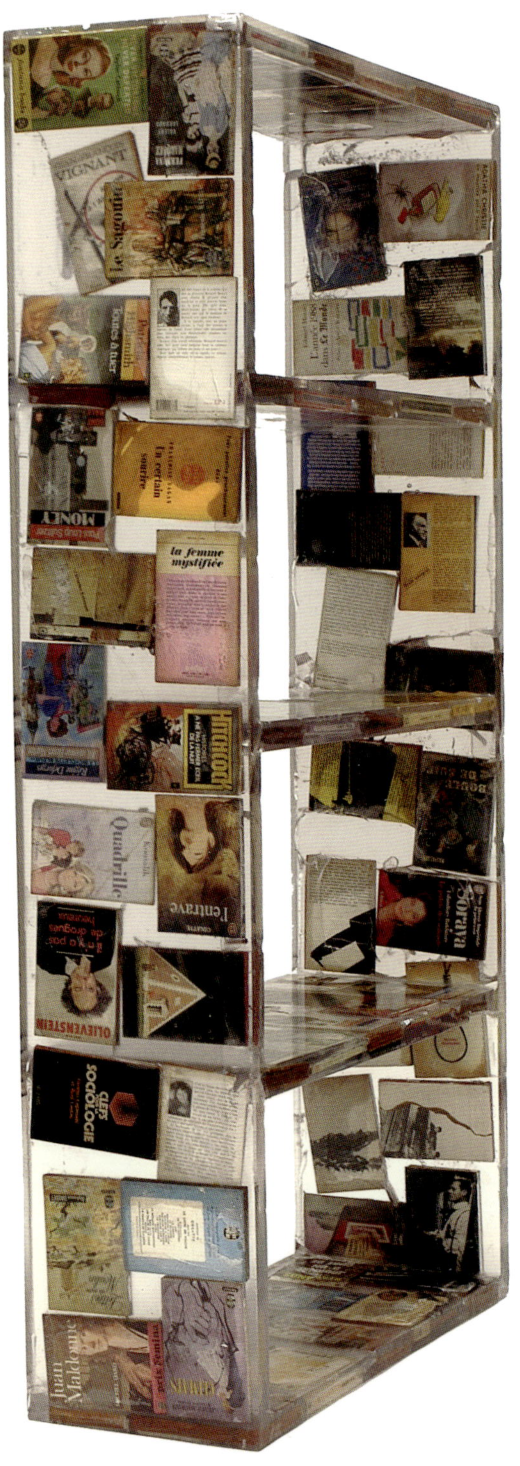

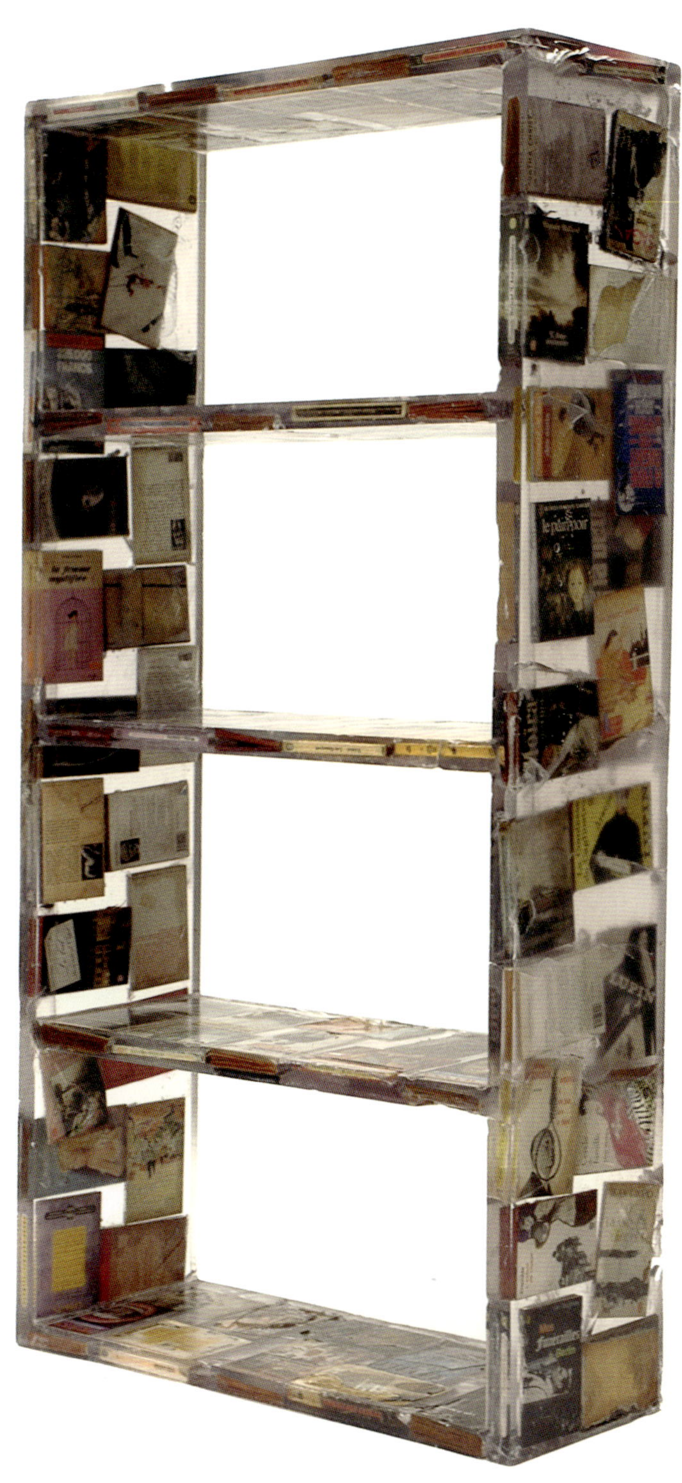

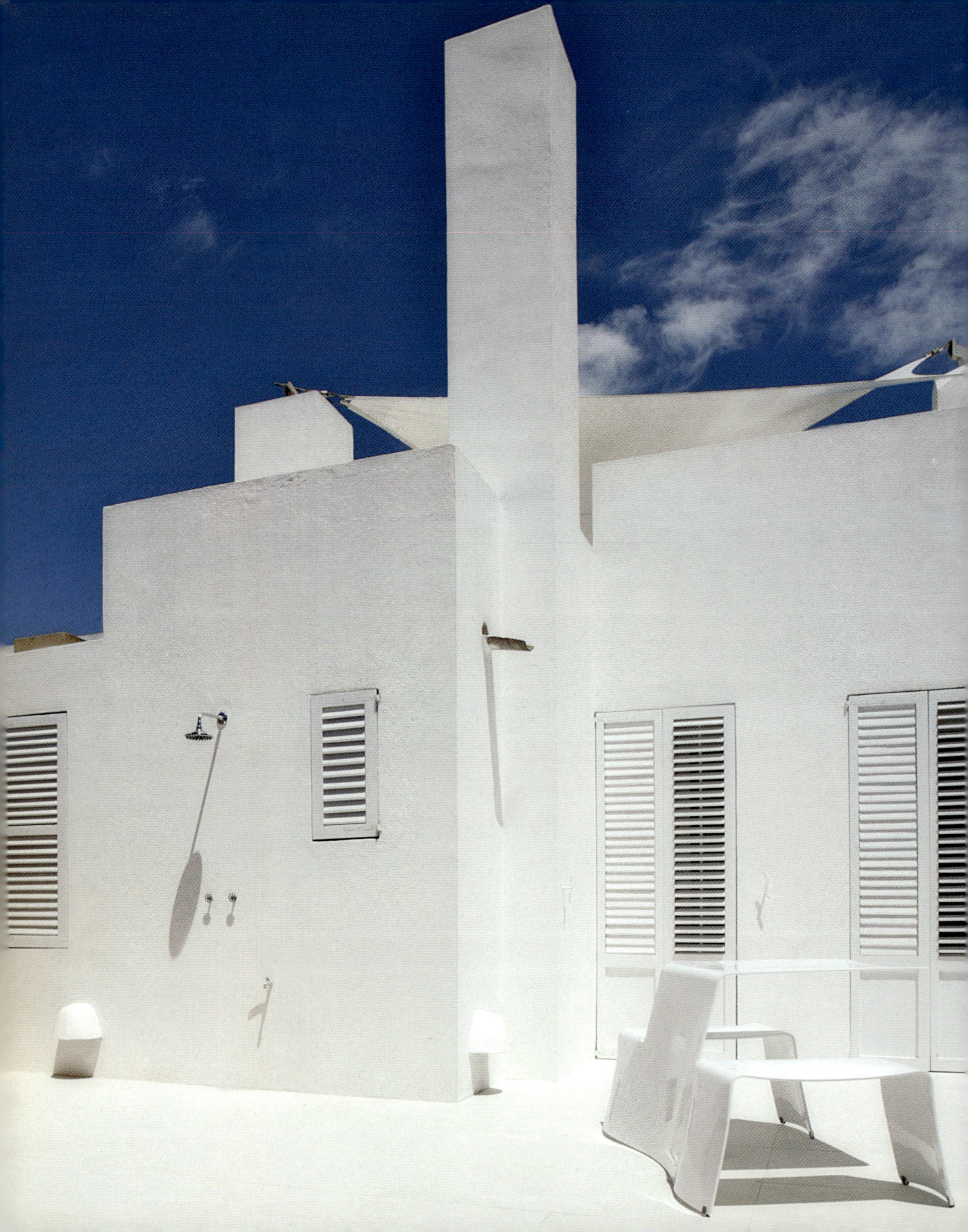

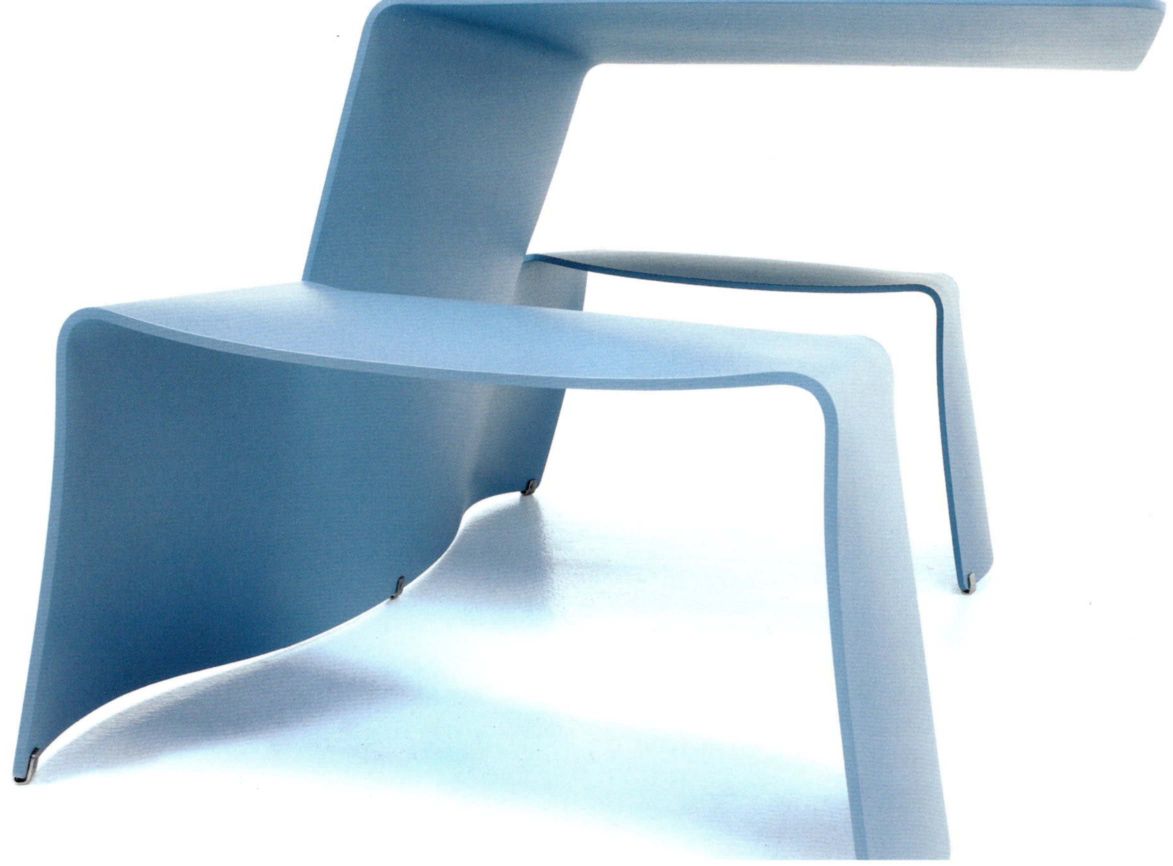

Xavier and I began our careers in the world of furniture design at the same time. He chose to work independently, while I wanted to gain some experience in the furniture industry before going solo. We had come across each other many years ago and had occasional contact over the years. In the meantime, we were both successfully working away at our craft.

I recognized an innovative and surprising folding technique in one of Xavier Lust's designs, 'Le Banc'. This technique, that he calls '(de)formation of surfaces', would be the perfect technical and aesthetic solution for the 'PicNik' table and chairs combo, which I started making earlier, around 2000. The first prototype, made of half of a standard plate, cut and folded into a table with two chairs, was not very rigid. Later versions did not do its original simplicity any justice. Both of us felt that design is about making good products, so Xavier was happy to collaborate on this project.

His plate distortion technique is surprisingly simple. Good designs stand out because they are simple, and the most obvious things are more often than not the most difficult to find. Although the reason for the process is purely mechanical – strengthening the thin material – it seems that the ergonomic and aesthetic qualities are, coincidentally also improved. I would call it sustainable design: pure, timeless and pared down.

However, this does not mean that it is easy to manufacture this product. Quite the contrary, an enormous amount of skill is needed when using conventional machinery. Thanks to the existing openness and cooperation between Xavier and the team of highly skilled experts, the production of the 'PicNik' was completed quickly.

The result is a design icon that became a significant piece in the evolution of the Extremis collection, and won various design awards. In addition, it has been included in many prestigious projects around the world, for example in the Tate Modern Museum in London.

Dirk Wynants, Extremis

Ongeveer gelijktijdig begonnen we onze carrière in de wereld van het meubeldesign. Xavier startte onmiddellijk als ontwerper in eigen beheer, ikzelf vond het beter om eerst wat ervaring op te doen in de meubelindustrie alvorens zelf iets op te zetten. In die context ontmoetten wij elkaar lang geleden voor het eerst en het contact bleef occasioneel bestaan. Intussen bouwden we beiden verder aan onze eigen weg, met succes.

Een innoverende en verrassende plooitechniek herkende ik in een ontwerp van Xavier Lust: 'Le Banc'. Deze techniek, die hij '(ver)vorming van oppervlakten' noemde, zou zonder twijfel zowel technisch als esthetisch de perfecte oplossing zijn voor 'PicNik', de tafel-en-stoelencombinatie die ik rond 2000 begon te ontwikkelen. Het eerste prototype had bijzonder weinig stijfheid. De latere versterkte versies die ik bedacht, deden afbreuk aan de originele eenvoud. Het maken van goede producten is voor ons beiden het enige waar het om gaat en Xavier was er dan ook dadelijk voor te vinden om dit product samen te tekenen.

Zijn plaatvervormende techniek is verrassend eenvoudig. Goede creaties zijn nog beter als ze eenvoudig zijn; het meest voor de hand liggende is vaak het moeilijkst te vinden. Hoewel de ingreep in de eerste plaats een puur mechanische reden heeft, namelijk het dunne materiaal meer sterkte geven, verbetert het tegelijkertijd en schijnbaar toevallig de ergonomische en esthetische kwaliteiten. Ik zou het een duurzame vormgeving durven noemen: zuiver, tijdloos, niets is overbodig.

Dit wil niet zeggen dat dit stuk op een eenvoudige manier te vervaardigen is. Het vereist bijzonder veel vakmanschap om dit met conventionele machines voor elkaar te krijgen. Door de reeds bestaande openheid en samenwerking tussen Xavier en zeer gespecialiseerde vakmensen kon de uiteindelijke realisatie dan ook snel ingevuld worden.

Het resultaat is een designicoon die een belangrijk stuk werd in de ontwikkeling van de Extremis-collectie, talrijke design awards kreeg en gebruikt werd in prestigieuze projecten wereldwijd, o.a. in het Tate Modern Museum in Londen.

Dirk Wynants, Extremis

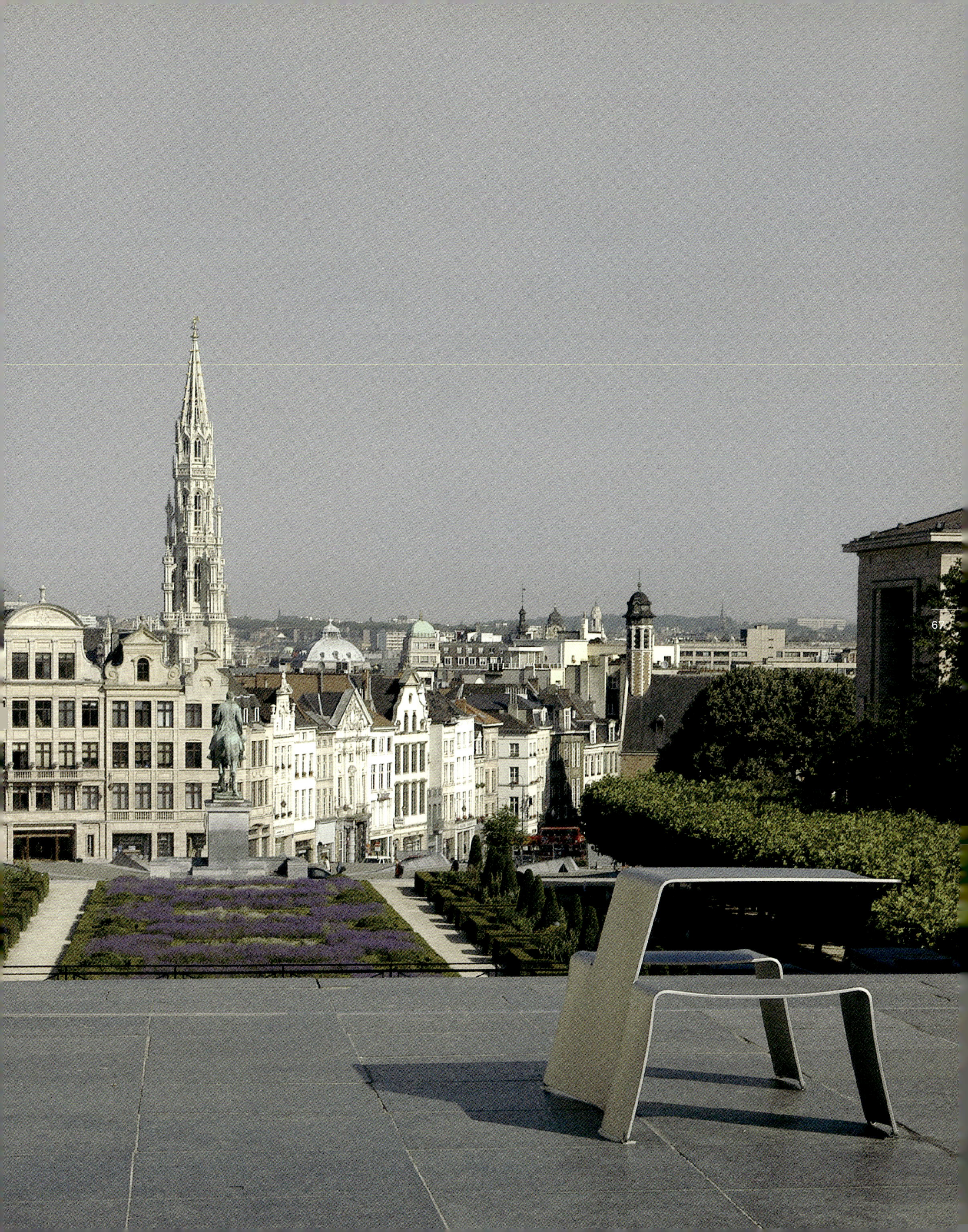

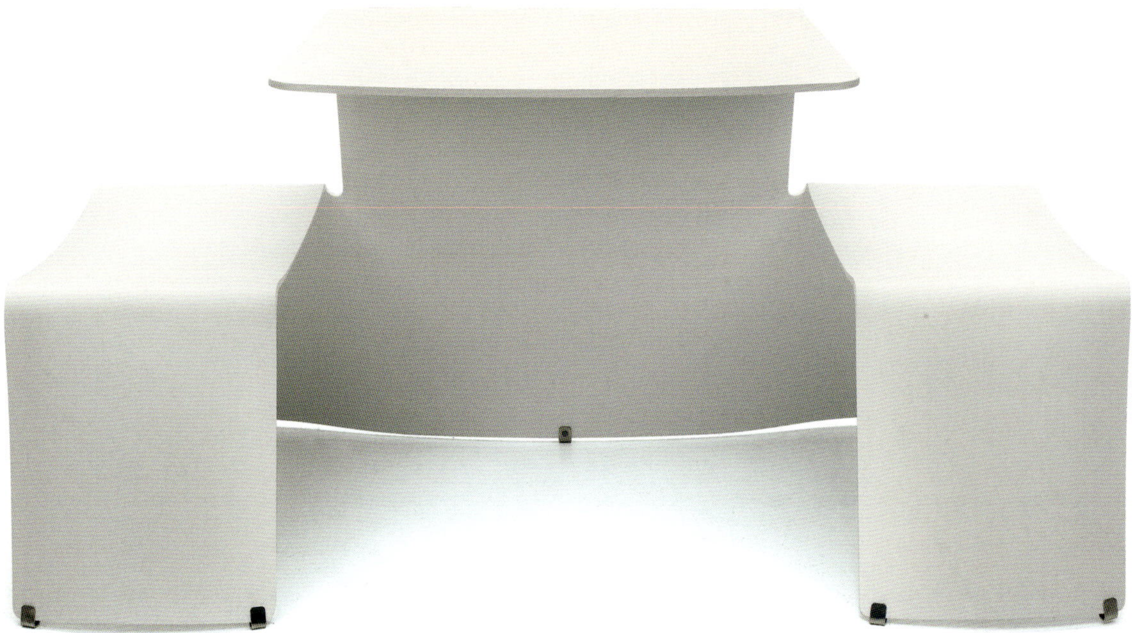

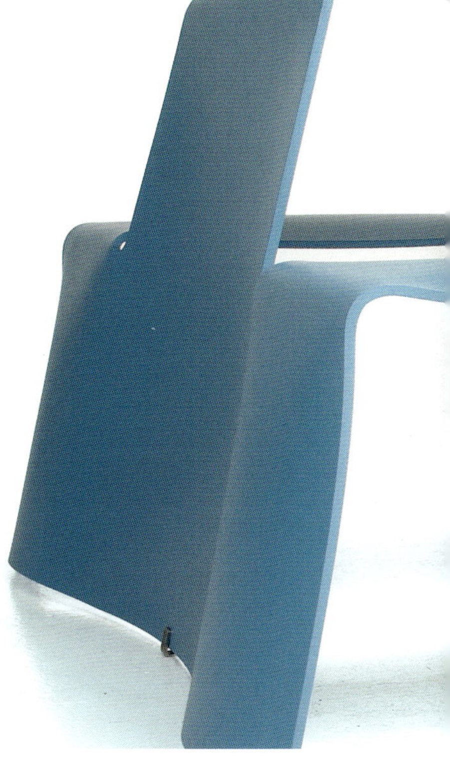

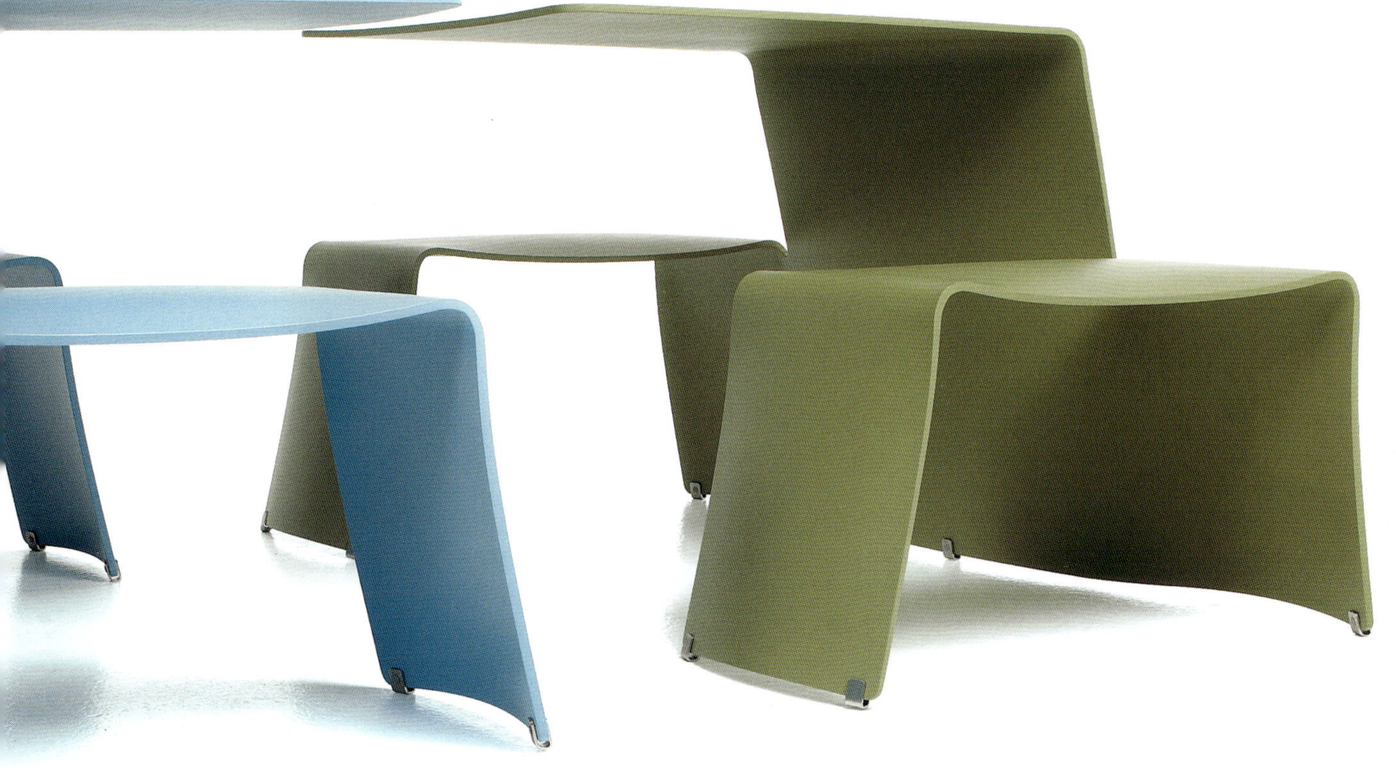

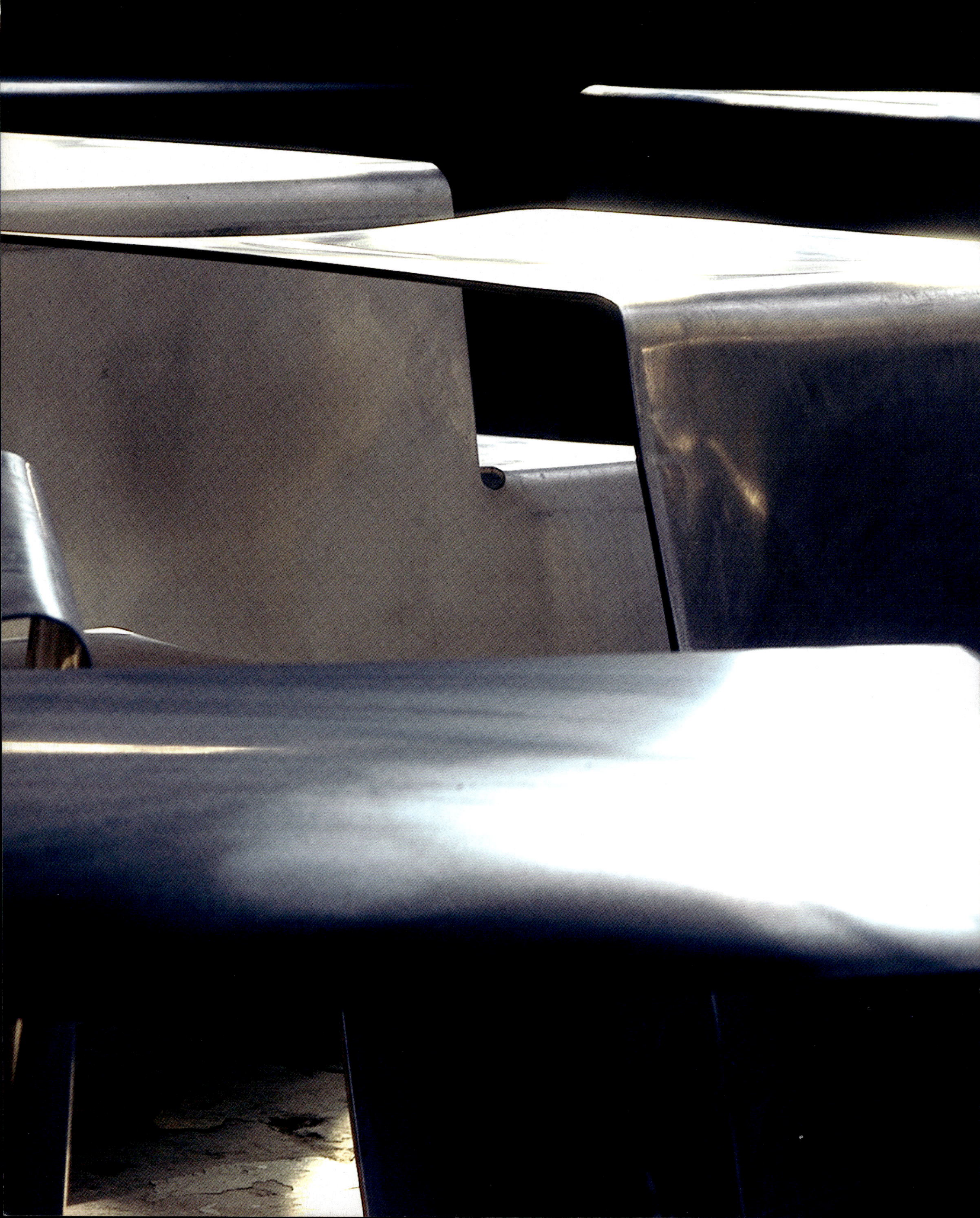

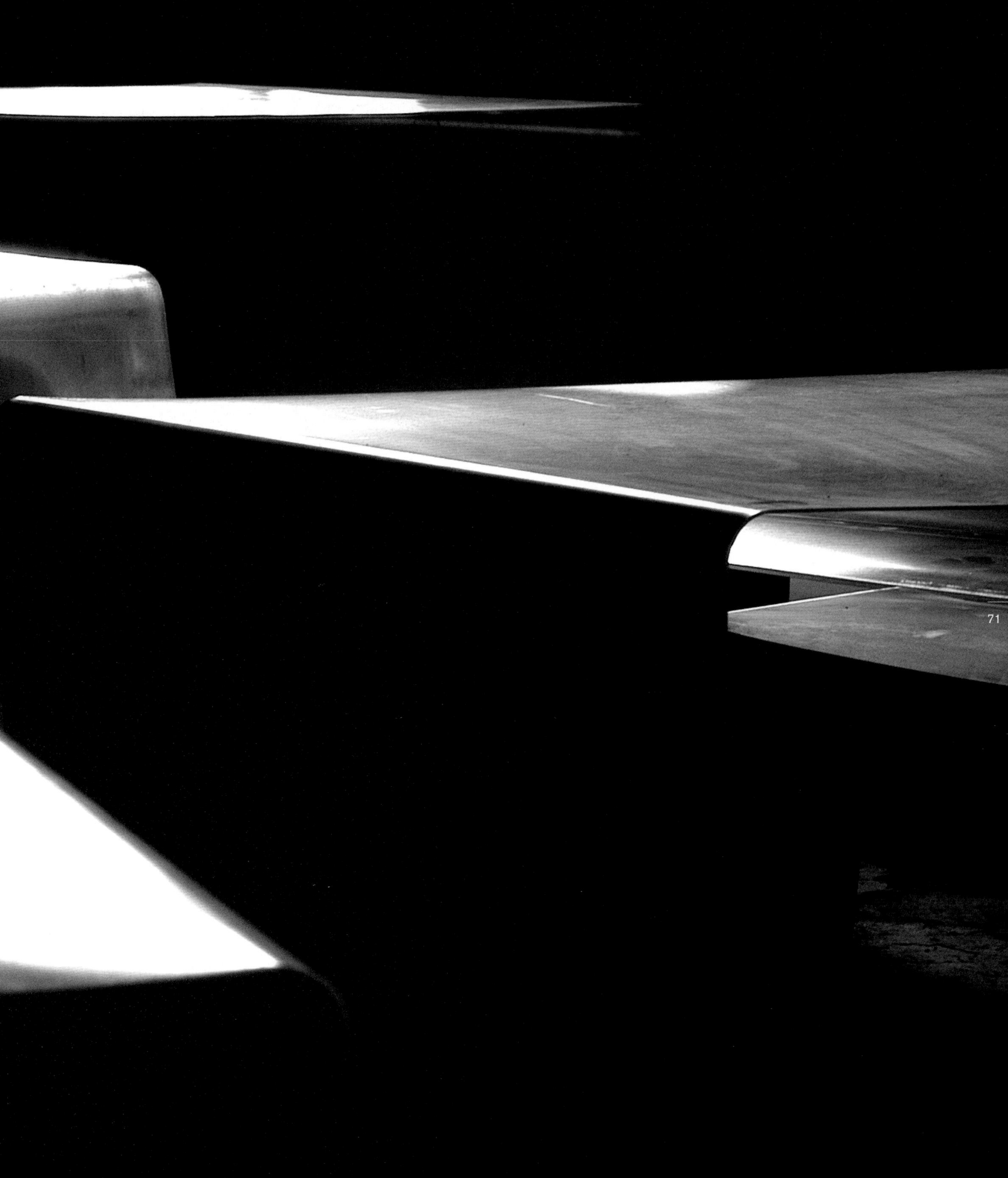

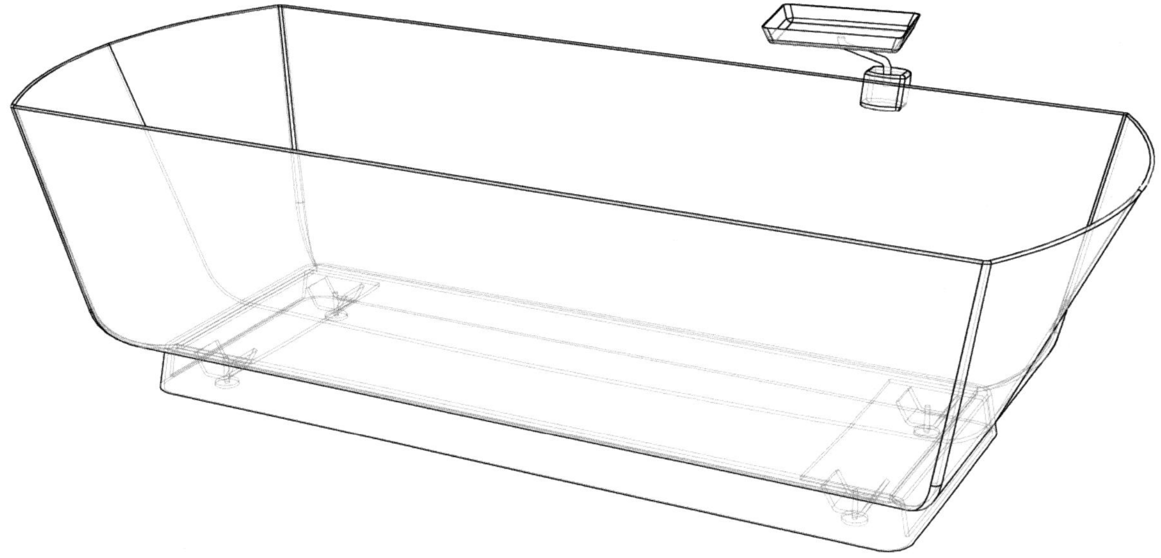

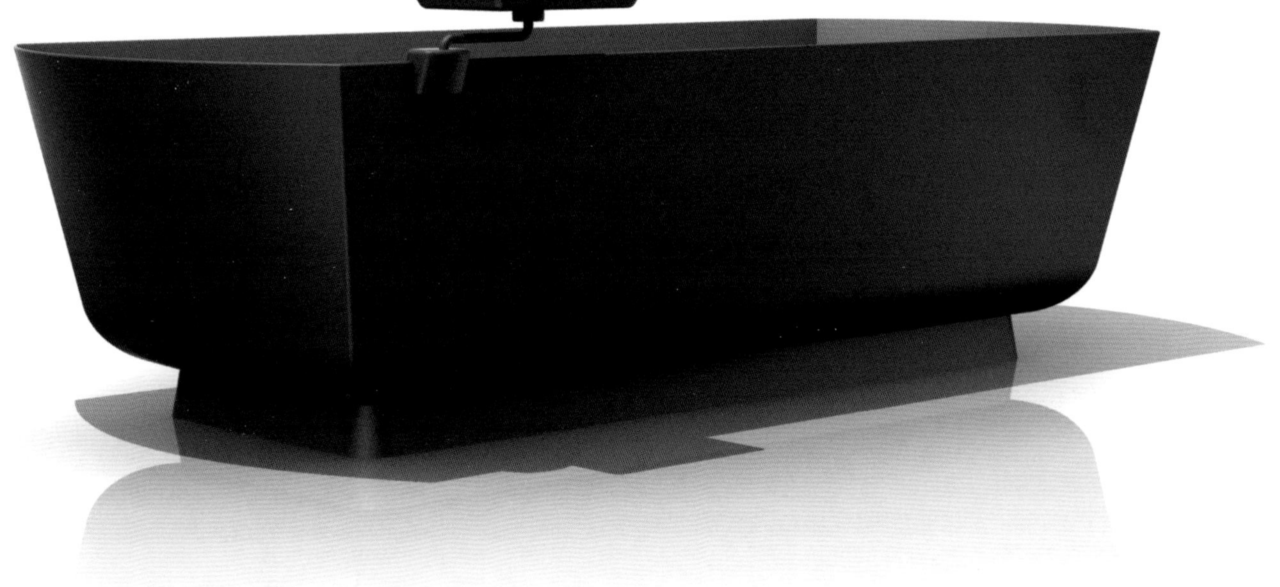

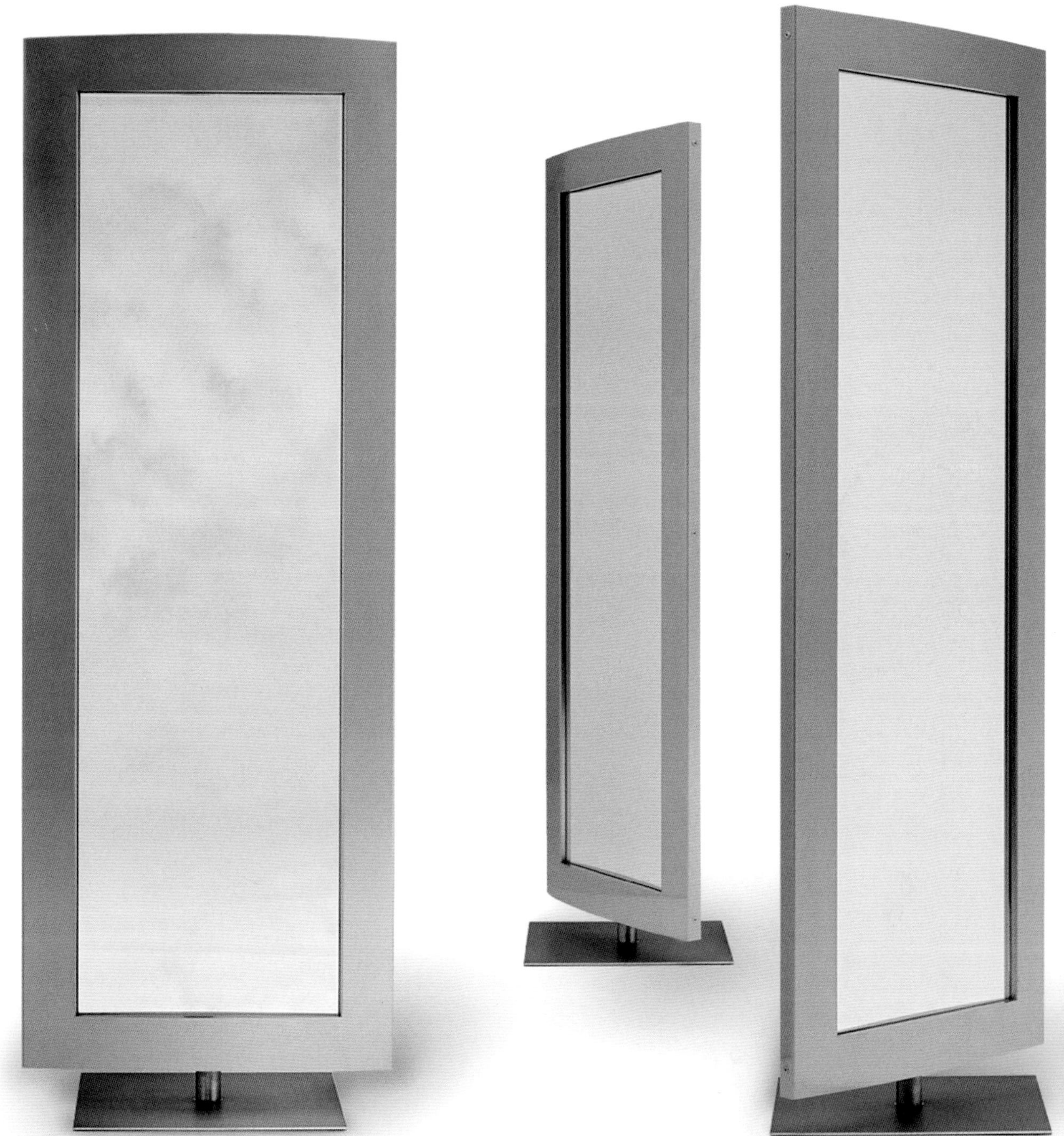

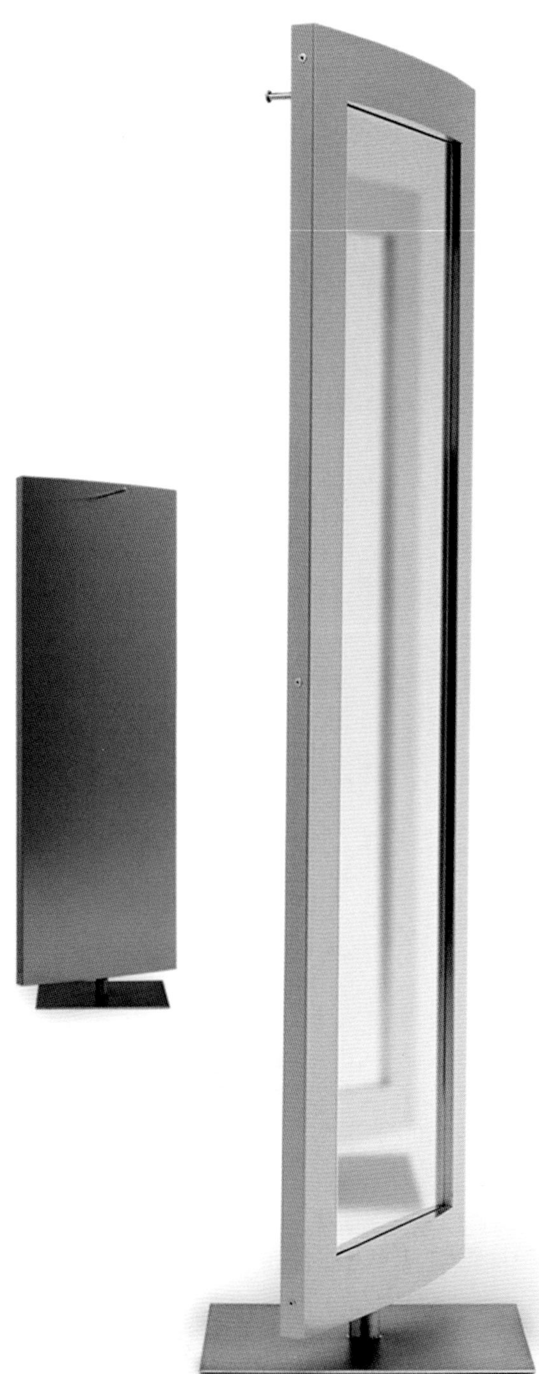
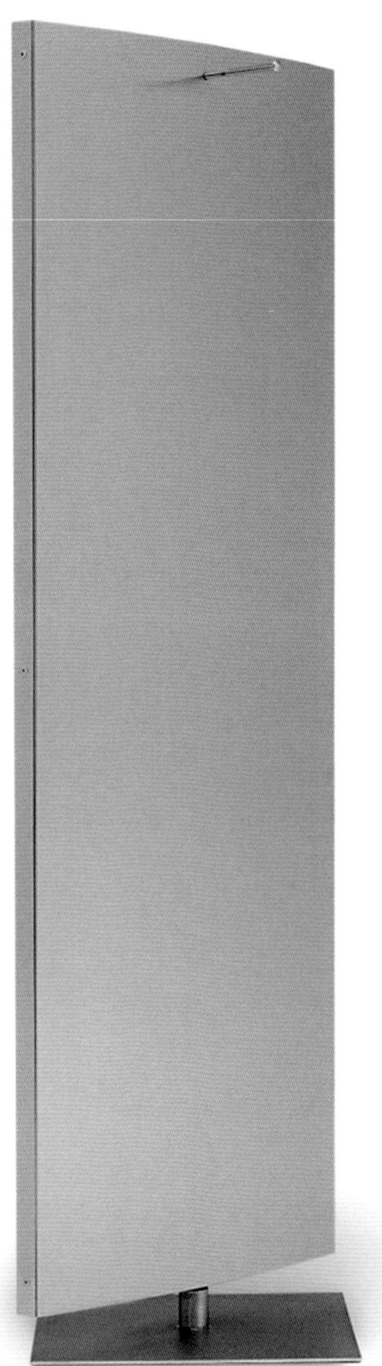

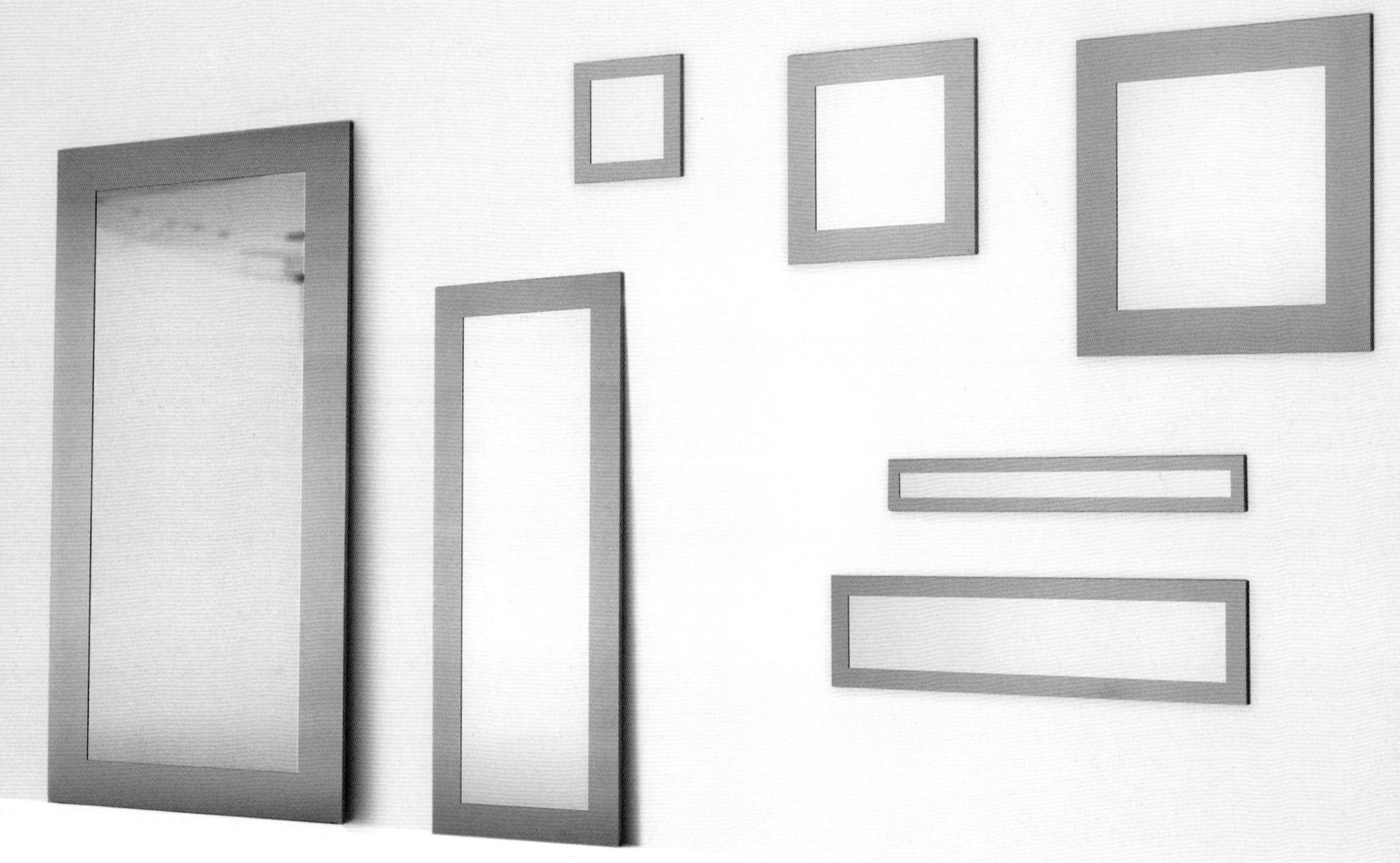

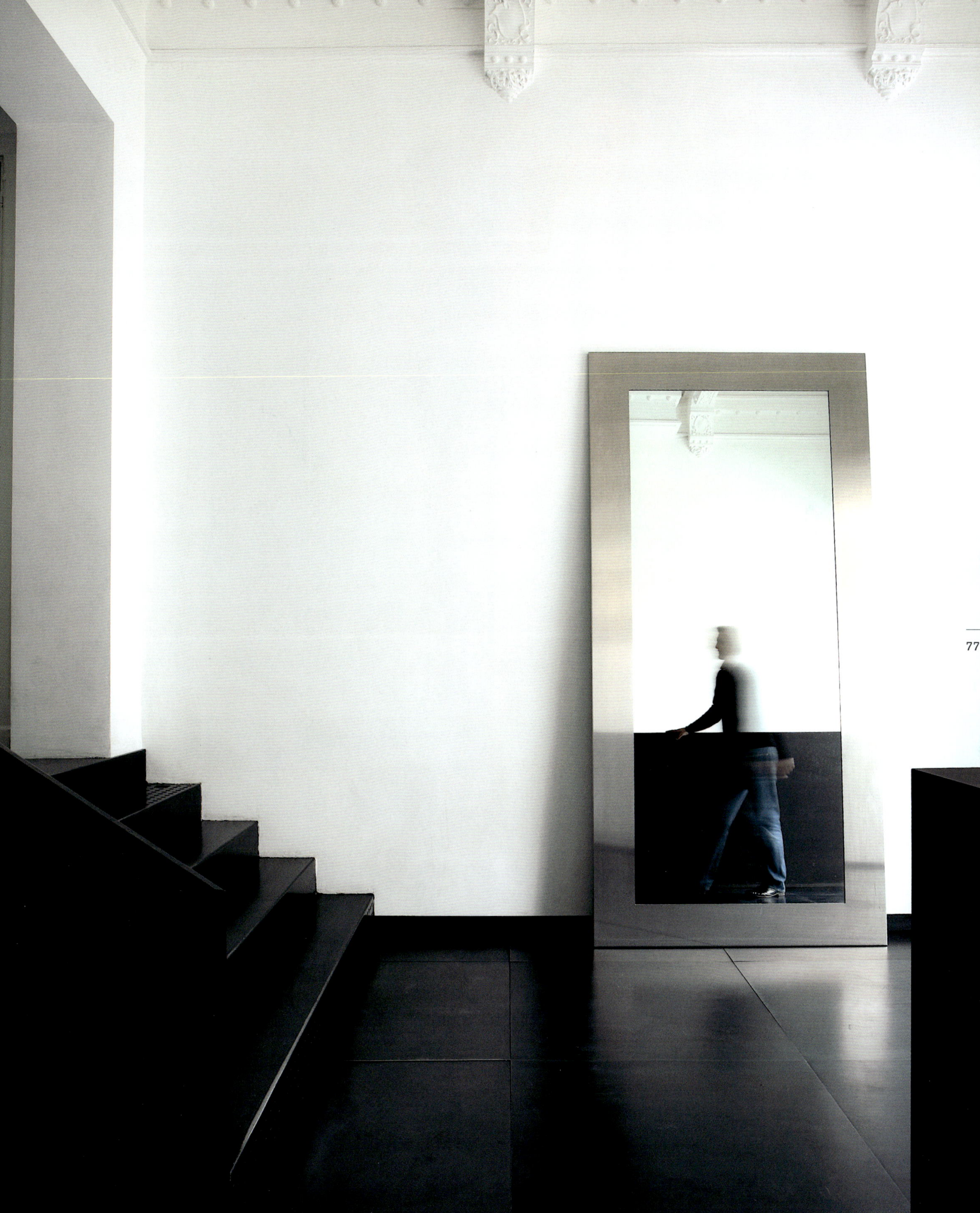

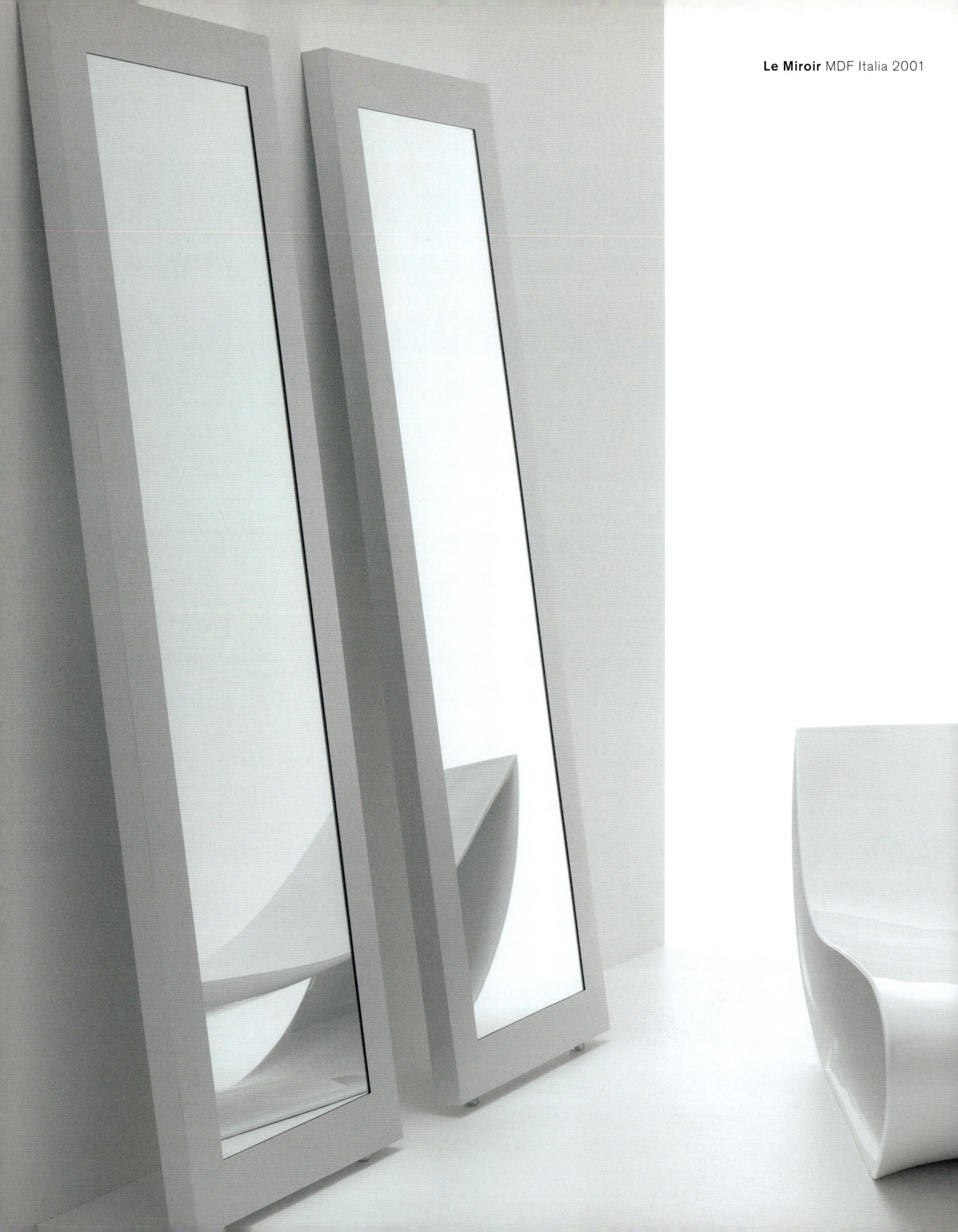

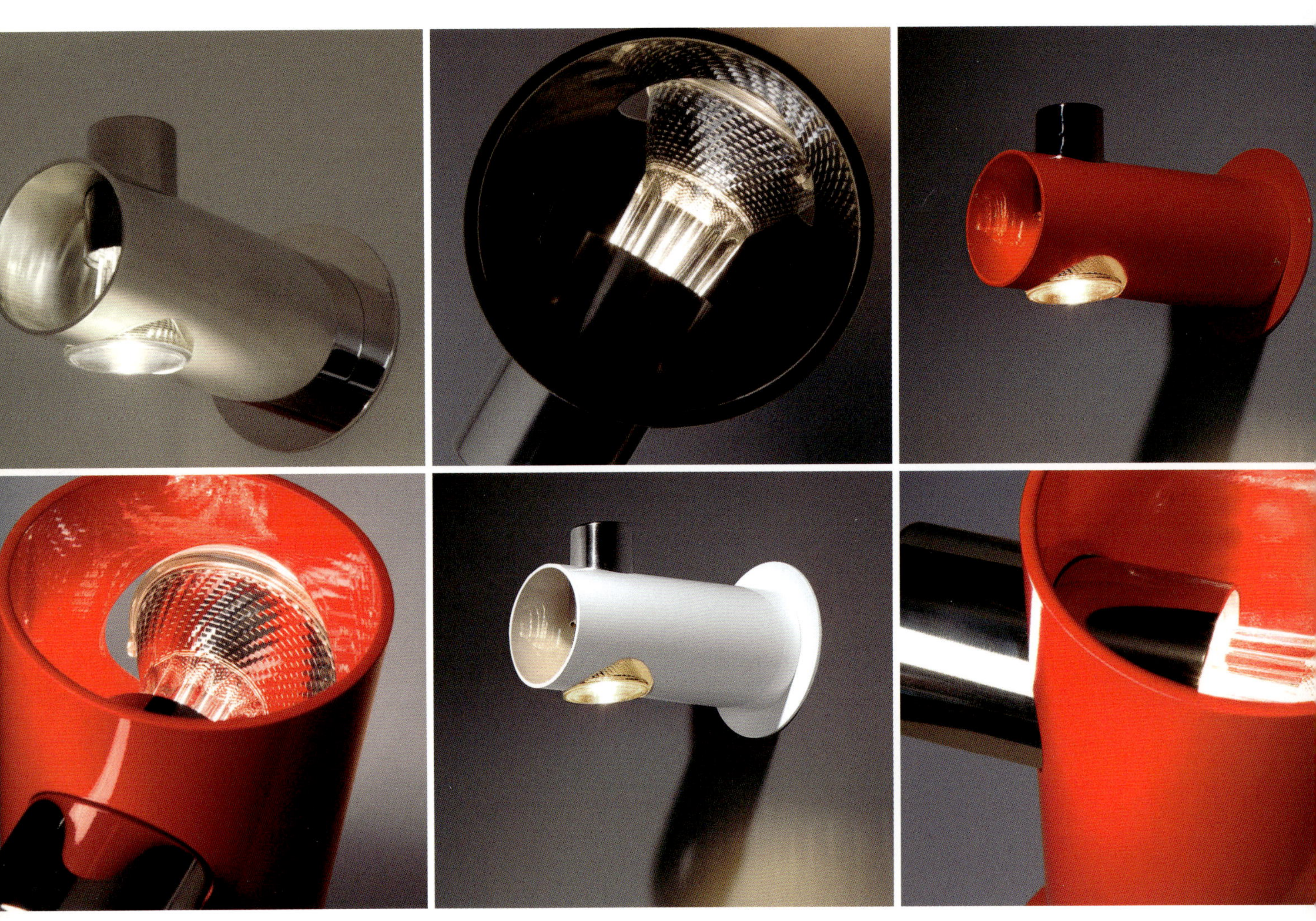

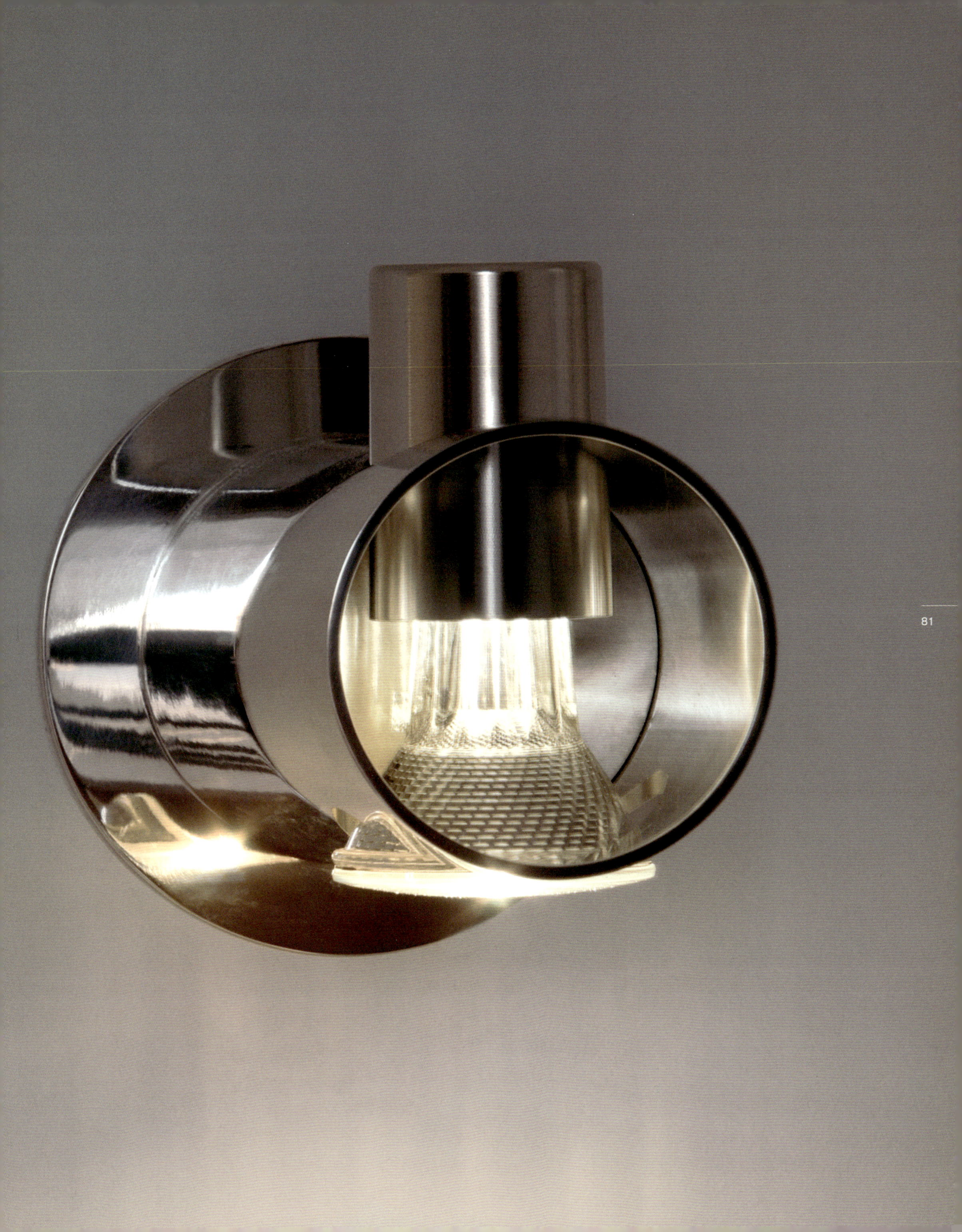

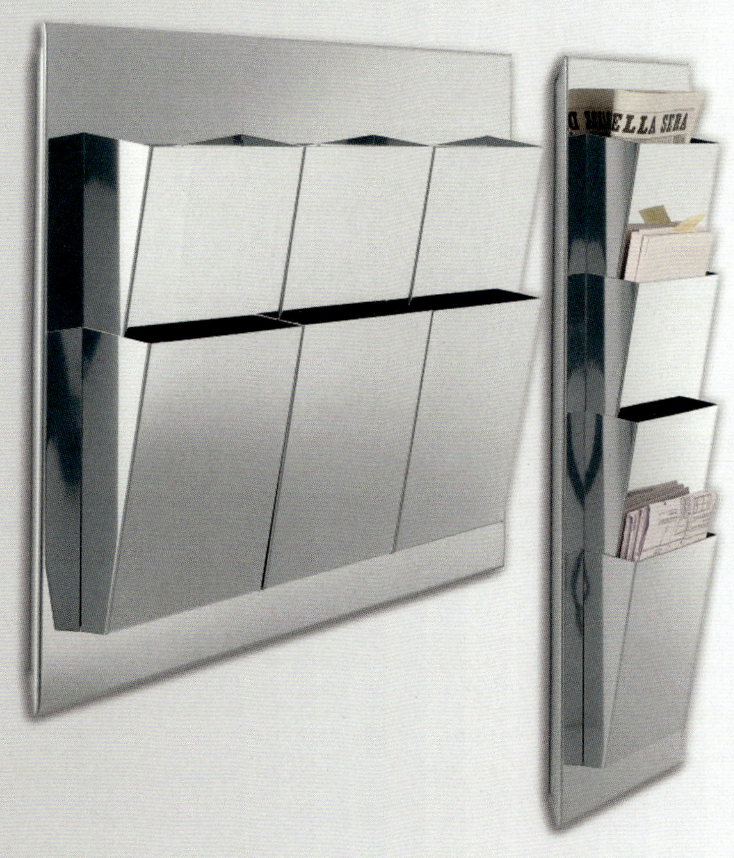

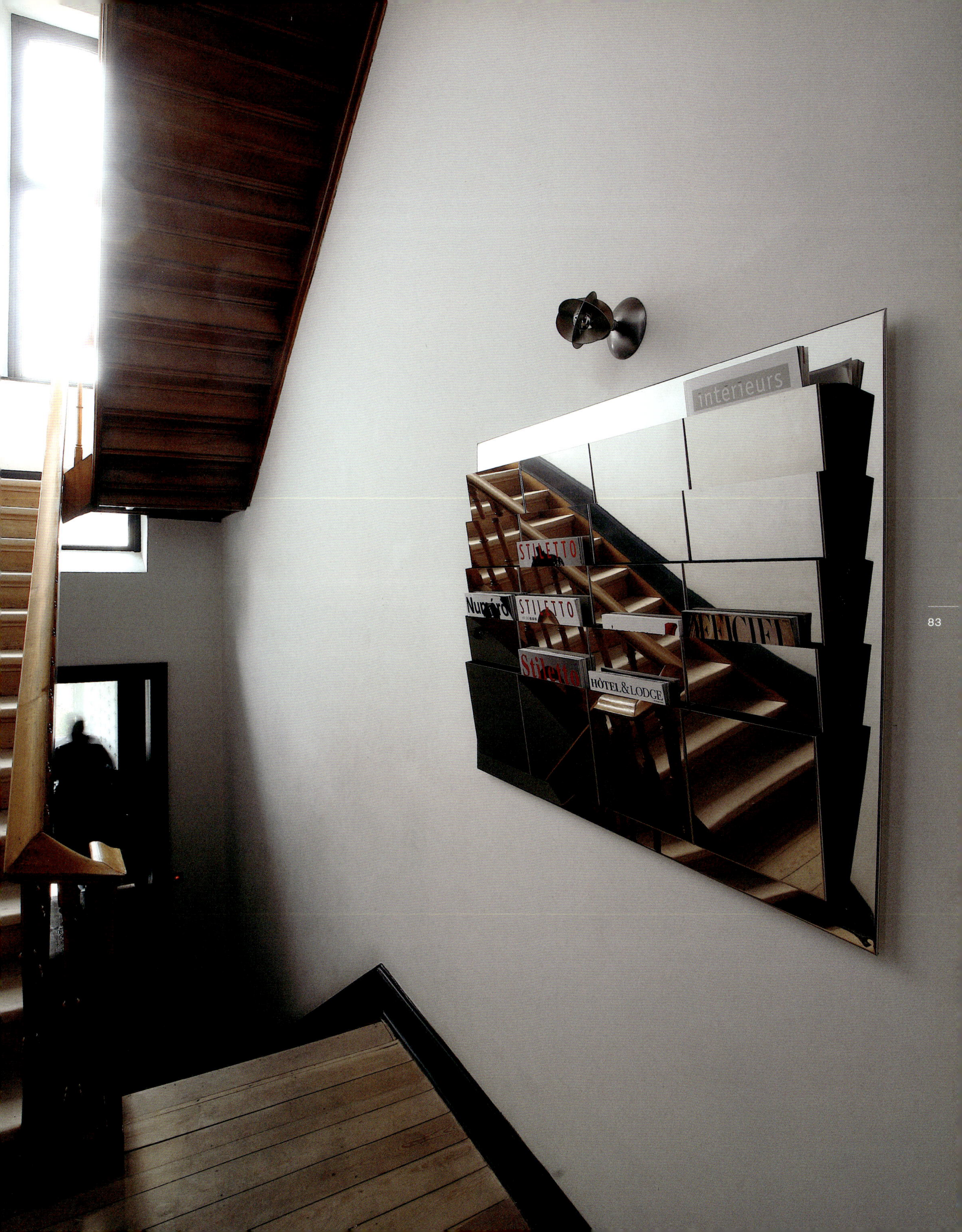
intérieurs
STILETTO
Numéro STILETTO
Stiletto
HÔTEL&LODGE
OFFICIEL

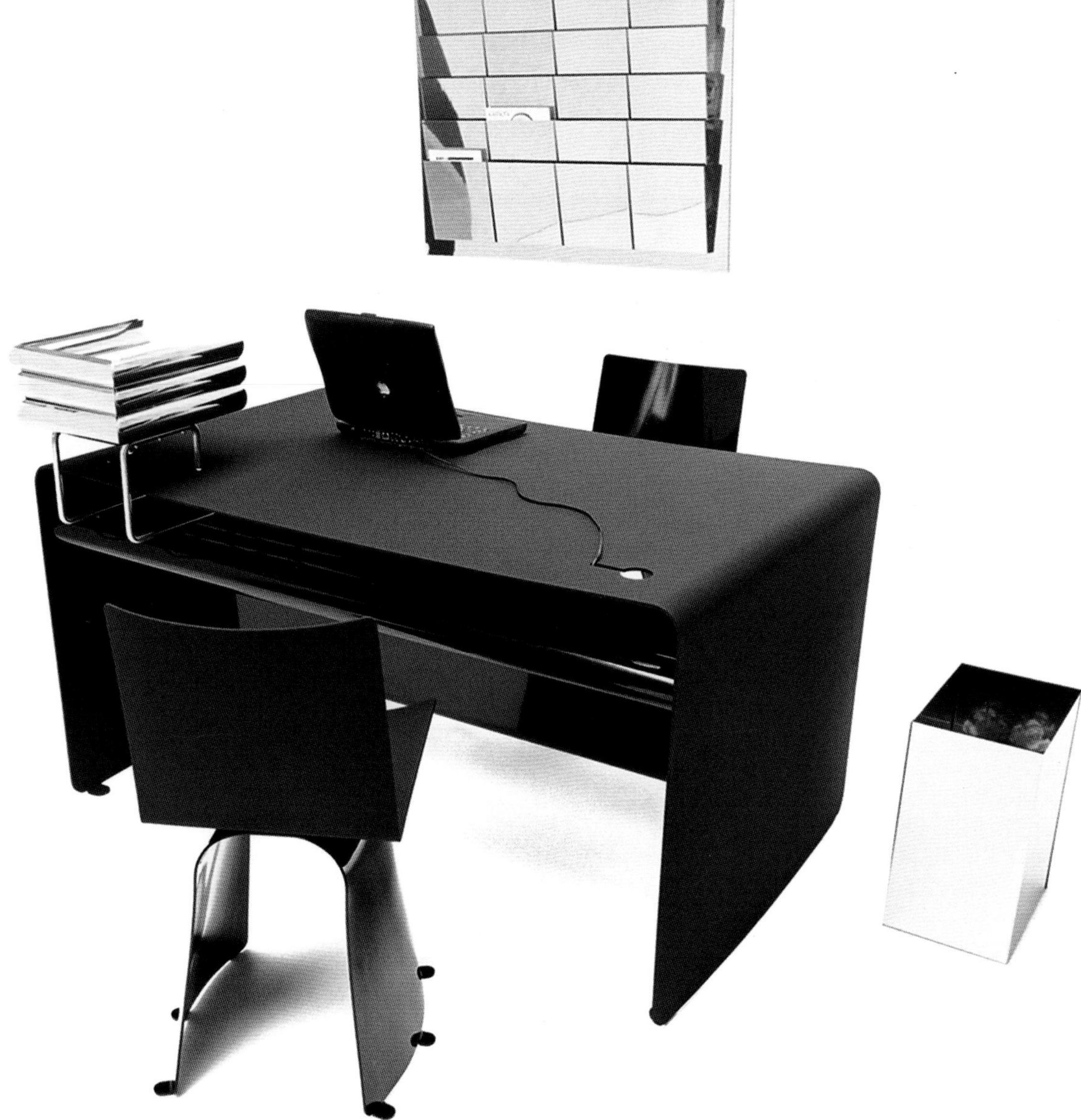

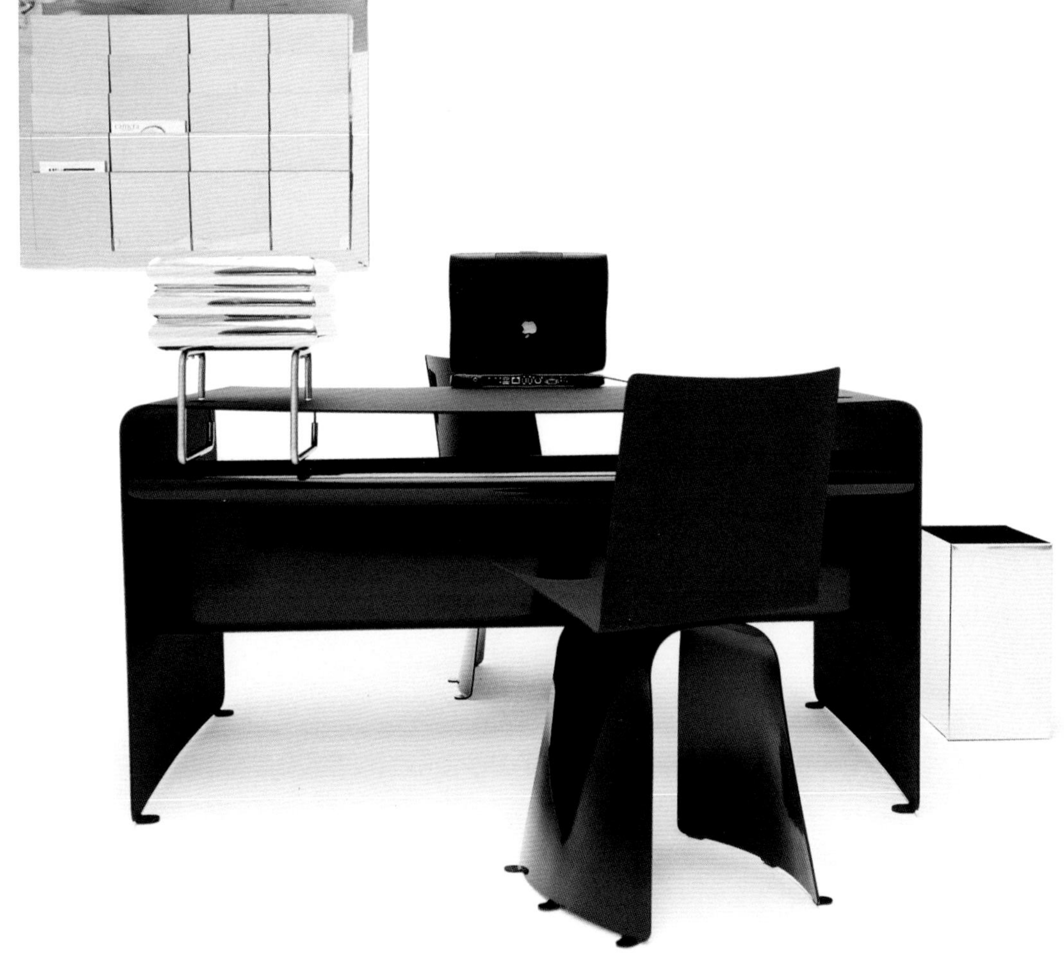

Xavier and I first met at the *Salone Satellite* in Milan in 2001. Mr. Fattorini from MDF had already taken the beautiful bench in folded aluminum, which I had found a very striking piece of work. But there was also 'Finder', a wall-mounted, stainless steel magazine rack that my mother had brought to my attention: an object that made a strong visual impact!'

Xavier's style is largely influenced by his extensive experience of industrial carpentry costs and techniques, which he gained first hand having worked in the field after completing his studies.

A highly unusual route for a young designer. His in-depth knowledge of industrial methods enabled Xavier to refine his stylistic code, thereby creating highly original forms through folds, scrolls and curves. These forms are perhaps imaginable in other materials, but certainly not in metal, and without resorting to welding.

During our initial collaboration, I discovered another side to Xavier's character: his determination to aim higher. I needed to use all my powers of persuasion to get him to accept the inclusion of 'Finder' in the Zoltan collection, which, at the time, had a smaller distribution. Xavier would rather have preferred his piece be included in the De Padova collection.

Xavier wins you over by his enthusiasm and his manner: determined, yet full of likeable human qualities.

Luca De Padova, Zoltan / De Padova

Con Xavier ci siamo incontrati la prima volta al Salone Satellite a Milano nel 2001. Il Signor Fattorini della MDF aveva già preso la bellissima panca di alluminio piegato che aveva molto colpito la mia attenzione. C'era però anche un portariviste in acciaio inossidabile appeso al muro che mi era stato segnalato da mia madre; un complemento di un certo impatto visivo!

Lo stile di Xavier derivava tutto dalla sua peculiare esperienza delle tecniche e dei costi industriali di carpenteria che si era fatto sul campo dopo gli studi e che era un percorso piuttosto inusuale per un giovane designer. La conoscenza approfondita della pratica gli ha permesso di affinare il suo codice stilistico, dando vita a forme inaspettate fatte di pieghe, volute, curve immaginabili forse su altri materiali ma non sui metalli; e ovviamente senza ricorrere alla saldatura. Dalle nostre iniziali relazioni di collaborazione ho poi percepito un'altra caratteristica di Xavier, la sua tenacia nel puntare in alto. In effetti ho dovuto usare tutte le mie doti di convincimento per fargli accettare l'inserimento del 'Finder' nella collezione Zoltan che, a quel tempo, aveva una distribuzione molto più ridotta, mentre Xavier avrebbe preferito fosse inserito nella collezione De Padova.

Xavier è convincente anche per il suo entusiasmo e il suo modo determinato ma pieno di umana simpatia.

Luca De Padova, Zoltan / De Padova

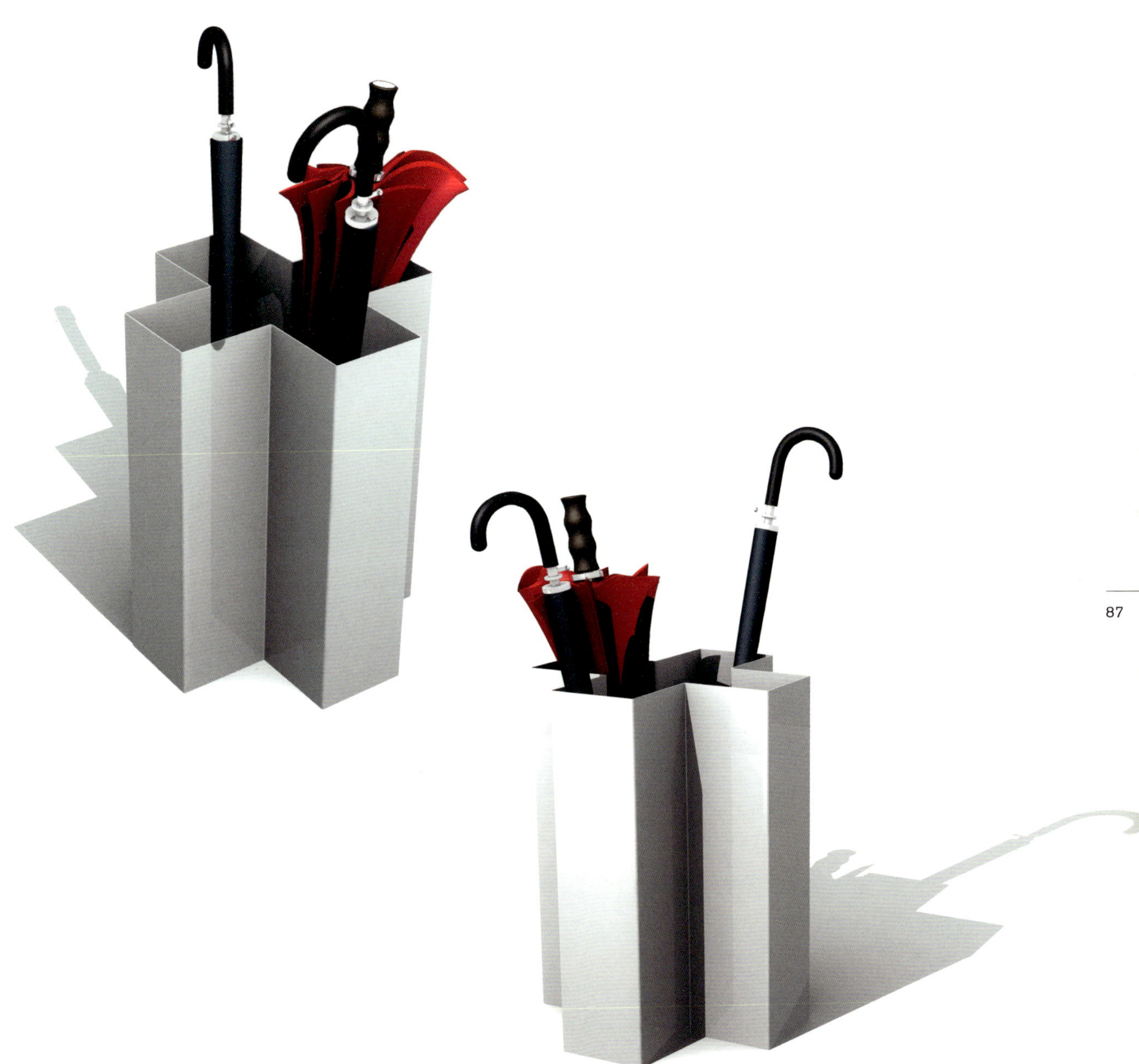

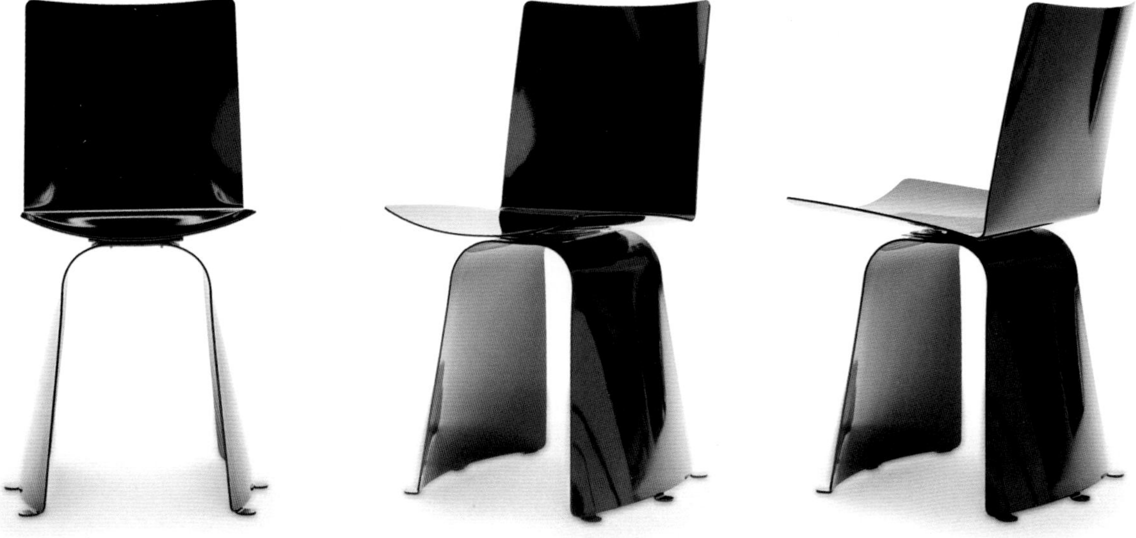

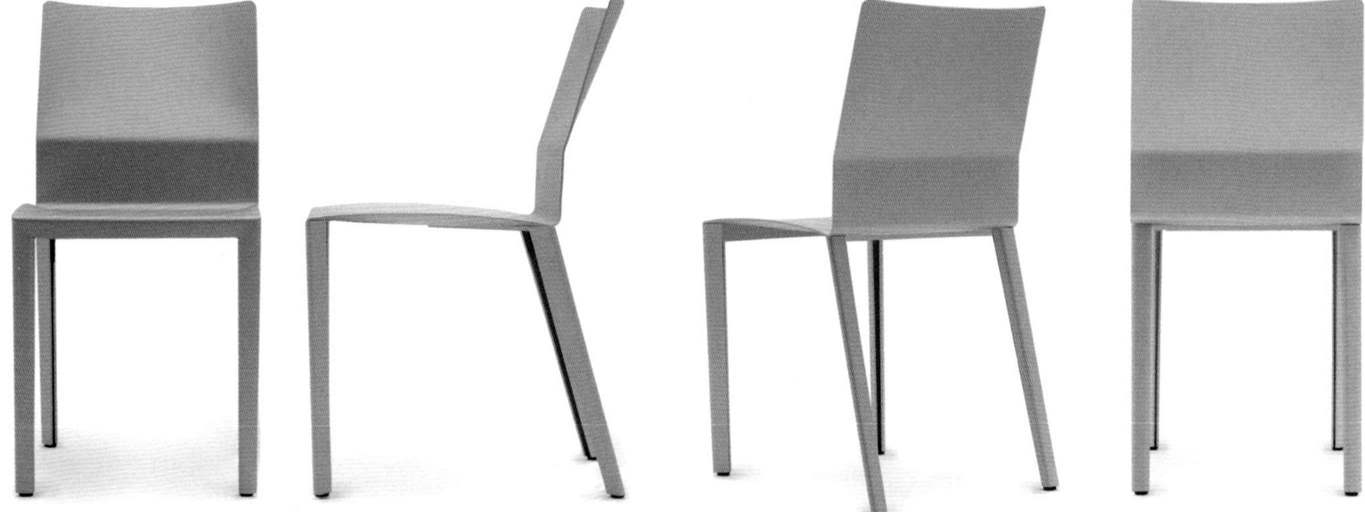

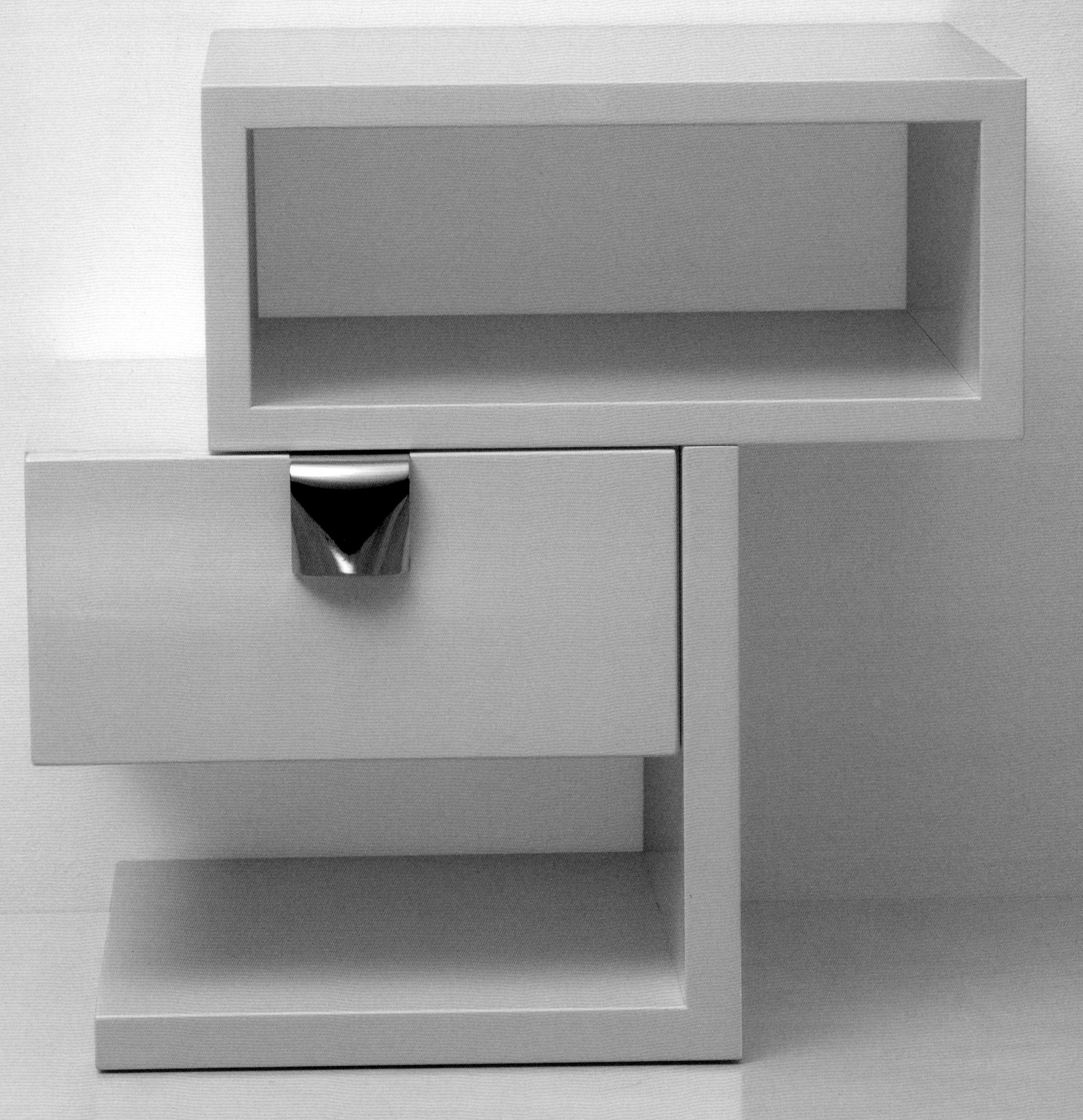

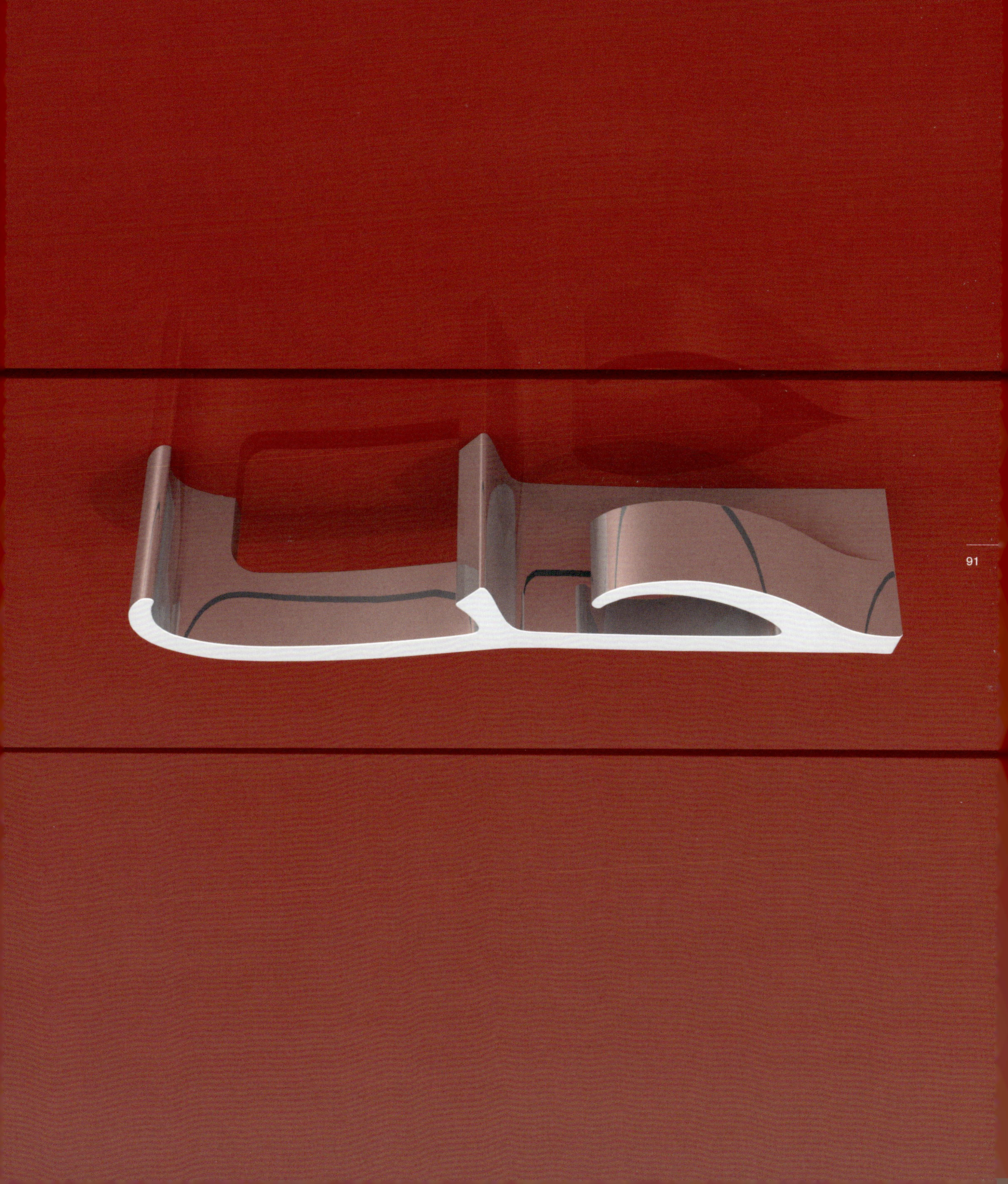

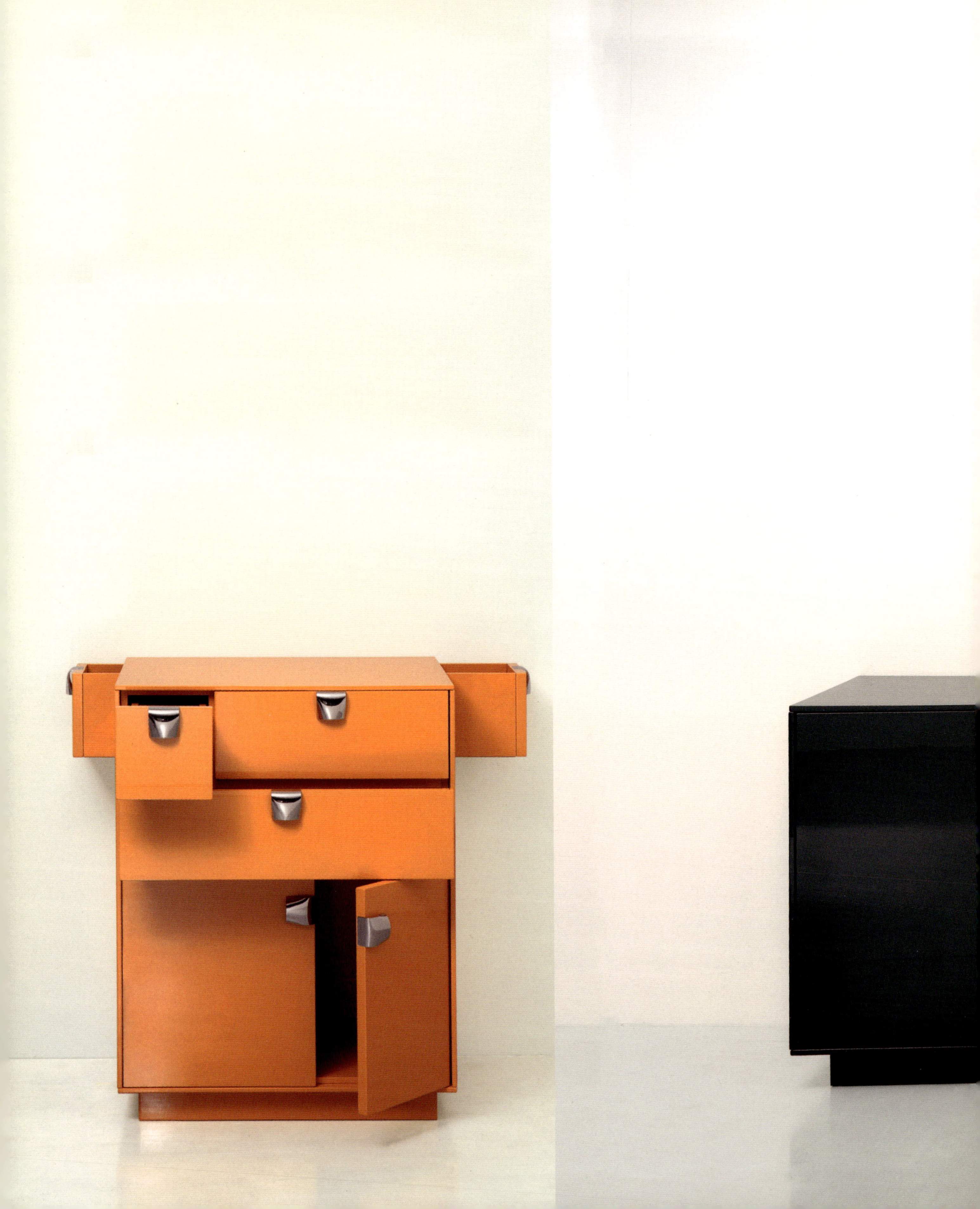

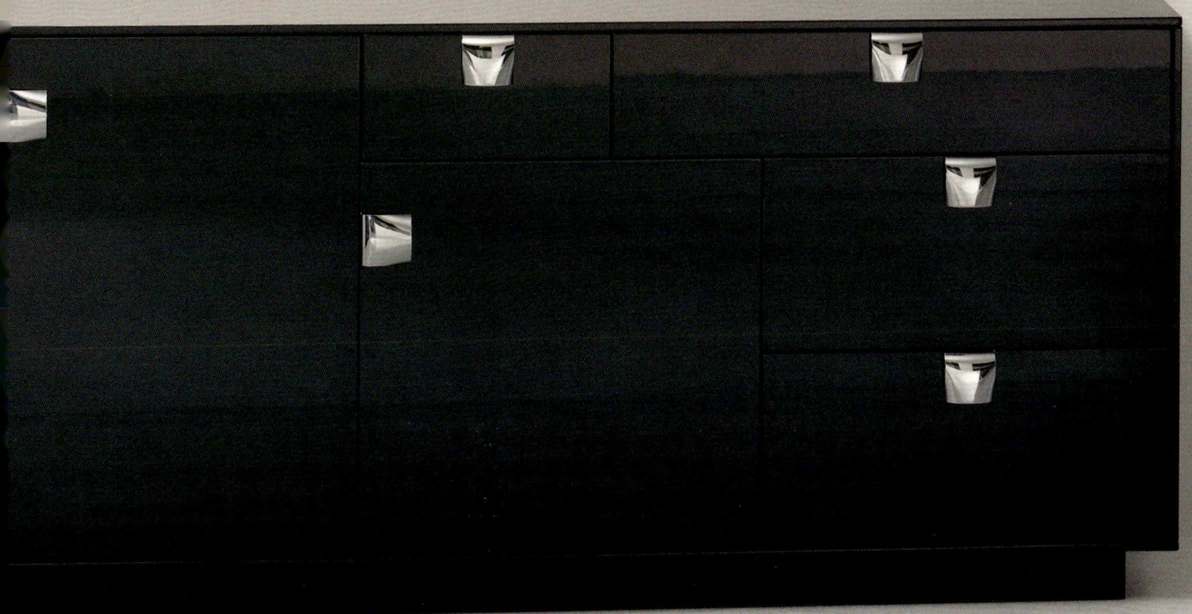

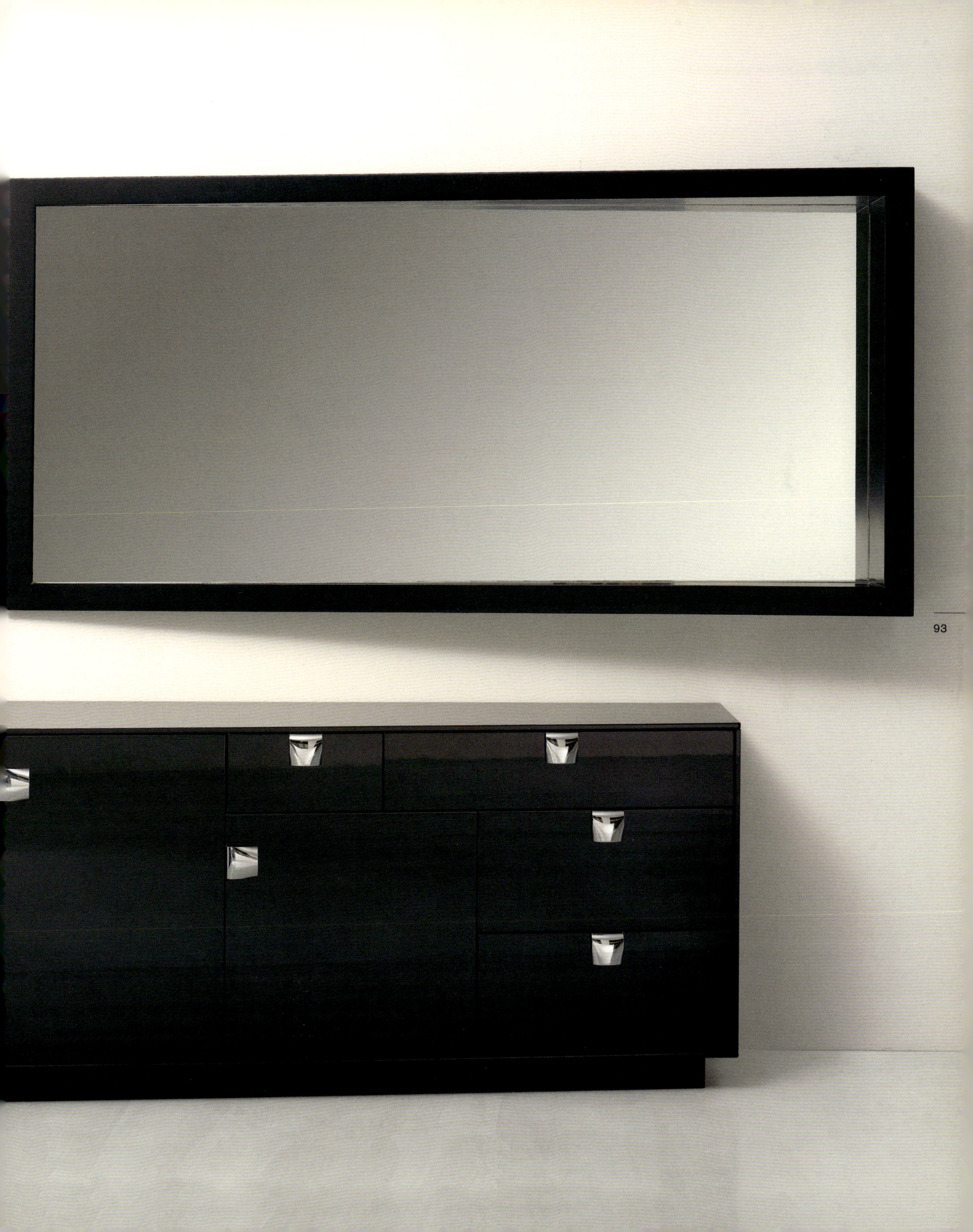

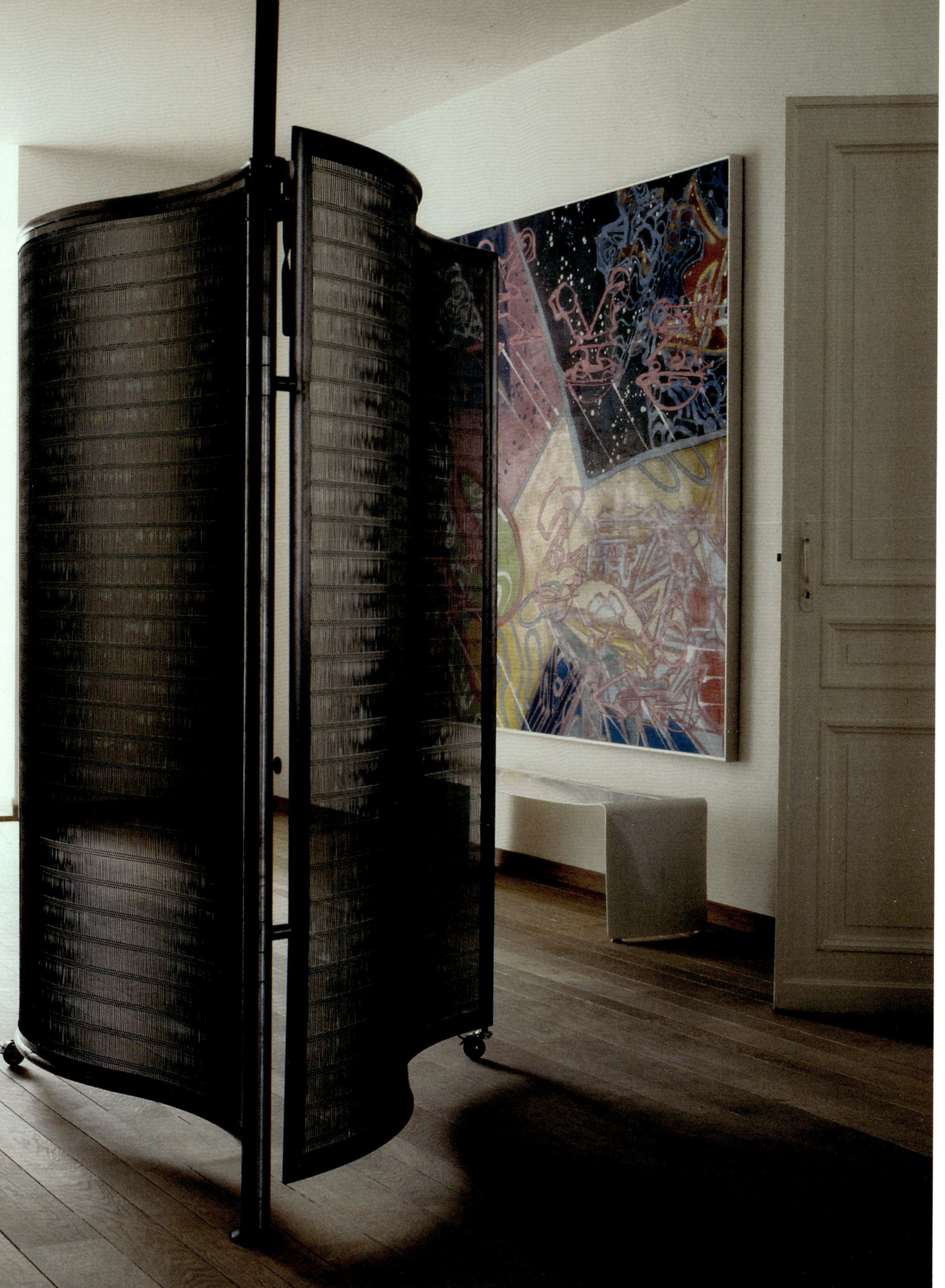

House in Ibiza, Spain 2007

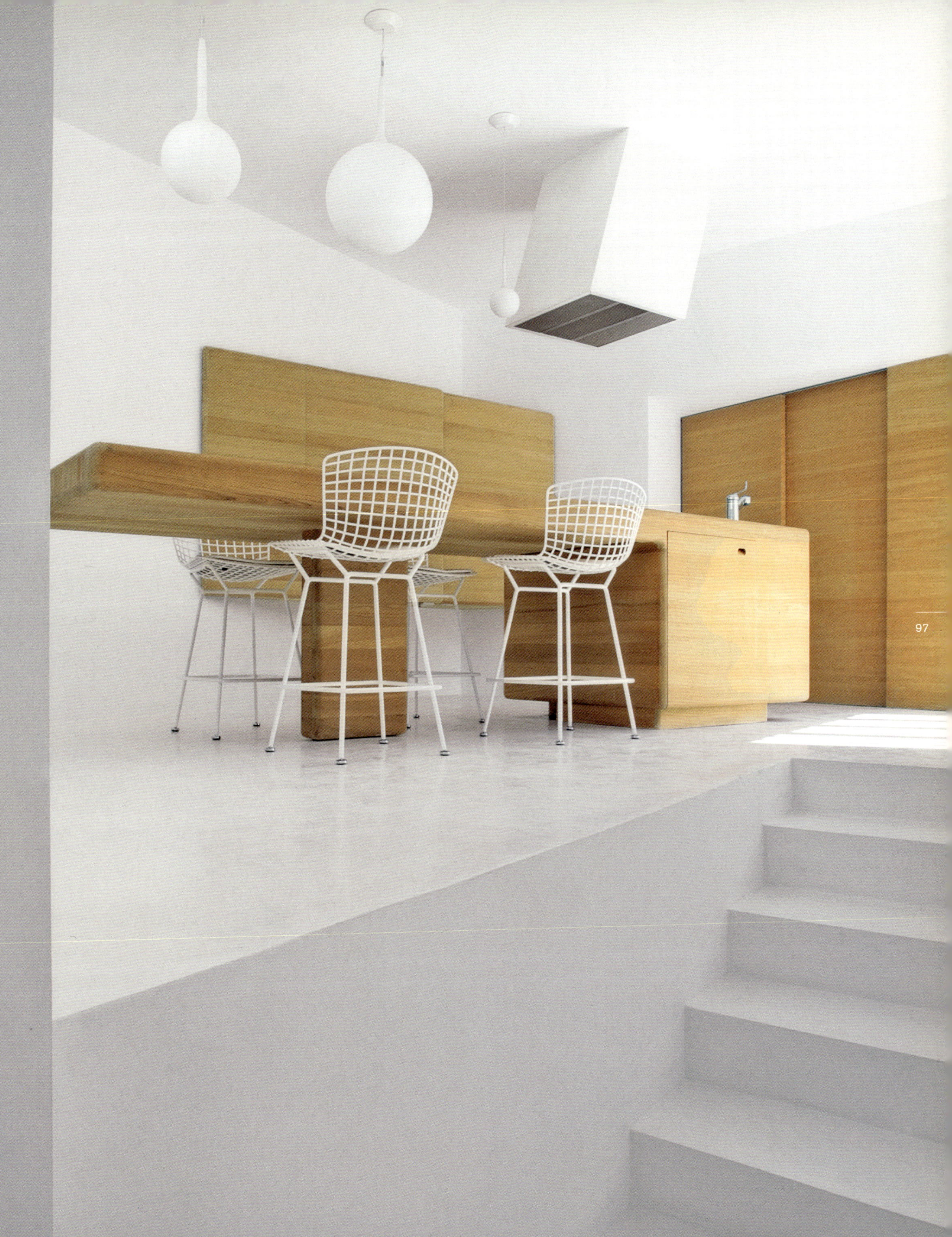

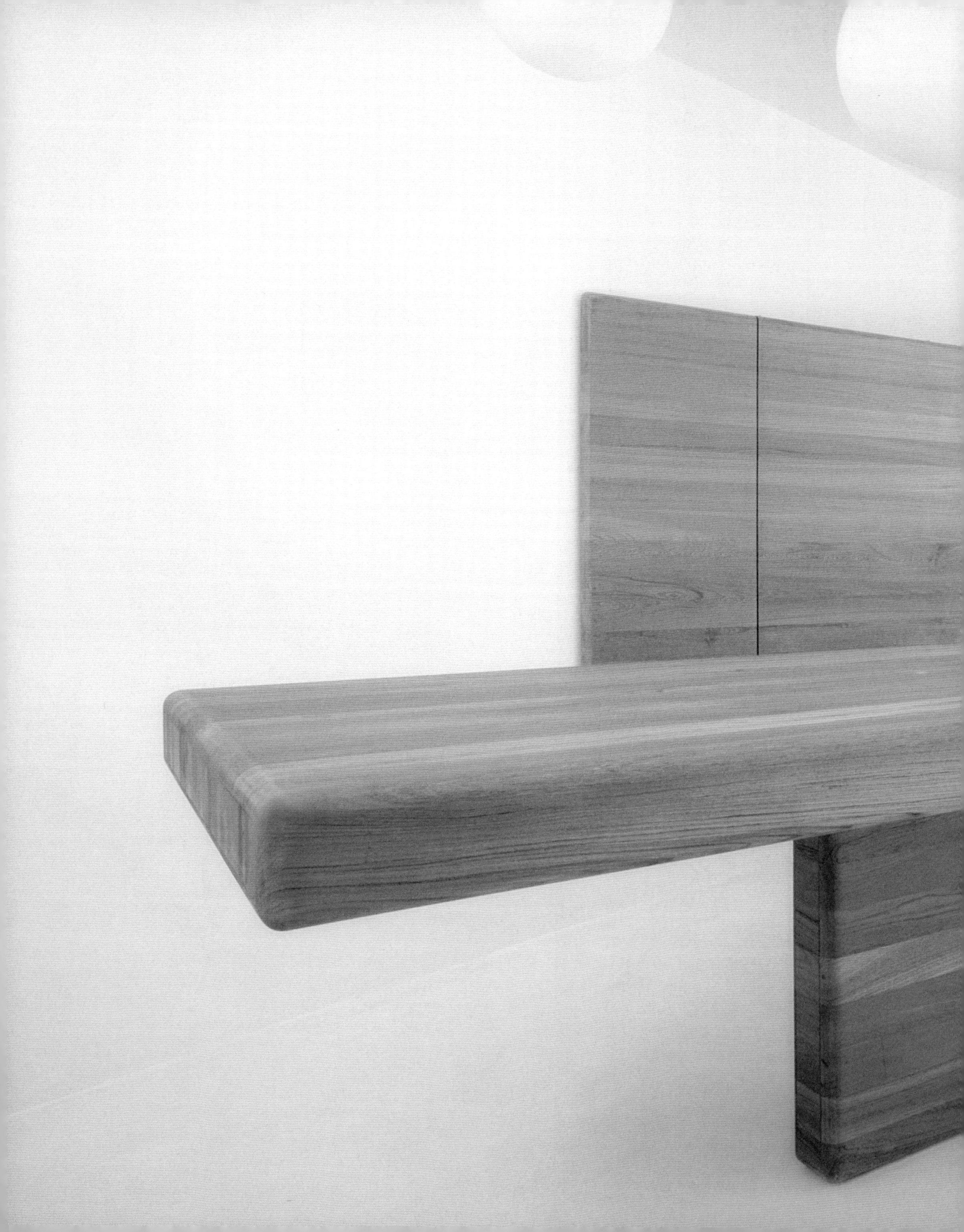

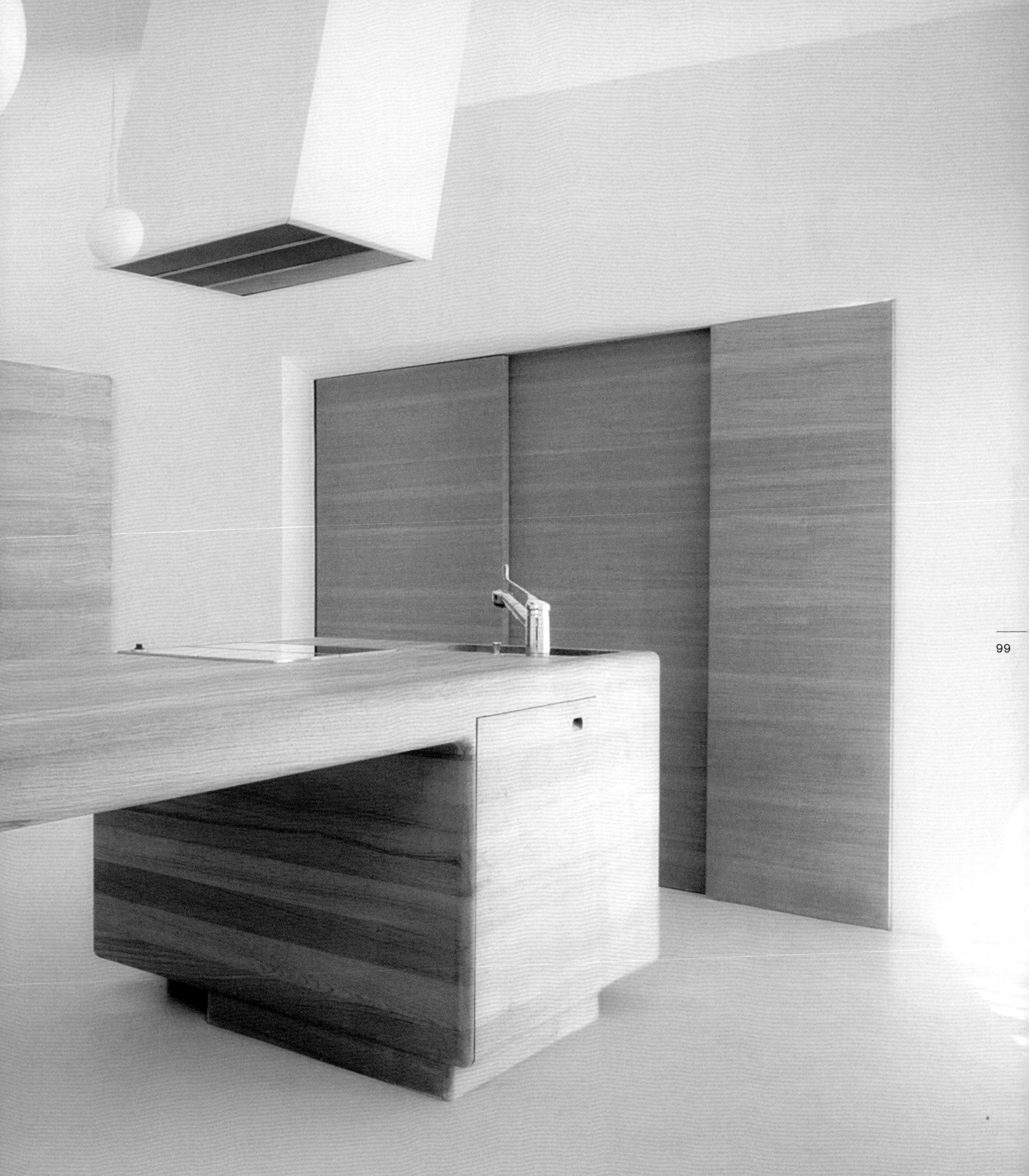

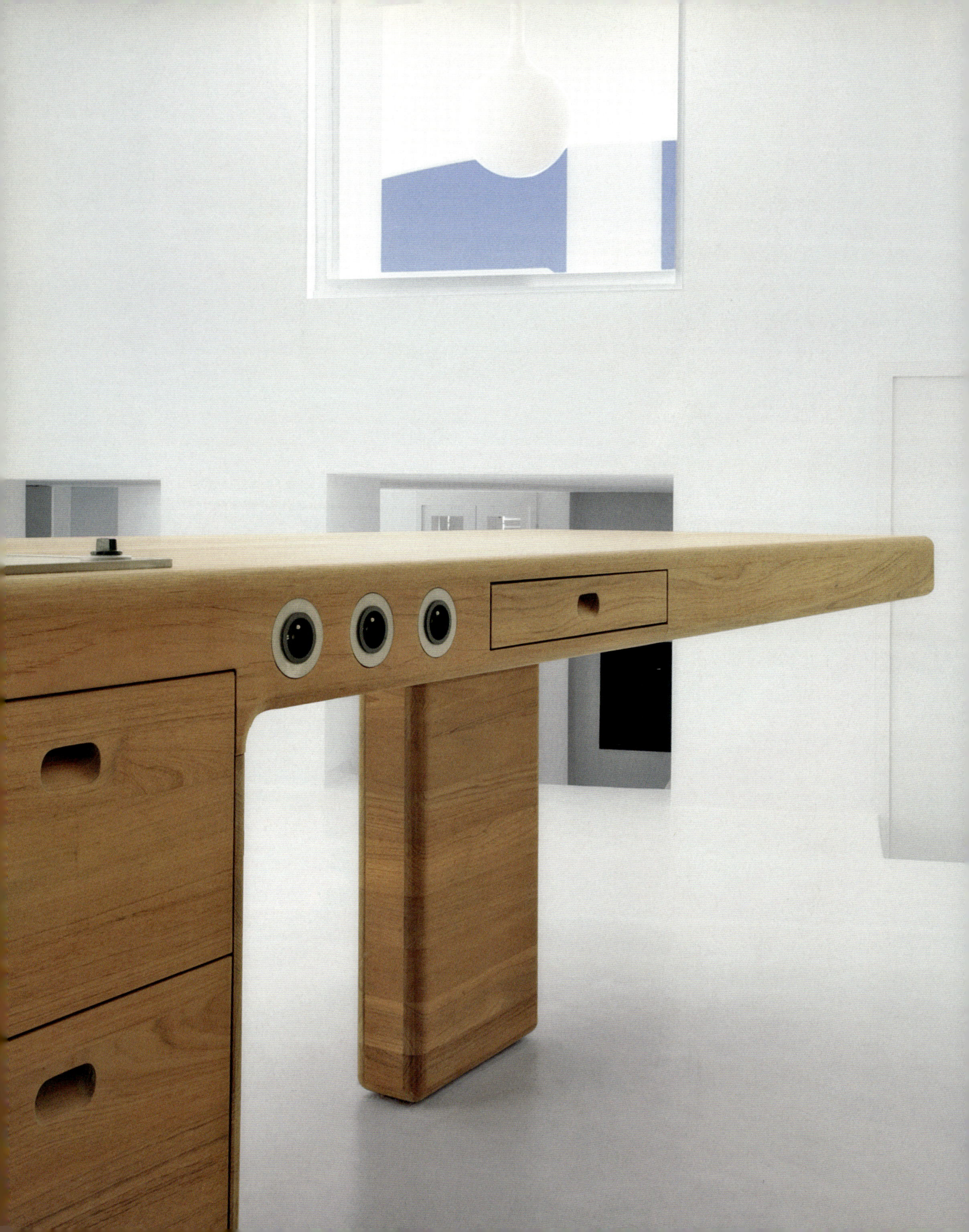

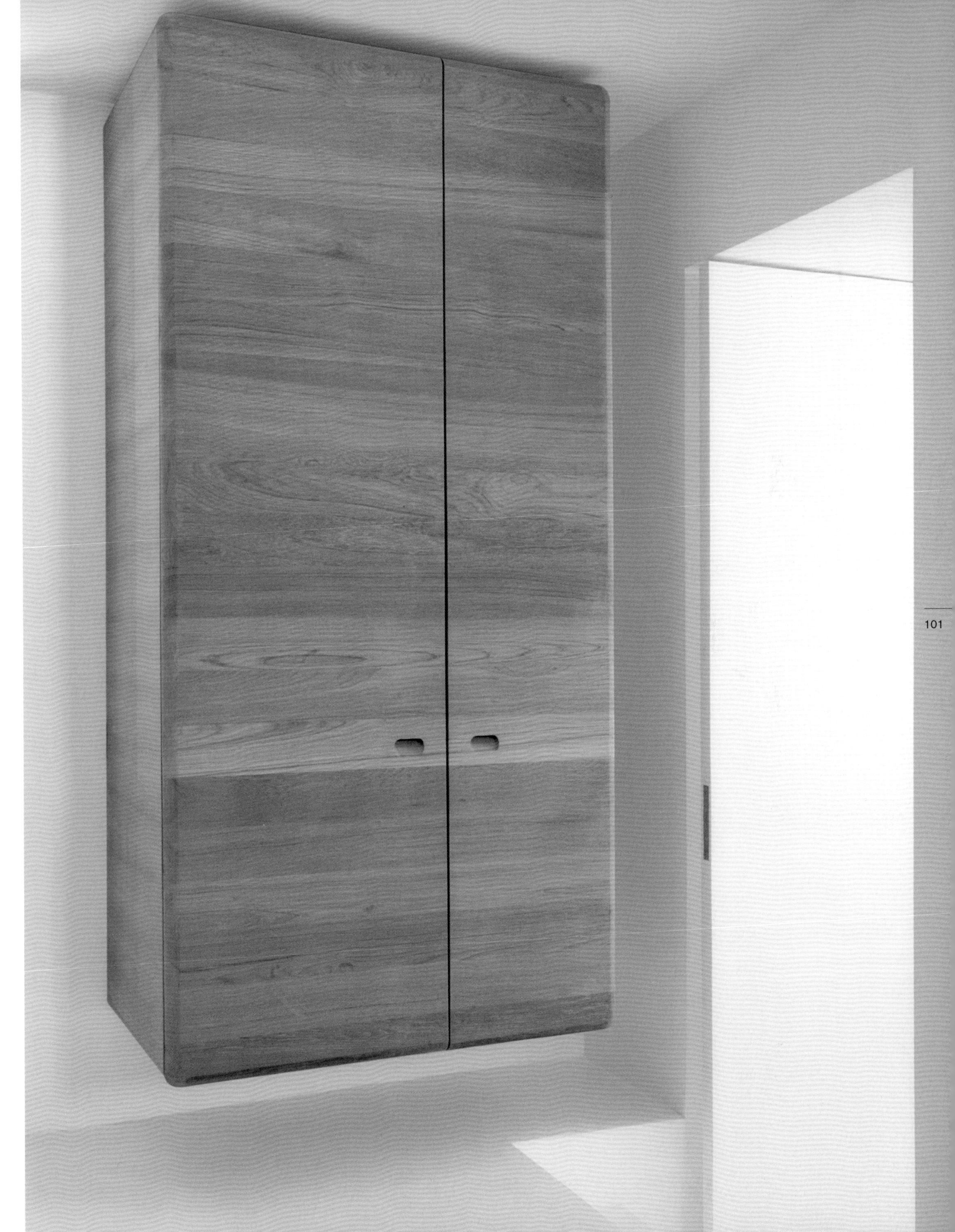

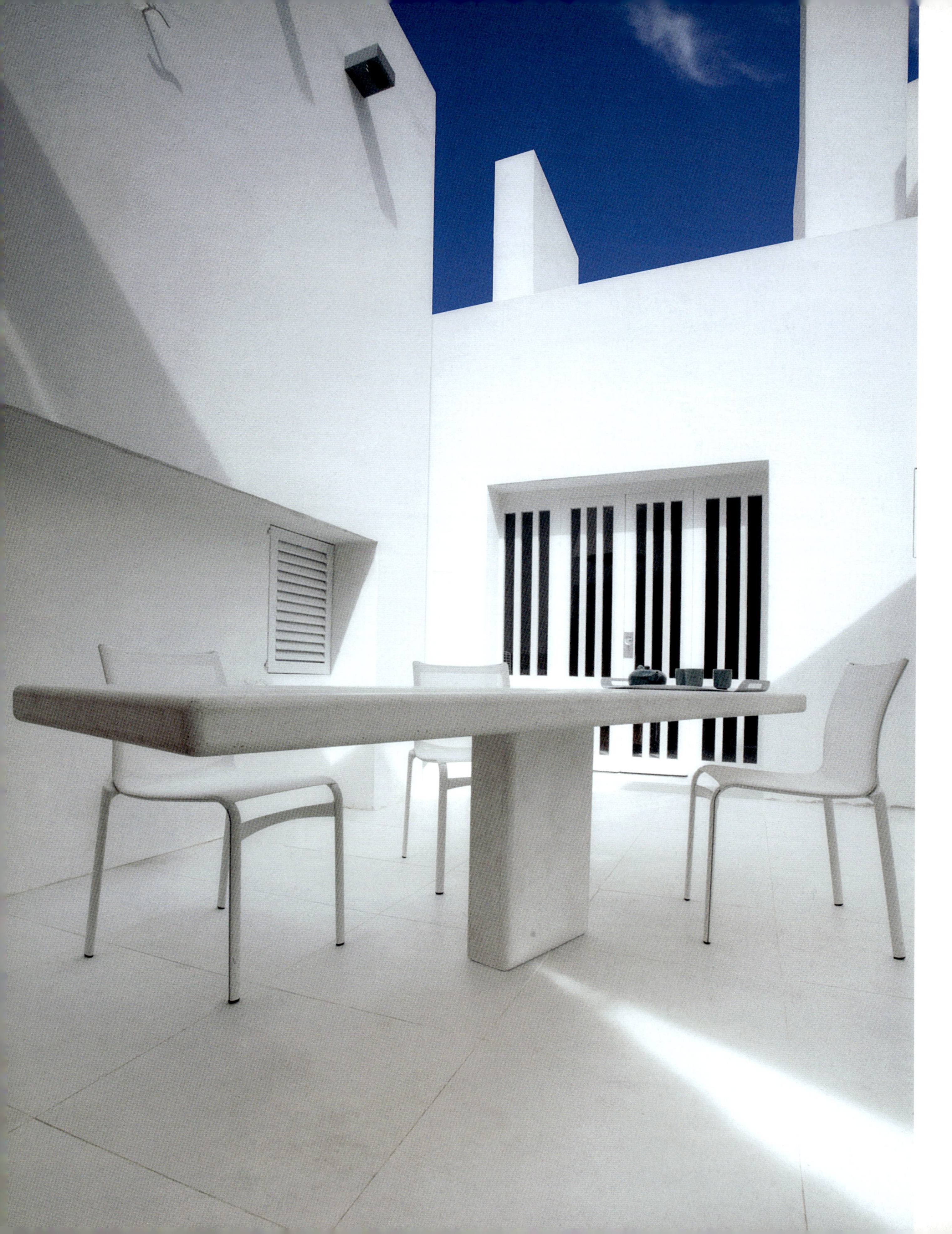

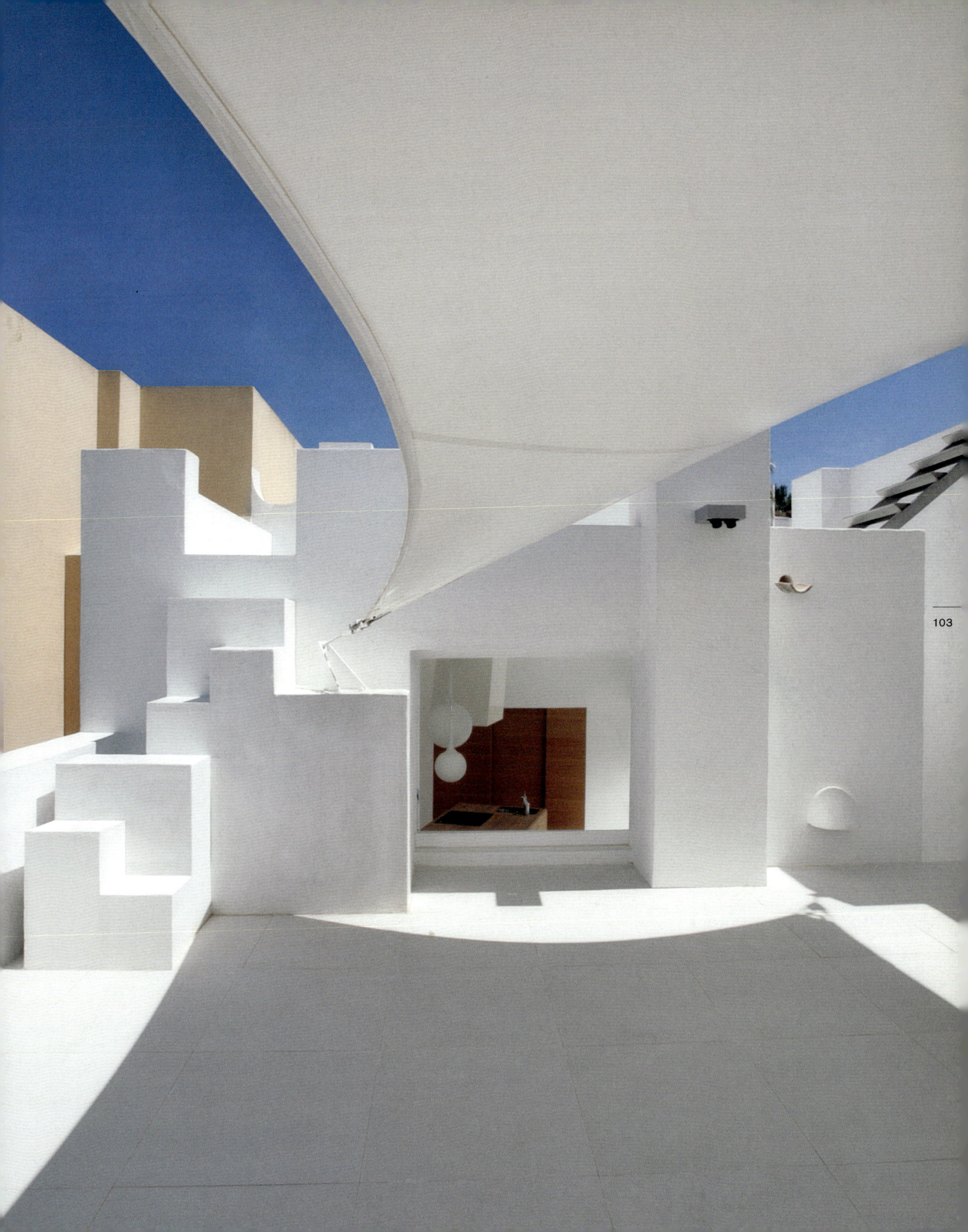

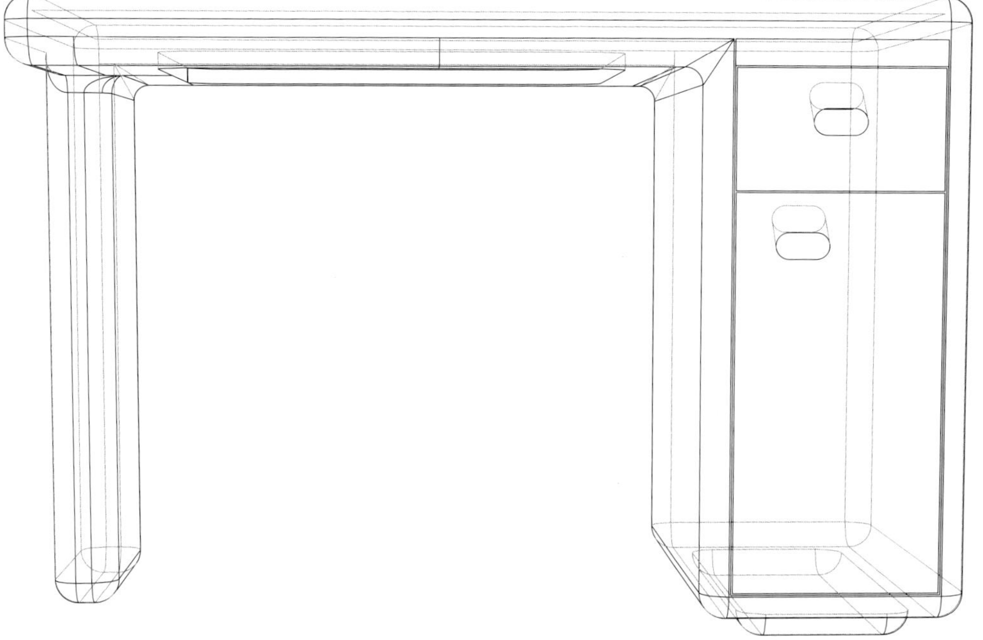

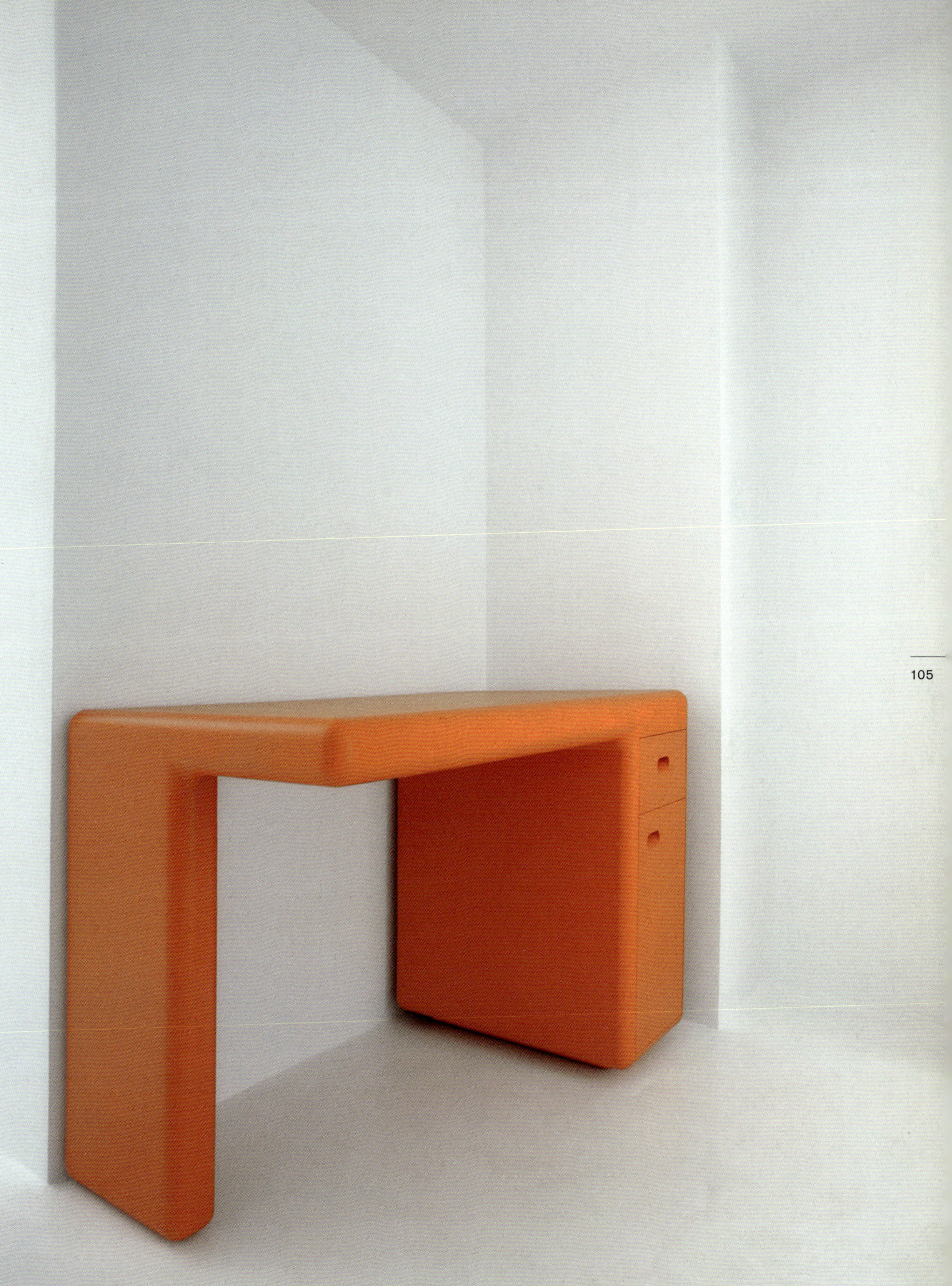

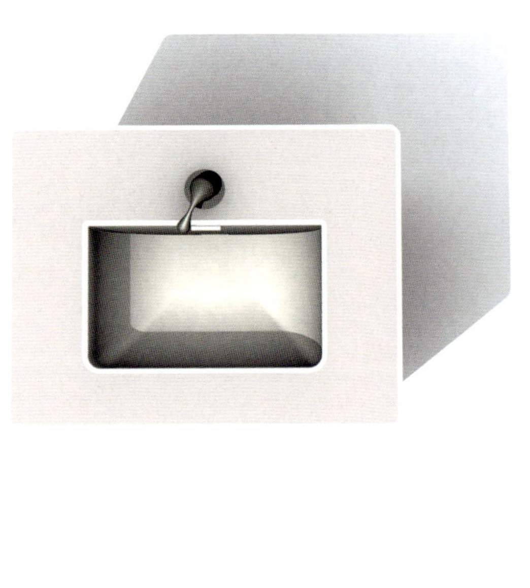

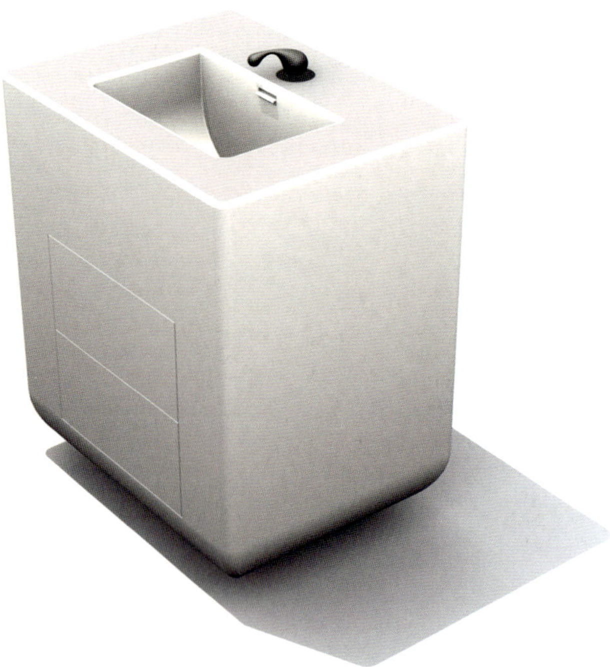

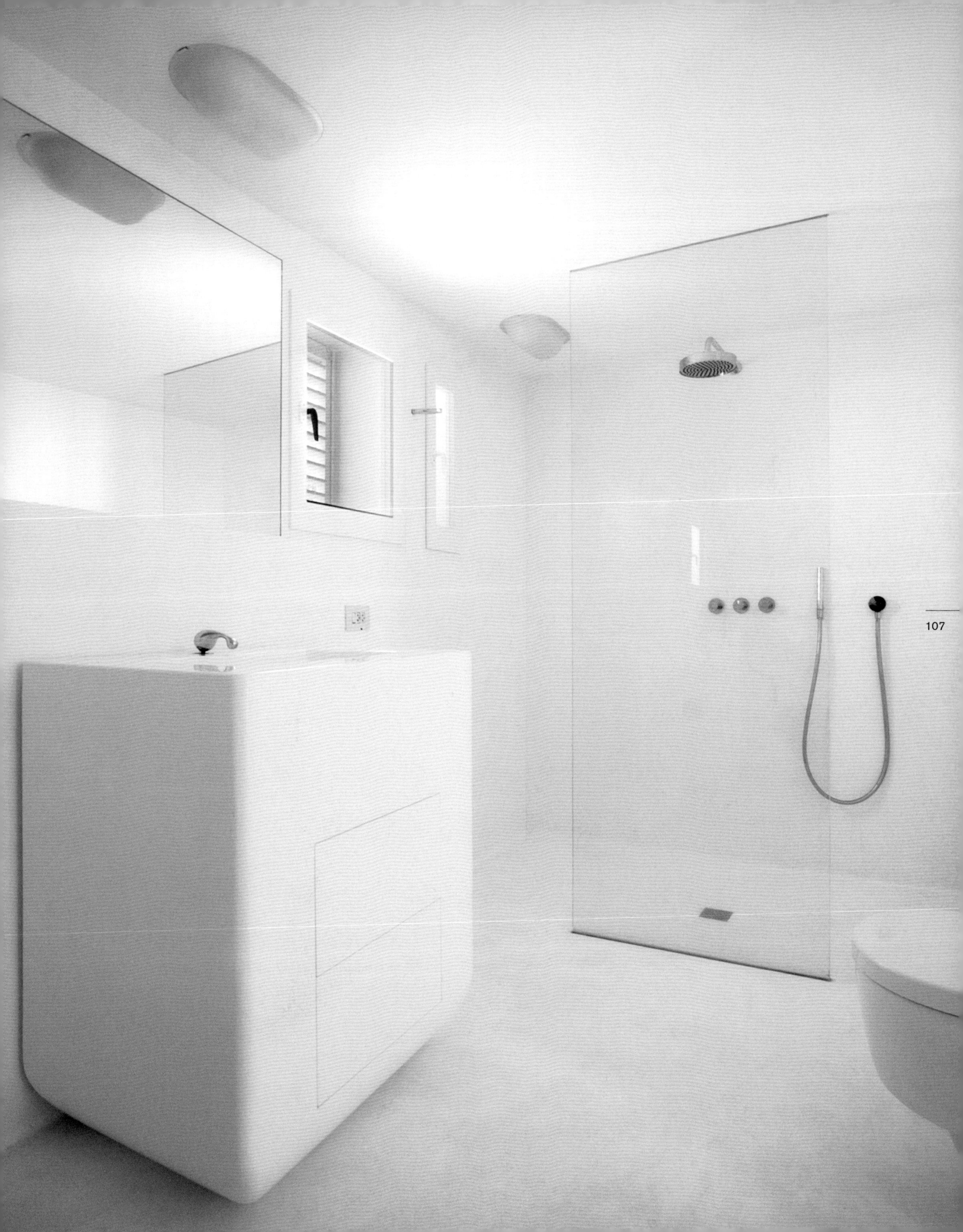

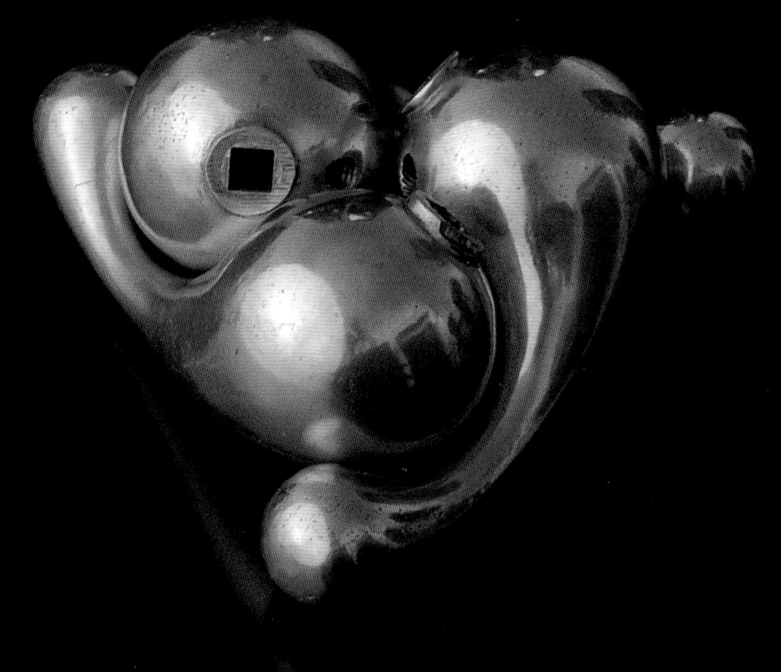

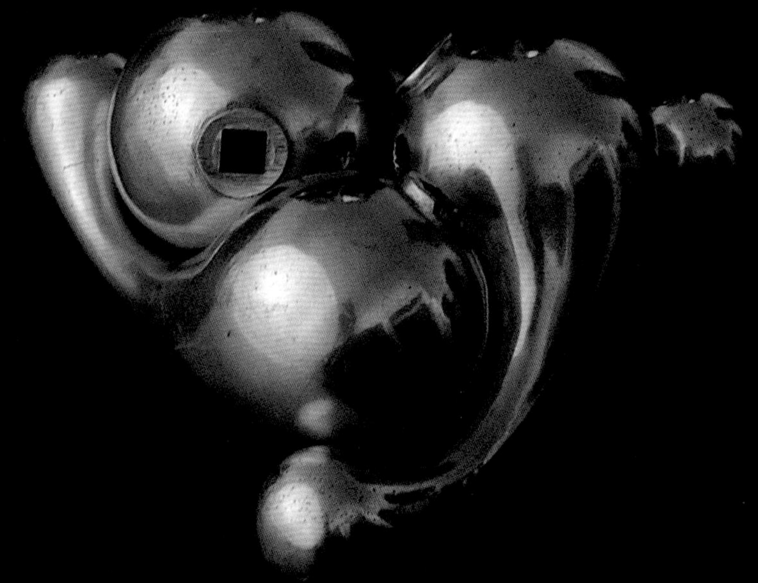

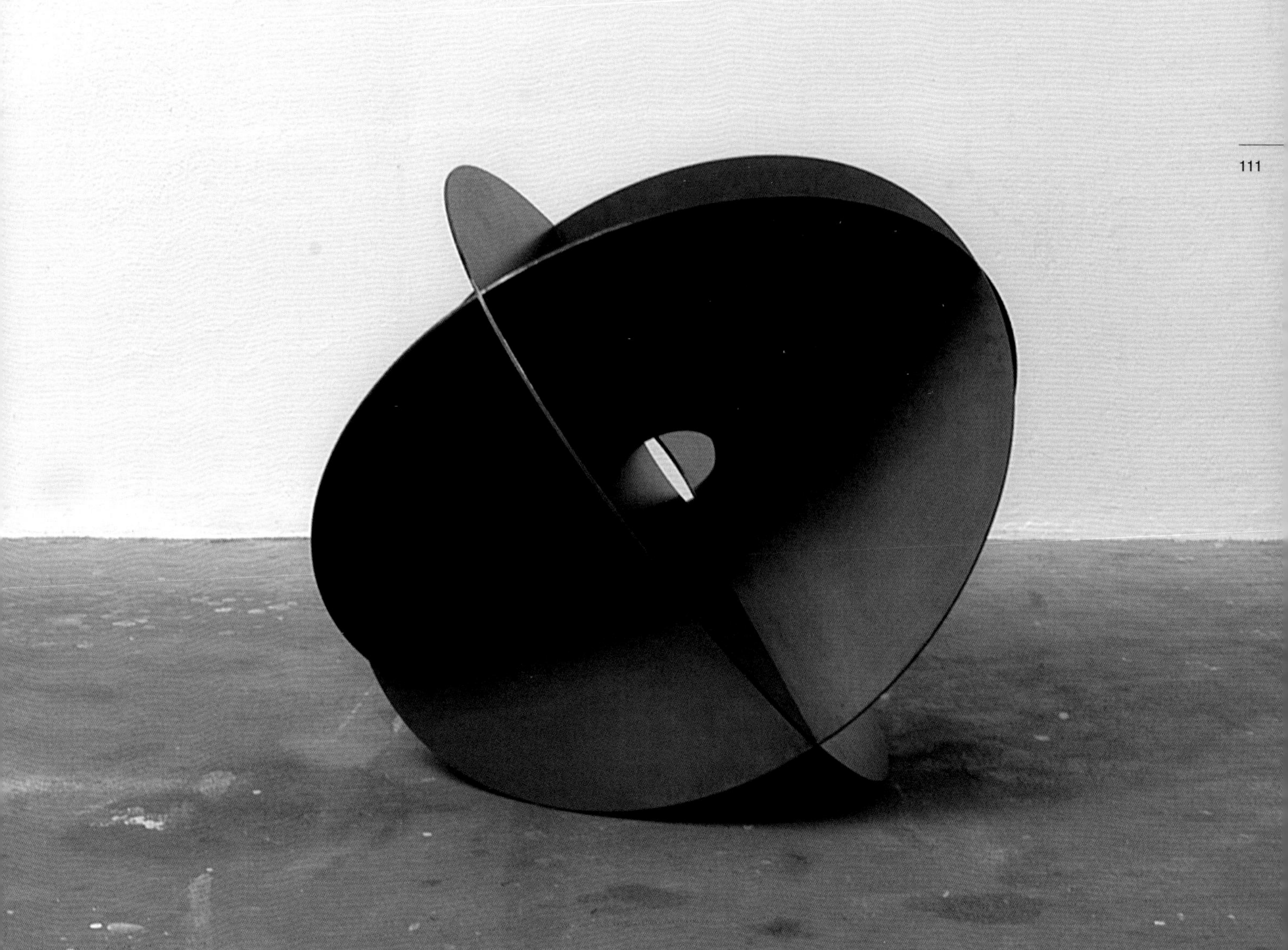

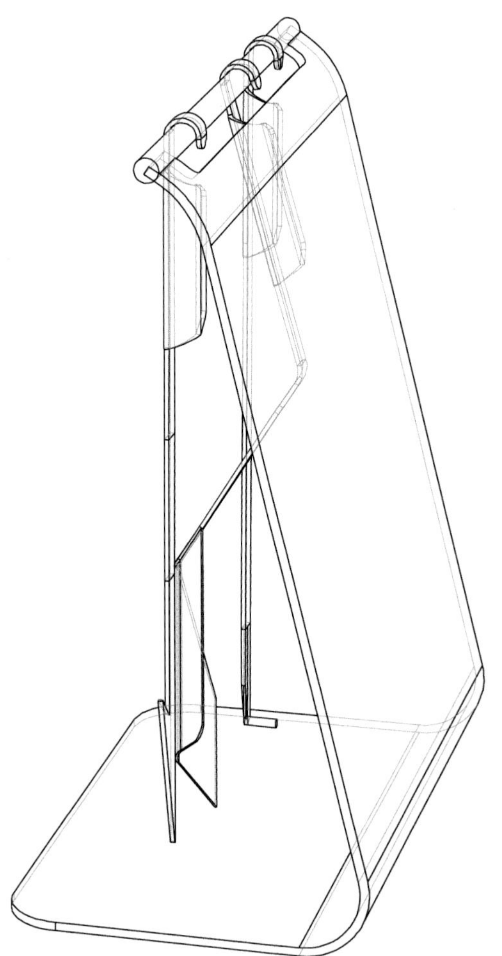

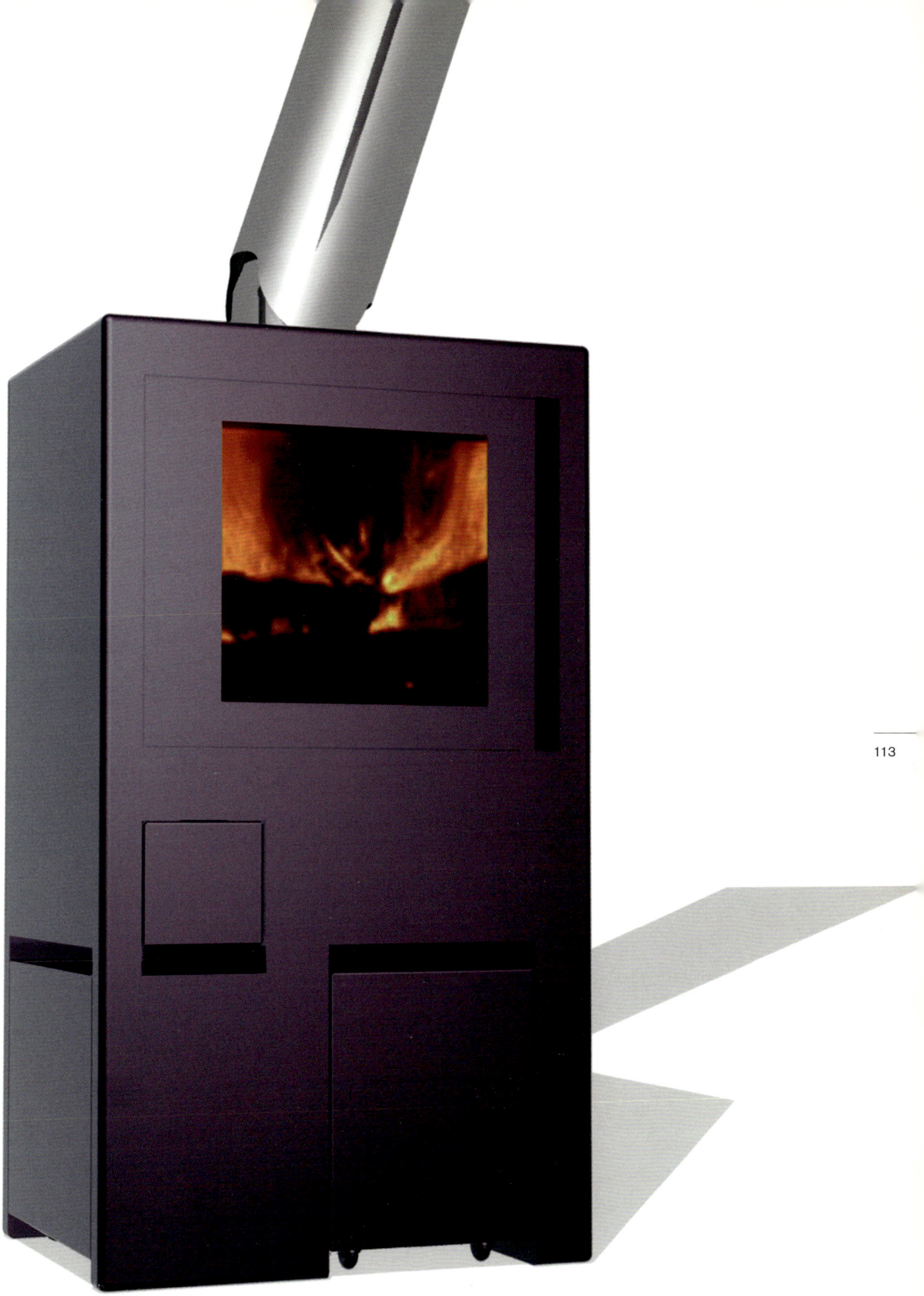

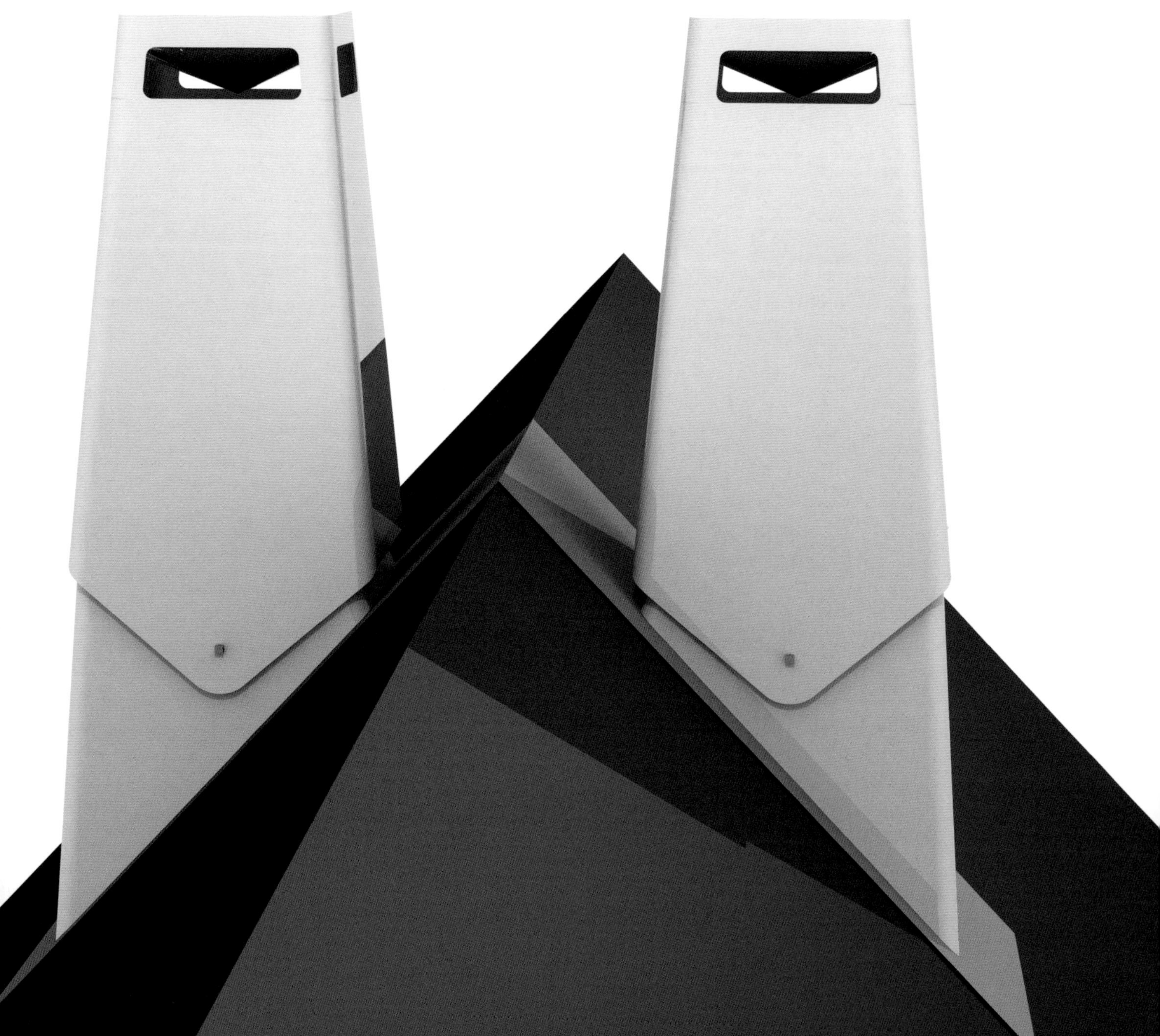

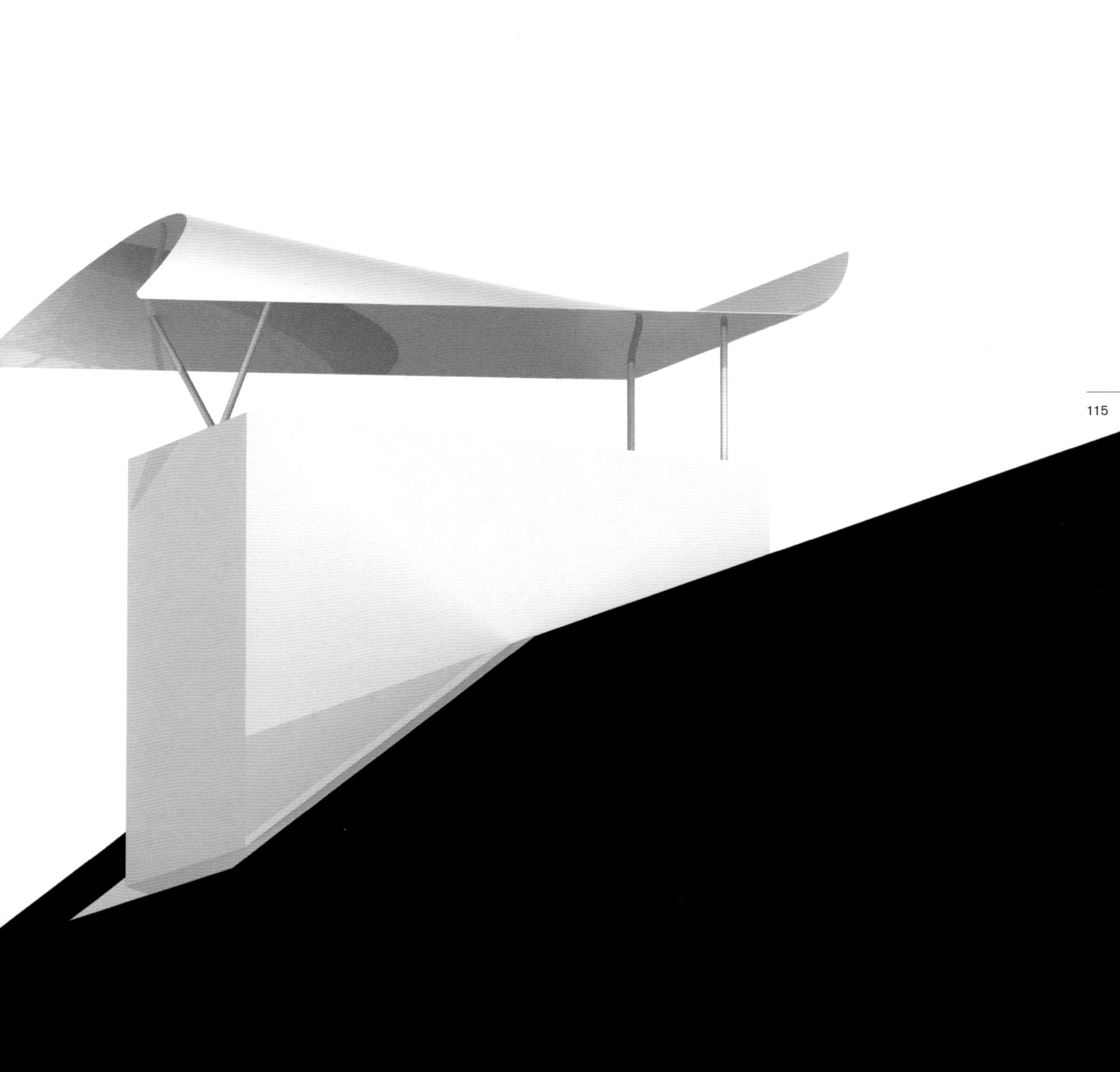

Abri-Voyageurs
Corbeille urbaine
Banc-Vélo
Abri-Vélo

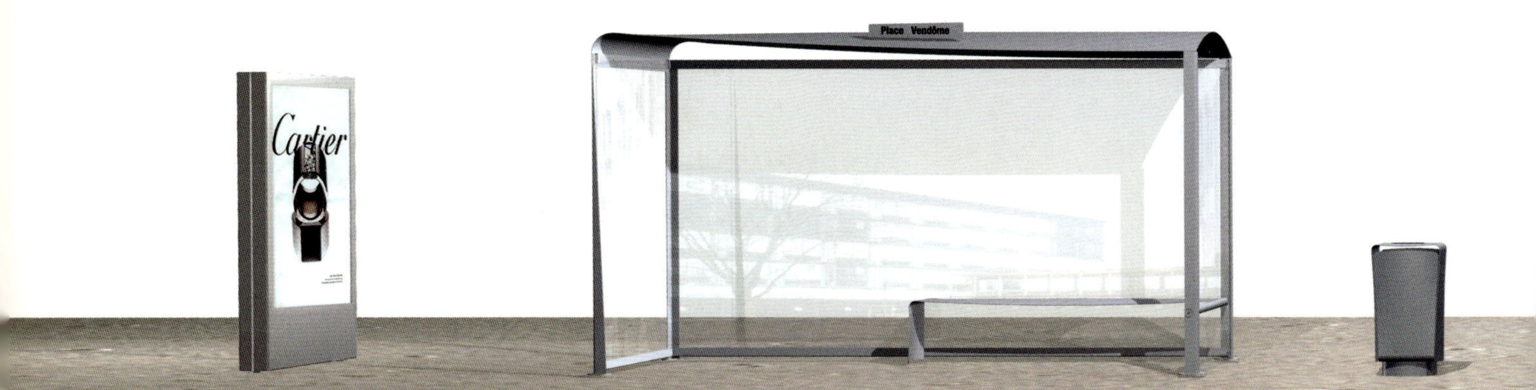

Cartier
Place Vendôme

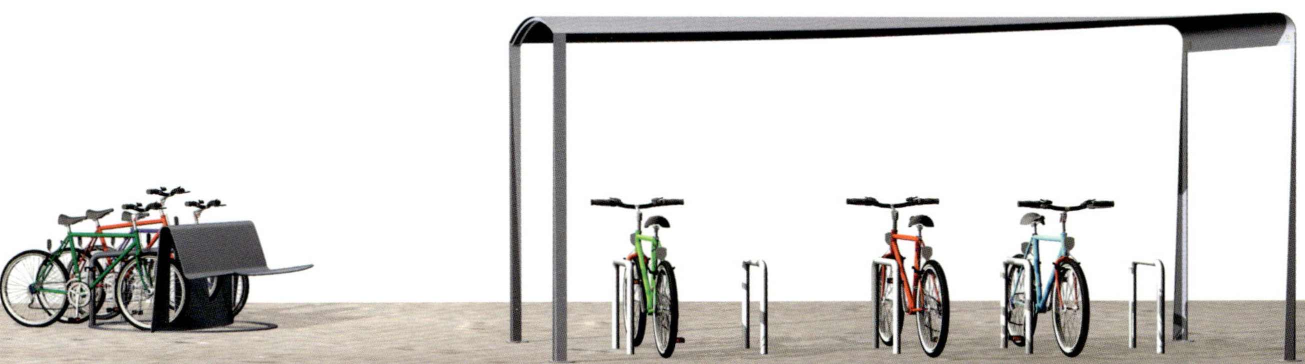

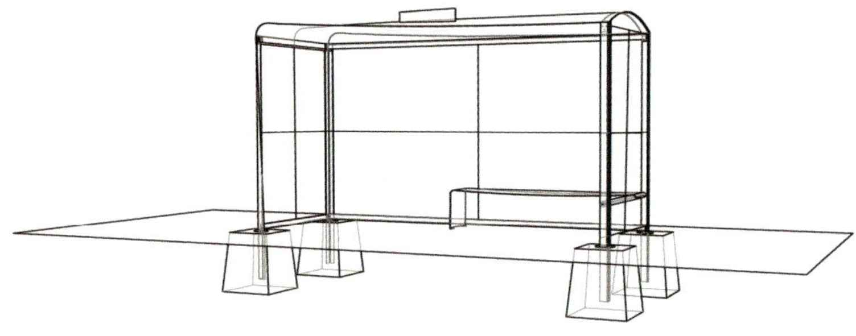

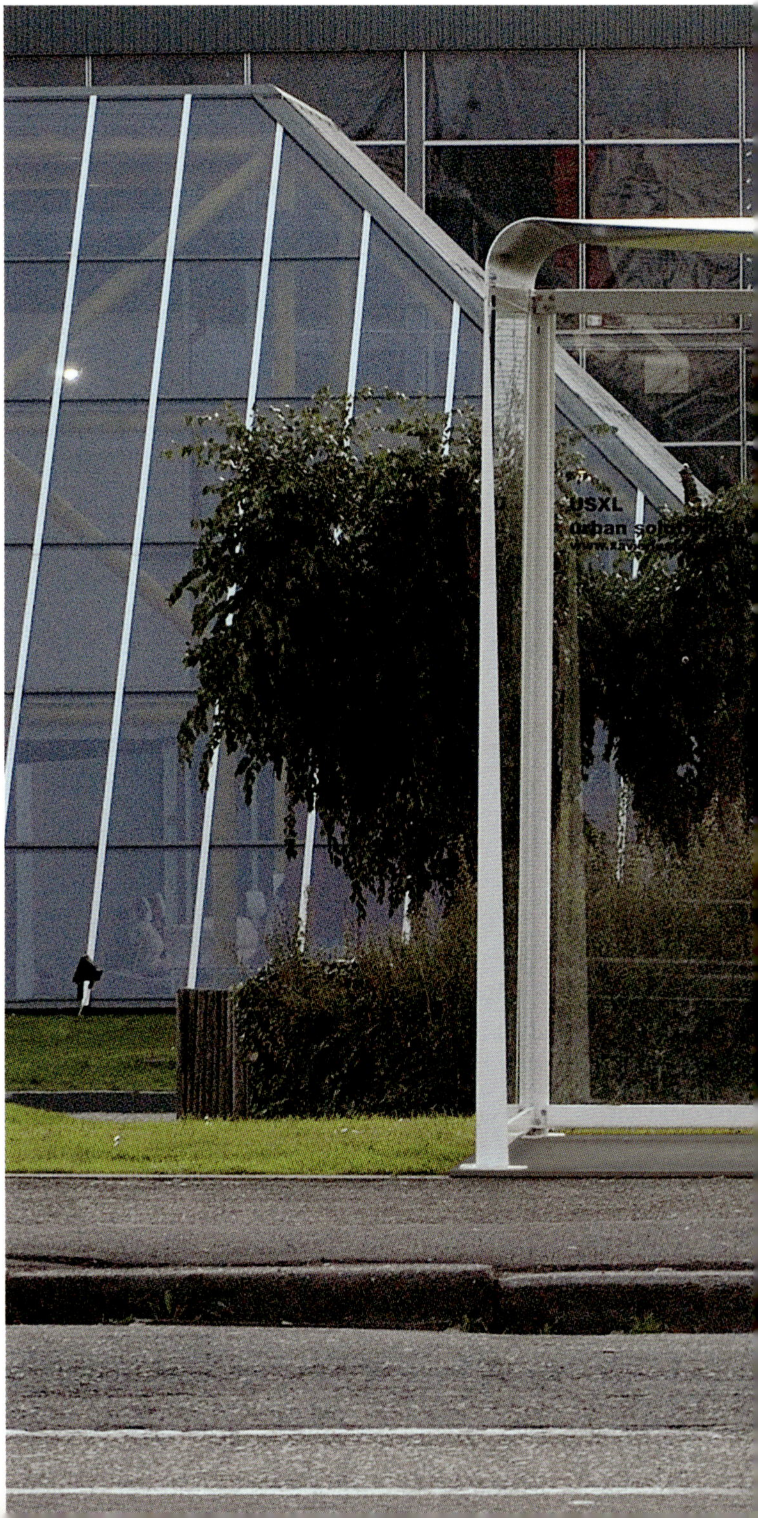

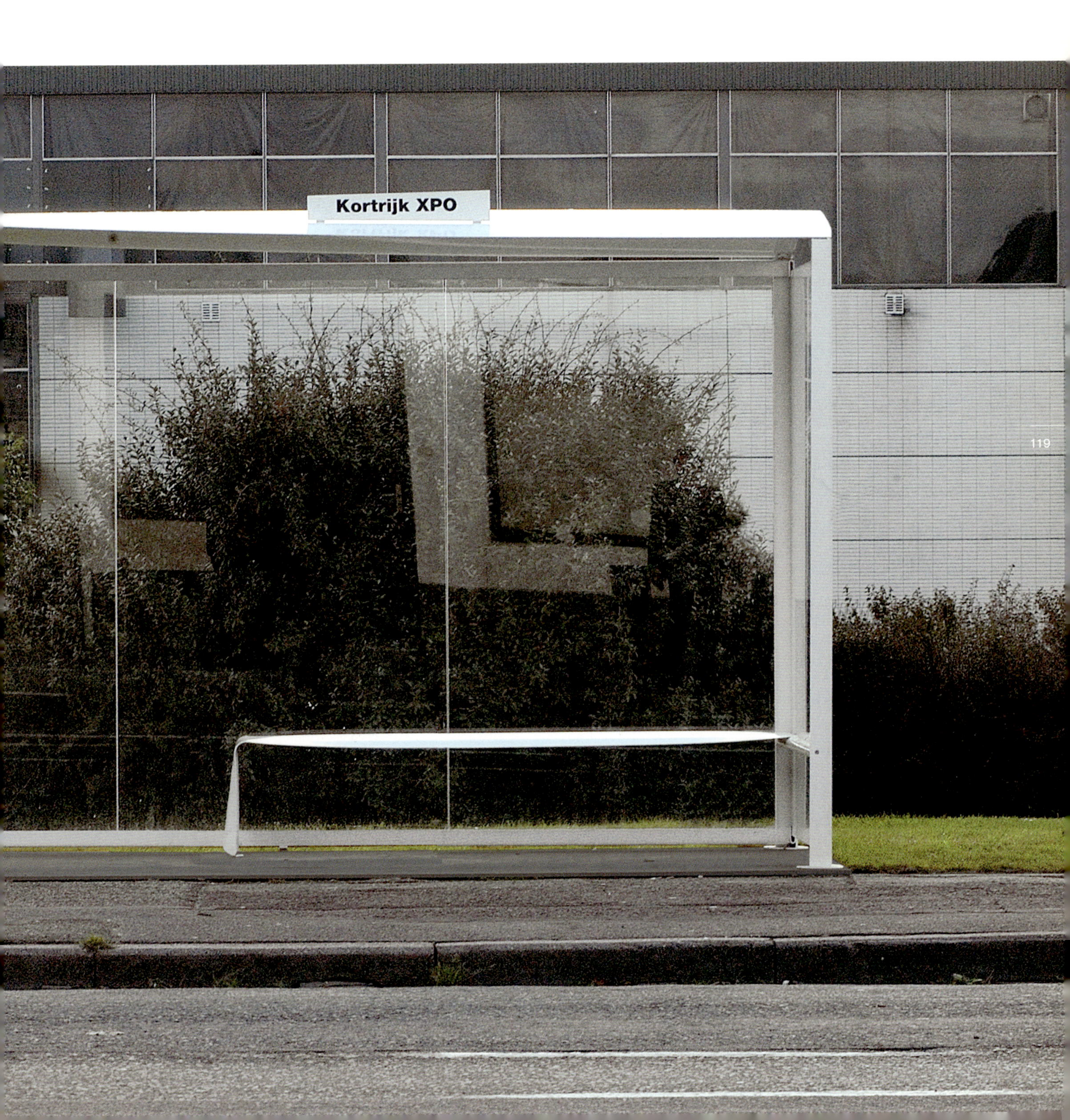

Kortrijk XPO

Dance, dance, dance

Olga Bozhko

Beauty can't be explained. It can be revealed and confirmed, but it's very difficult to describe it. Have you ever tried to capture the beauty of a human body in simple words? The only thing you would get is mere tautology. Beautiful – and that's that!

An easier way to describe beauty is to give a consequent description of shapes and proportion, but this method suits objects better than people. The process of getting the right shape is a beautiful process on its own. When you see the perfect result, you might think that it looks so easy. You get a similar impression when you see a smiling ballerina, who seems to jump effortlessly. Somehow you know that she had to endure extremely hard work and hours of torture in order to obtain such flexibility.

Working with a sheet of metal can be compared to working with a human body. When you try to fold it, it unbends. You have to be precise and insistent to 'teach' the sheet to maintain a certain shape. Xavier Lust knows exactly how to educate the material and to make your eye feel this education.

A wonderful aspect of Xavier's works is the illusion of lightness and … motion. In his designs he manages to express what seems impossible. No hidden details and connections: they are not necessary. His pieces breathe and whirl like ballerinas. Xavier Lust is able to show the capacity of movement in different ways. Even if it is just a park bench or a city bicycle stand … it exudes a certain motion or is related to it in a certain way. A tray seems to be ready to fly. A cupboard seems to want to get filled with garments and open its doors. It is a gentle hint about the life, value and character of an object.

Design critics often say that a designer must be brave each time he creates a new piece. Their concerns are irrelevant when true talent is involved. The resulting designs are distinguished by high quality. This is most certainly true for Lust's designs: they are not created … they are born.

Танцующий металл

Ольга Божко

С красотой непросто. Ее можно опознать. Указать на нее, сказав – да, красиво. Описывать ее в деталях куда сложнее. И уж совсем невозможно объяснить. Попробуйте в простых предложениях передать красоту человеческого тела. Получается одна тавтология. Красиво – и все.

Помогает, если последовательно описывать собственно форму и пропорции. Но этот метод все же больше подходит к предметам, чем к людям. Когда видишь правильную гармоничную вещь и понимаешь, как она сделана – думаешь: да это очевидно, иначе нельзя. Из-за этой очевидности возникает иллюзия, что это легко повторить. Примерно так же, когда смотришь на балерину, с улыбкой взмывающую вверх. Что тут такого. Идешь и прыгаешь. Головой понимаешь, что за легкостью скрыты ежедневная работа и часы мучений по достижению такой гибкости.

Работать с листом металла почти как с телом. Пытаешься его согнуть – он назад распрямляется. Чтобы «приучить» его к определенному положению, нужно быть очень настойчивым и точным. У Ксавье Люста, бельгийского дизайнера, это получается. Но что поражает в его работе больше всего – именно заветная иллюзия легкости. И еще движения. В вещи ему удается передать то, что передать как кажется невозможно, да и не особенно нужно. Они дышат, кружатся, как балерины. Даже если это всего лишь скамейка или городская стойка для велосипедов – они подразумевают движение или определенным образом соотносятся с ним. Поднос кажется готов взлететь. Комод – переполниться вещами и открыть дверцы. Такой тонкий намек на внутреннюю жизнь вещей, их достоинство и характер.

Одно из общих мест критики дизайна – обилие нового. Однако новое различается по качеству. Если это новый талант – он может оставаться новостью вечно.

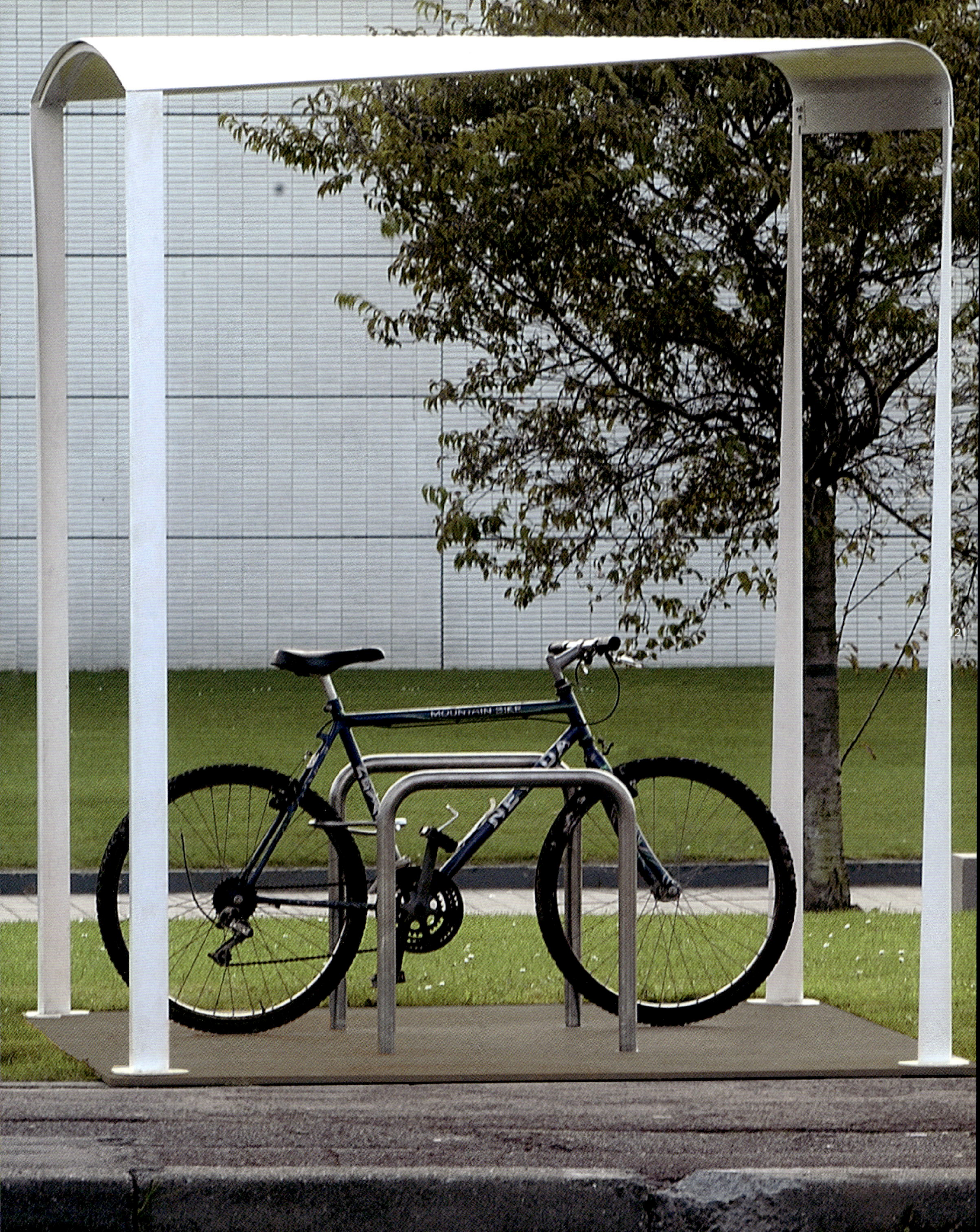
MOUNTAIN BIKE

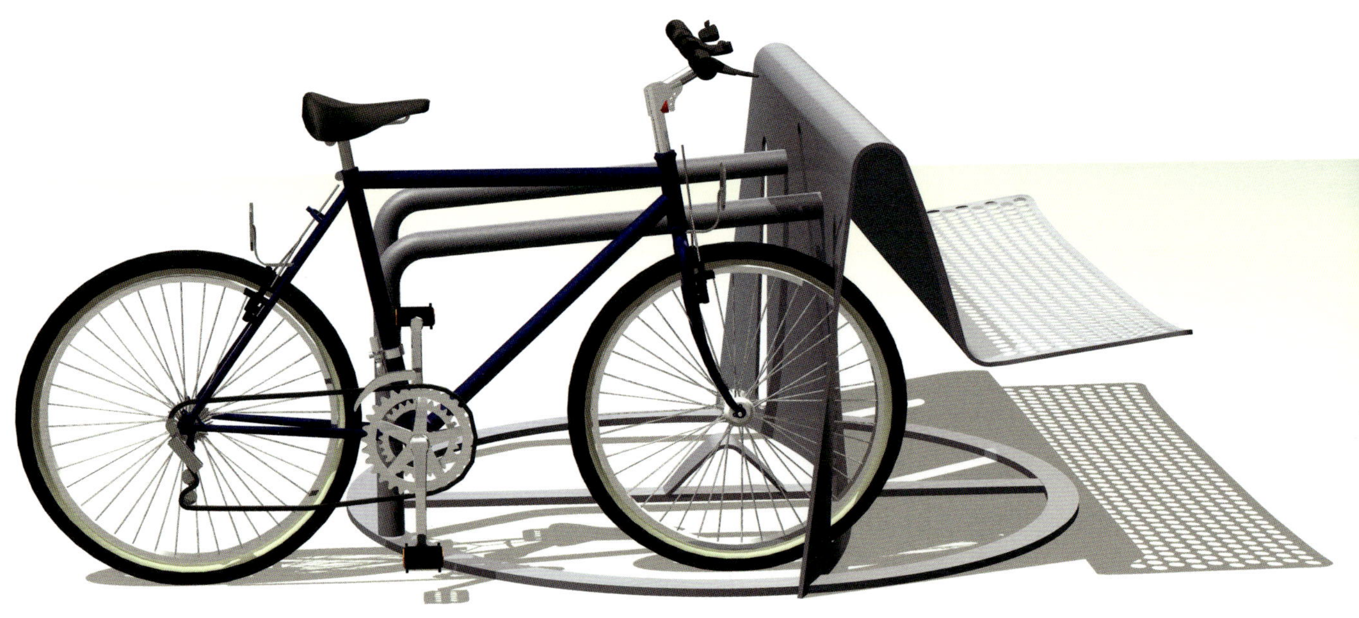

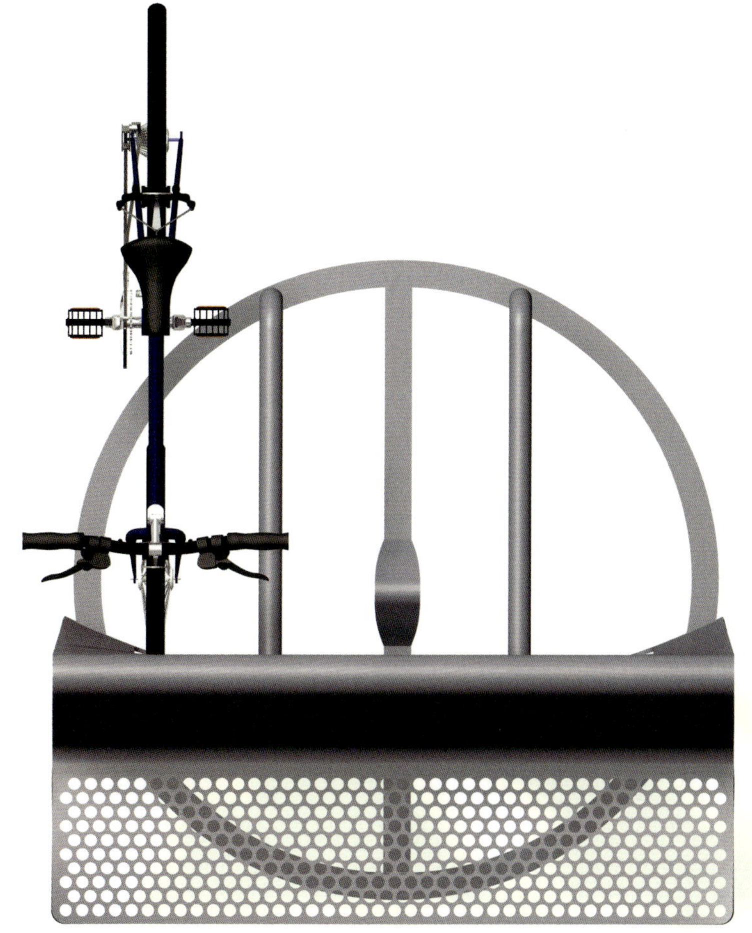

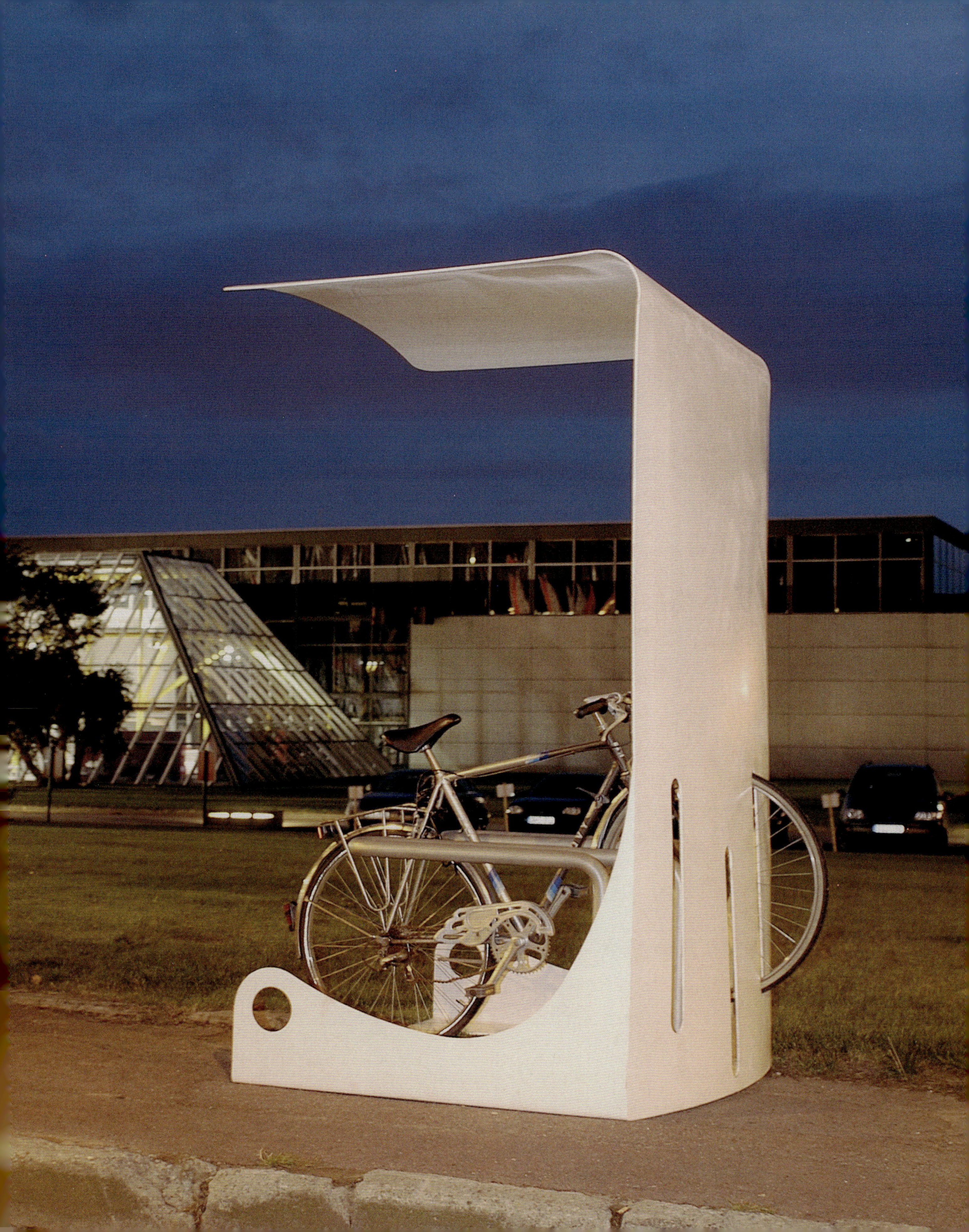

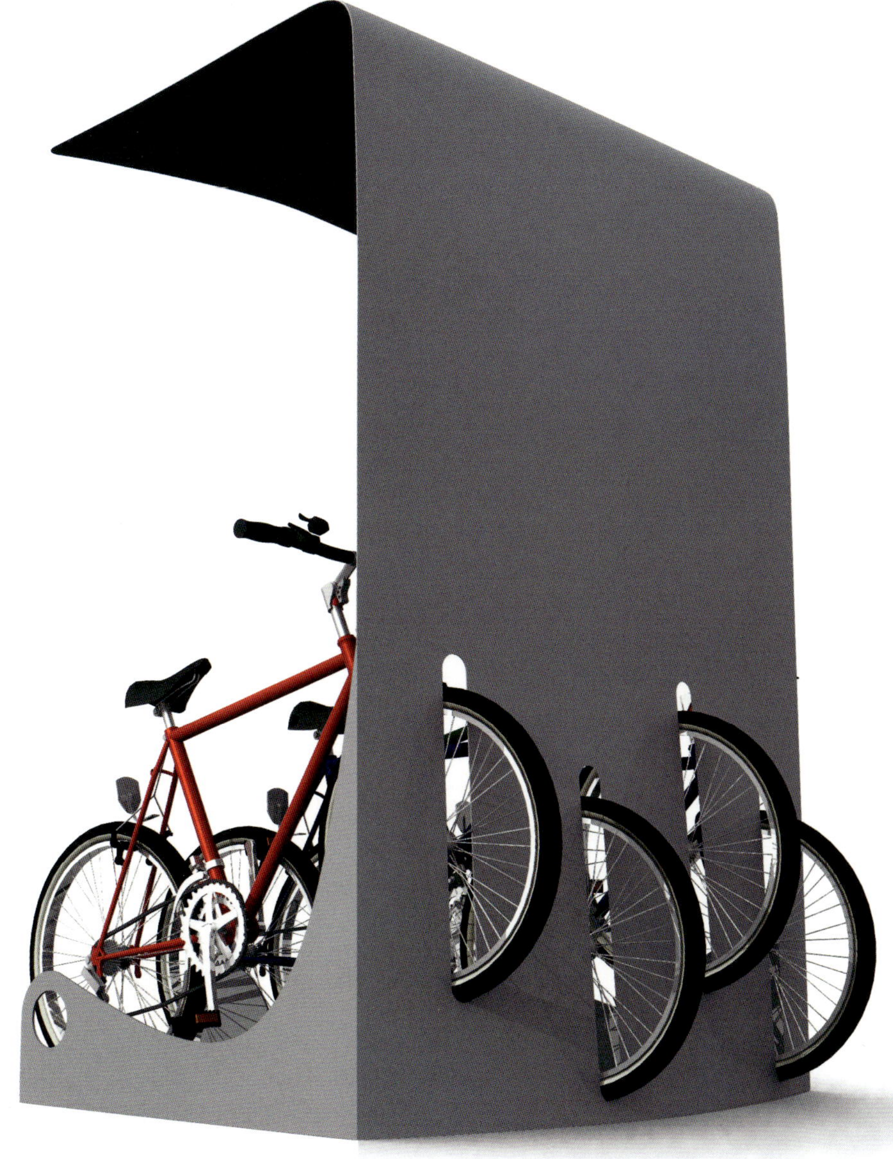

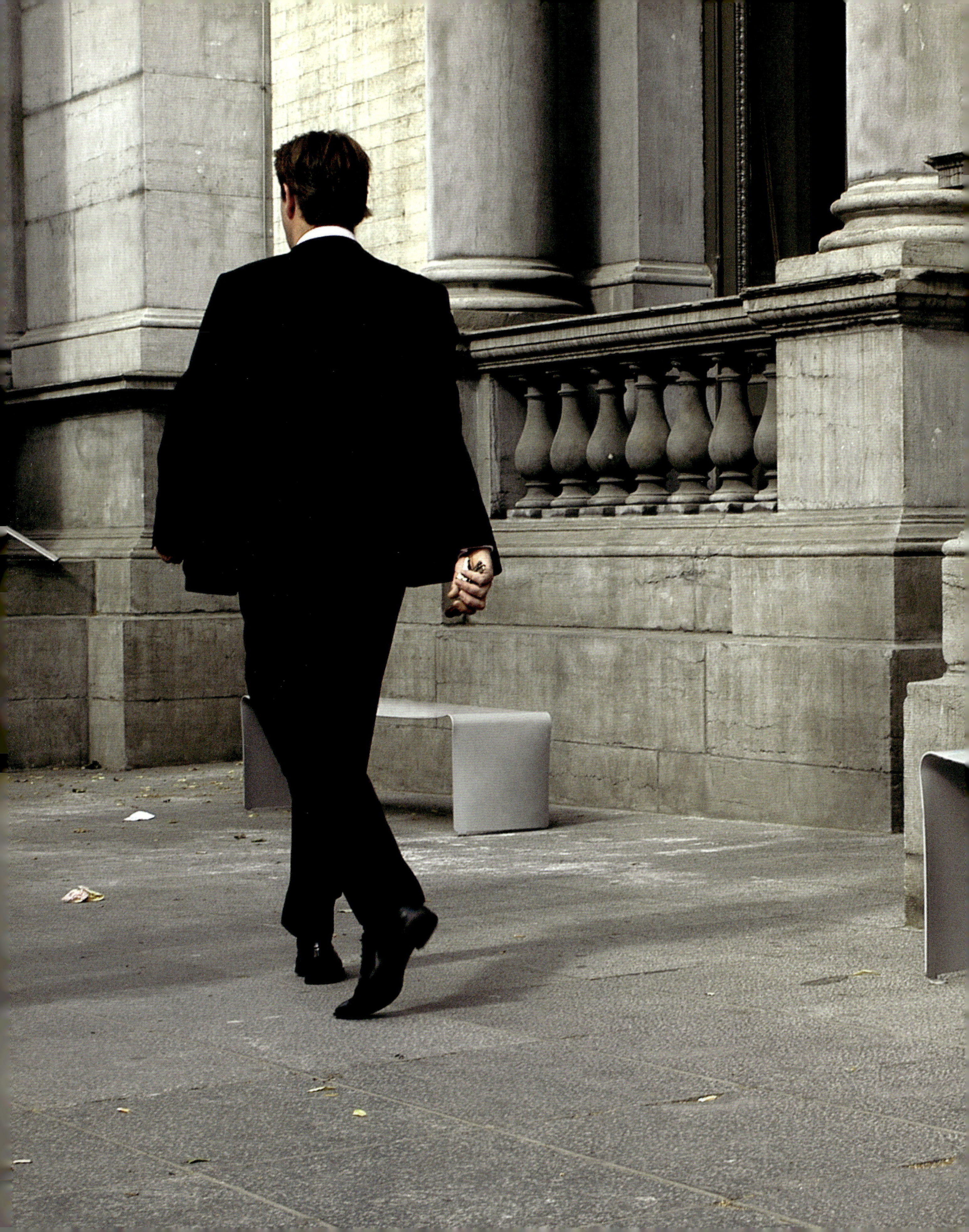

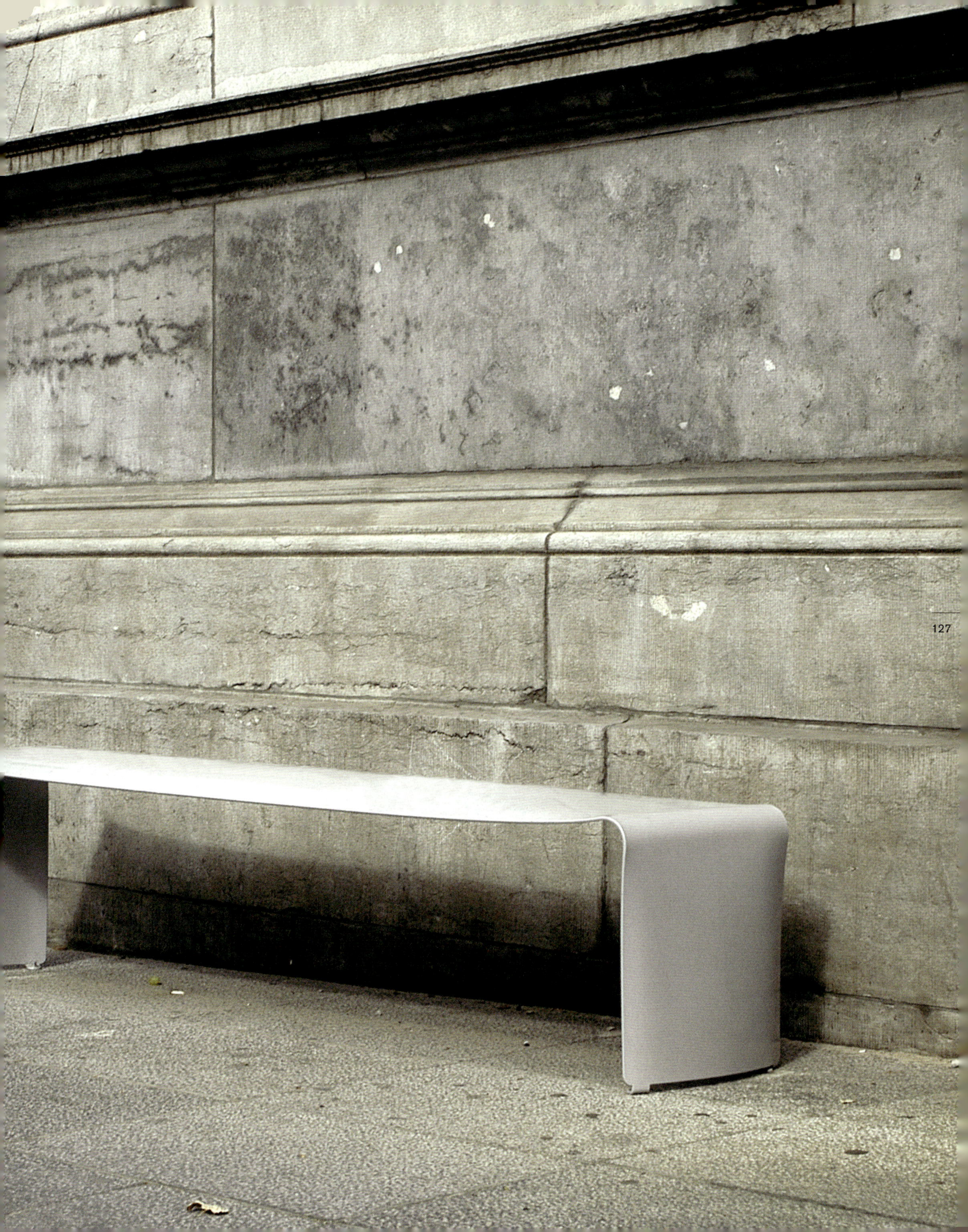

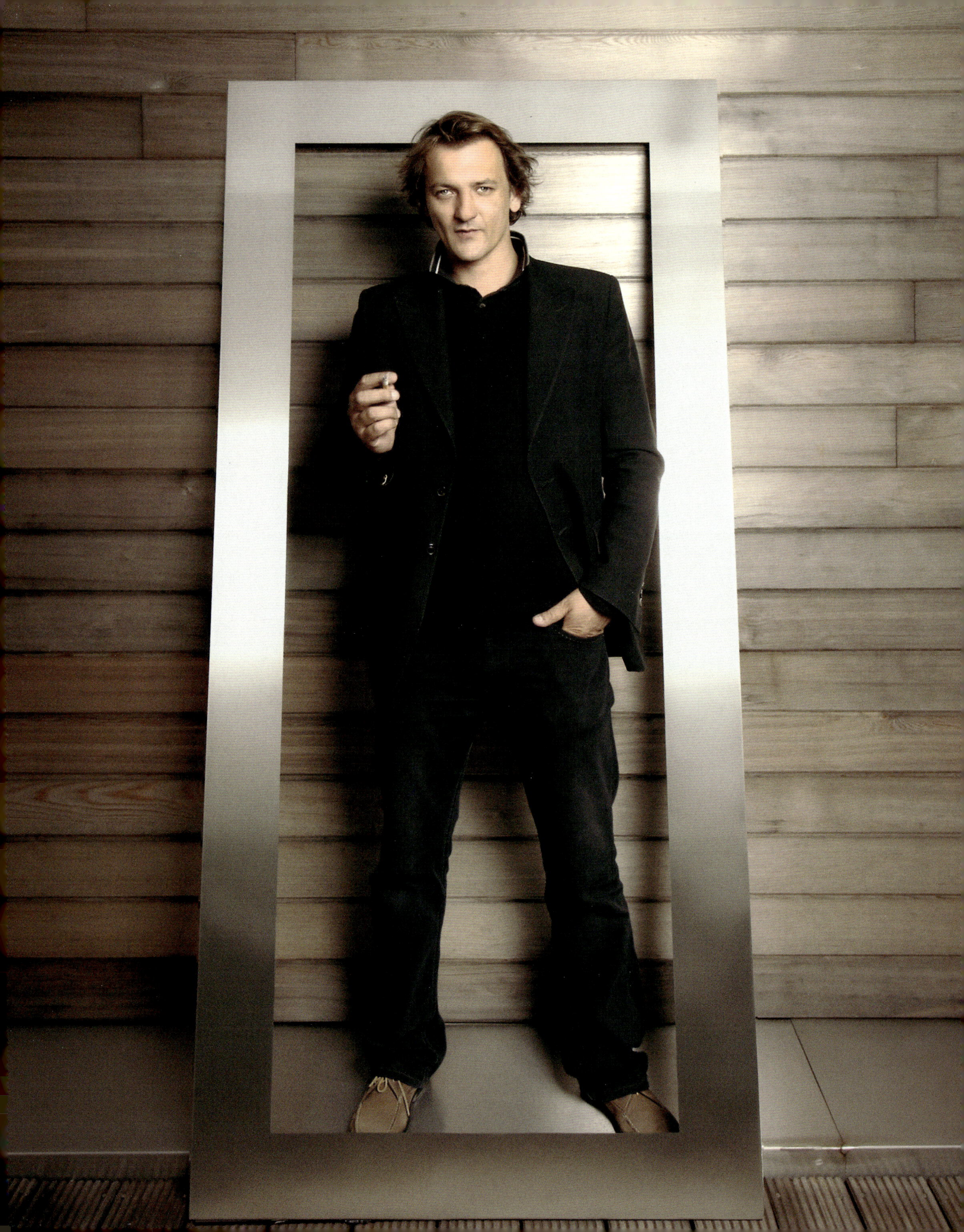

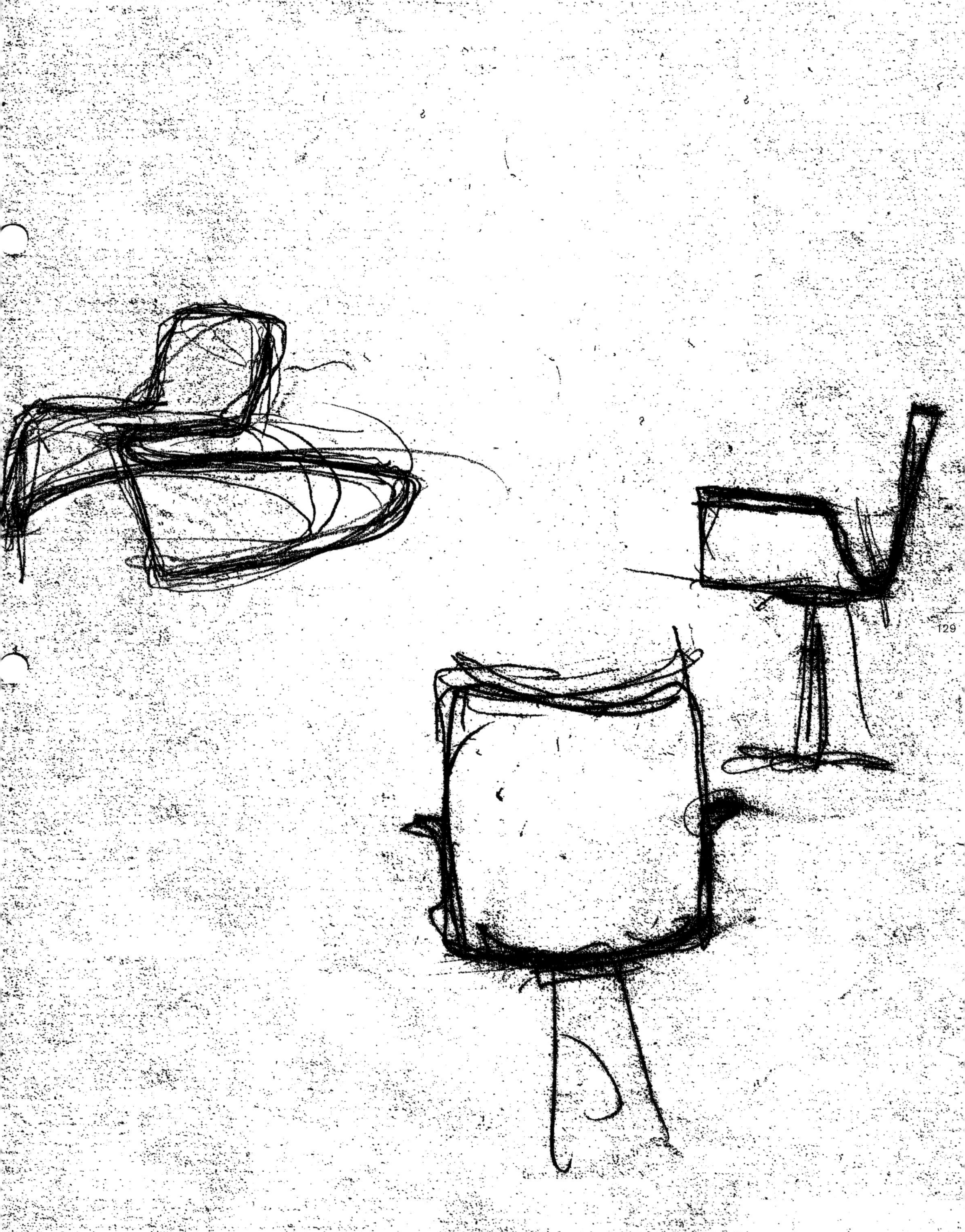

An aesthetic equation
Lise Coirier

Interior architecture studies at the Saint Luc Institute, Brussels provided Xavier Lust with a universe of forms that he has continuously tapped to create his own strong, highly recognizable identity and expressive language. An icon of contemporary design, 'Le Banc' was acclaimed by many international collectors. It marked the beginning of Xavier's elevation to a designer working with some of the great names in Italian furniture production.

After fifteen years as a creative designer, this independent and very articulate artist is a man with a mission. He is passionate about the ideal of functional beauty, a view he expresses as the free spirit he is, tempered, however, with a certain restraint and balance. Throughout his career, Xavier has maintained an authenticity thanks to the clear, uncompromising language with which he expresses his concept of furniture and visionary environments.

What are the artists and techniques that have had the greatest influence on your own creative talent?

Like many of my predecessors, I consider designing an aesthetic equation underpinned by four essential axes that should be part of any design project: function, aesthetics, technology and culture.

Having said that though, when you're developing a project, simplification is the decisive element to get the right balance.

Do you think it was destiny that you were born under a fortuitous star in the year 1969?

Who knows? It's true I was born in 1969, the 'erotic' year, under the sign of Virgo on 27th August. My name, Lust, is of German origin and is a synonym for 'Epicurus'. In English, the name has a slightly more licentious ring! But don't we create in happiness and joy? (laughs).

What are the essential challenges in design?

Embarking on a new project forces you to shed preconceived ideas and conventions and return to the essential, to the human being and objects in their primary form as tools. We sometimes attribute a certain style to a designer, but it's essential that each creation be considered independently, without any genre bias. The real challenge lies in finding an innovative formula while offsetting the constraints; that's the underlying theme of the equation I mentioned before.

Une équation esthétique
Lise Coirier

Des études d'architecture intérieure à l'Institut Saint-Luc à Bruxelles ont donné à Xavier Lust un univers de formes qui n'a cessé d'évoluer vers une identité forte et reconnaissable qu'il a traduit par un langage qui lui est désormais propre.
'Le Banc', devenu icône du design contemporain, a été apprécié par de nombreux collectionneurs internationaux. Il fut le point de départ d'une reconnaissance et d'une ascension au sein du cercle des grands éditeurs italiens.

Après une quinzaine d'années de création, avec une personnalité indépendante doublée d'un talent d'orateur, Xavier Lust suit une trajectoire particulière. Cultivant avec passion l'idéal de la beauté fonctionnelle, il allie une personnalité libre à un sens de la mesure et de l'équilibre. Au fil de ce parcours professionnel, il a su préserver l'authenticité de son talent par un langage clair qu'il transmet au travers de la conception de mobilier et d'environnements visionnaires.

Quelles sont les influences artistiques et techniques de votre démarche créative ?

Comme nombreux de mes prédécesseurs, je considère le travail de conception comme une équation esthétique qui est régie par quatre axes de réflexion essentiels que l'on devrait retrouver dans tout projet de design : fonction, esthétique, technologie et culture.

Cependant, lors de l'évolution du projet, la simplification est le facteur décisif pour atteindre le meilleur équilibre.

Y a-t-il un destin à être né sous la belle étoile de l'année 1969 ?

Qui sait ? Il est vrai que je suis né en 1969, l'année érotique, sous le signe de la vierge — le 27 août. Mon nom, Lust, d'origine allemande, est synonyme de 'Epicure'. En anglais, le sens est plus connoté et s'apparente davantage au libertinage. Ne créons-nous pas dans la joie et la bonne humeur ? (rire)

Quels sont les défis existentiels appliqués au design ?

Aborder un projet nous oblige à nous libérer des conventions et des idées préconçues pour revenir à l'essence, à l'homme et à l'utilisation de l'objet qui s'apparente à un 'outil'.
Il arrive que l'on attribue un style à un designer, mais il est essentiel

Innovation, be it technical, formal or conceptual, is important because it guarantees the authenticity of the project and avoids the risk of ending up with something that's *déjà vu*.

What are the fundamental values you defend?

Simply human nature.

I'm an ardent defender of the authenticity of innovation as opposed to copying, and I'm against all-out industrialization geared simply to making money on account of consumer gullibility and lack of forethought. It's interesting to see how a product with little innovative content can be promoted to the stars, becoming the market winner, while an original product just gets forgotten. I'm always the first to applaud a project that has a purpose and real reason for existing. Good projects assure the respect and good name of their creator.

The 'microcosm' of design lived by this ethical approach until a few years ago. But now there has been a certain drift. At this beginning of the new millennium, the design world is undergoing deep change, and will probably become increasingly an object or tool of marketing, and so become more like the consumer goods industry.

A well designed object takes on a soul; it has a place in posterity thanks to the underlying values it transmits: aesthetic quality, ergonomics, performance, ecology, solidity, ease and pleasure of use, joy and happiness and where possible, accessibility to as wide a public as possible.

What's your attitude to the question of making money and being part of the economic system in general?

Ever since I began my career in 1992, I've wanted to create my own projects. Just designing is not enough for me. I have no wish to subject myself to the hierarchy of an architectural office.

At the beginning of the Nineties, to my knowledge at least, there was no promotional or subsidy system for design as there is today in Belgium, which would have allowed me to communicate my intentions and projects.

So I created my own workshop where I made prototypes for my own satisfaction. They were not sculptures but always models that could be industrially reproduced and so they really followed the principles of industrial design. That's why I am so particular about production details, as it's often these that make the difference. At that time I was

que chaque création soit considérée indépendamment de tout préjugé de genre.

Le vrai défi de cette réflexion est d'apporter une formule innovante en jonglant avec les contraintes, véritable fil conducteur de cette équation que j'évoquais précédemment dans notre discussion.

L'innovation, qu'elle soit technique, formelle ou conceptuelle, est importante puisqu'elle garantit l'authenticité du projet et élimine le risque de se retrouver en bout de course face à un projet 'déjà-vu'.

Quelles sont les valeurs fondamentales que vous défendez ?

Elles sont simplement de nature humaine.

Je suis un fervent défenseur de l'authenticité et de l'innovation face à la copie, et je m'oppose à l'industrialisation forcenée lorsqu'elle est basée sur le seul profit et mise sur la crédulité et le manque de réflexion du consommateur.

Il est parfois curieux de voir à quel point un objet peu innovant et promu à outrance sur le marché peut s'imposer et faire oublier le modèle original. Je suis toutefois le premier à applaudir un projet qui a du sens et une réelle raison d'exister. Les bons projets sont garants du respect et de la notoriété qu'acquiert spontanément leur créateur.

Le 'microcosme' du design est resté, jusqu'il y a quelques années, proche de cette ligne éthique. Mais il faut constater une certaine dérive. La planète design se trouve en ce début de millénaire en pleine mutation et elle va probablement devenir de plus en plus objet et outil de commercialisation pour se rapprocher de l'industrie de consommation.

L'objet juste acquiert une âme et une garantie de postérité qui soustend ses caractères fondamentaux et les valeurs qu'il véhicule : qualité esthétique, ergonomie, performance, écologie, solidité, facilité et plaisir d'utilisation apportant de la joie et du bonheur et, si possible, un accès aisé au plus grand nombre.

Quel est votre rapport à la rentabilité et au système économique en général ?

Lorsque j'ai débuté ma carrière en 1992, j'avais une grande envie de réaliser mes projets, le dessin ne me suffisait plus. Je n'avais aucune disposition pour me soumettre à la hiérarchie d'un bureau d'architecture.

Au commencement des années 90, il n'y avait, à ma connaissance, aucune structure de promotion ou d'aide au design comme actuellement en

hardly concerned at all with making it worth my while. Having to make money seemed superfluous and I was confident about the future. Gradually though, with the everyday pressures, the need to make some money became increasingly compelling …

What are your sources of inspiration?
After traveling abroad, I realized that discovery and getting away from things are indispensable values in our profession. We are 'sponges'; our experiences nourish our internal universe, becoming the source of inspiration.
When I returned from a trip to India, I designed the 'Virgo' bookcase, which I batch produced myself for several years, and was distributed by Tradix, a Belgian importer of Italian furniture. That was my first self-production experience. Afterwards, I produced the 'Vice Versa' mirror in stainless steel, then the '4 pattes' in aluminum, all distributed by the same firm until 1999.
I look back at that period without bitterness as a time when I spent a great deal of energy, had many human experiences and made products that financially proved not very profitable. As time developed I was forced to look for new means of production. I developed a new technique I called '(de)formation of surfaces' as a means of substantiating an idea. In that way, apparently unreconcilable opposites come together: rupture and tension, forms of the infinite, take shape in the finite. Contradictions are resolved without conflict, and there is nothing more to add.
After that, at the age of 30, I began meeting with Italian producers, presenting my best models at the 'Salone Satellite' of the Milan *Salone Internazionale del Mobile* in 2000.
It was essential that the specialist and potential producers actually saw what my work looked like.

After MDF Italia, De Padova and Driade followed, and in Belgium Xavier worked with Extremis, Aquamass and Modular.

His name features now among the famous in the design world. He is one of the 135 international designers included in the Perpetual Design Calendar, *published by Designboom, and considered the most likely to influence the 21st century. He appears in many other publications. Then there is the long list of awards and prizes, the most*

Belgique, qui m'aurait permis de relayer correctement mes intentions et mes projets.
C'est alors que j'ai créé mon propre atelier dans lequel je réalisais pour mon plaisir des prototypes, pas des sculptures mais toujours des modèles reproductibles en série qui étaient donc fidèles aux principes du design industriel.
Pour ces diverses raisons, je suis très attaché aux détails de fabrication, car ce sont souvent eux qui font la différence. J'étais, à cette époque, peu préoccupé de rentabiliser mon temps, l'obligation du gain me paraissait superflue et j'étais confiant dans l'avenir. Petit à petit, par les contraintes du quotidien, le besoin de rentabilité est devenu de plus en plus nécessaire…

Quelles sont vos sources d'inspiration ?
Lors de voyages à l'étranger, je me suis rendu compte que la découverte et l'évasion sont des valeurs primordiales dans notre métier.
Nous sommes des 'éponges' et c'est notre vécu qui nourrit notre univers intérieur, et devient la source de notre acte de création.
Au retour d'un voyage en Inde, j'ai dessiné l'étagère 'Virgo' que j'ai produite personnellement en série pendant des années, diffusée par Tradix, l'un des importateurs belges de mobilier italien. Ce fut ma première expérience d'auto-édition. J'ai produit par après le miroir 'Vice Versa' en acier inox, puis la table '4 pattes' en aluminium, tous diffusés par le même distributeur jusque 1999.
Sans amertume, je garde de cette période le souvenir de beaucoup d'énergie dépensée, de nombreuses expériences humaines et de productions finalement peu rentables financièrement. Le temps de l'évolution m'imposa la recherche de nouveaux moyens de production, et j'ai mis au point une nouvelle technique que j'ai baptisée '(dé)formation de surfaces', par laquelle j'objective l'idée dans la matière. Sont alors réunis les contraires apparemment irréconciliables, rupture et tension, qui forment une véritable figure de l'infini dans le fini. Ces contradictions se résolvent ensuite dans l'apaisement, il n'y a plus rien à ajouter.
Dès lors, je me suis lancé, à 30 ans, avec mes meilleurs modèles, à la rencontre des éditeurs italiens au *Salone Satellite* du Salon du Meuble de Milan en 2000.
Il était essentiel que les spécialistes et éditeurs potentiels puissent être confrontés physiquement à mes modèles.

noteworthy being the Compasso d'Oro special mention in 2004 awarded by ADI, the Industrial Design Association headquartered in Milan, to his aluminum 'La Grande Table' produced by MDF.

On the scope of design, what are your limits?
I'm currently working in five design areas:
- industrially produced furniture and accessories;
- limited series;
- interior architecture;
- urban furniture;
- industrial design.

Furniture and accessory design goes hand in hand with architecture projects for both public and private clients. Recent projects have been the Belgian Consulate General in Montreal, Canada, the library in Watermael-Boitsfort, the new Isy Brachot art gallery in Brussels, and a home in Ibiza.

Xavier has also entered new markets like urban furniture which is a means of getting his design aesthetic known to the general public and creating a dialogue between his concept of beauty and our often chaotic urban environment.

Luckily Xavier still has time left to mull over his many ideas about how to translate dream into reality. For that is still the equation to be solved. But for Xavier, quality remains the key goal for which there are simply no short cuts. Lust's professional 'design culture' reflects his own persona. The ease and energy he projects are incomparable. His approach to the concept is both open and honest: it is the thread that runs through his entire existence, the basic tenet he turns into tangible objects.

Tell me about being destined to design.
The choice of my profession became apparent at 19 when I began a higher education course in interior architecture. My father was in the business of original communications, often using printed, folded and glued paper (pop-ups, origami etc). I was good at that, figuring out the technical problems quite easily. I loved fiddling about and trying different things; I was truly happy when I liked the results. With time it became clear that this was what I should be doing in life; it was a gift

Après MDF Italia, les collaborations s'enchaînent, avec De Padova, Driade, et en Belgique avec Extremis, Aquamass et Modular.

Son nom est repris parmi les plus célèbres designers. On le retrouve dans le Perpetual Design Calendar *publié par Designboom, dans un ouvrage sélectionnant les 135 designers internationaux susceptibles d'influencer le XXIe siècle, et de nombreux autres. A cela s'ajoutent les mérites et les prix qui font l'objet d'une longue liste, tel le plus remarquable prix de design, le Compasso d'Oro délivré en 2004 par l'ADI (Association pour le Design industriel installé à Milan), qui attribue une mention spéciale à 'La Grande Table' en aluminium éditée par MDF Italia.*

LES TERRITOIRES DU DESIGN

Quelles sont vos limites ?
Actuellement, je développe 5 secteurs d'activités :
- design de meubles et accessoires produits en grandes séries ;
- design de séries limitées ;
- architecture intérieure ;
- mobilier urbain ;
- design industriel.

La conception de mobilier et d'accessoires s'accompagne de projets d'architecture auprès d'une clientèle privée et publique. Les réalisations récentes sont notamment le Consulat Général de Belgique à Montréal (Canada), la bibliothèque pour adultes de Watermael-Boitsfort et la nouvelle galerie d'art Isy Brachot à Bruxelles, ainsi qu'une résidence à Ibiza.

Il accède aussi à de nouveaux marchés comme celui du mobilier urbain, qui permet de faire apprécier au plus grand nombre l'esthétique du design dans l'espace public et de faire dialoguer sa vision du beau avec l'urbanité souvent chaotique d'une ville…

Il lui reste heureusement du temps et une multitude d'idées à traduire du rêve à la réalité. C'est sans doute là que réside encore l'équation à résoudre, mais Xavier Lust vise avant tout la qualité et ne cèdera jamais à la tentation de la facilité. Sa culture du design rejoint ses convictions personnelles. La liberté et l'énergie qu'il dégage sont en effet sans pareils. Une philosophie face au concept qui m'apparaît franche et honnête. Une ligne du temps, un fil conducteur qui le suit et qu'il traduit en objets tangibles.

from heaven. There are no idle moments, no fixed timetables. It's a job that involves sensitivity at all times. If you think of some of the Italian maestri I admire, people like Vico Magistretti and Achille Castiglioni, who at over 80 still create with such crispness. Then there are the pioneers of design like Maddalena De Padova with whom I've been lucky enough to establish a working relationship but also a real friendship. In these relations, as in creation, there are intelligent, inexpressible and hidden aspects.

SILENT BEAUTY
What is your view?
Beauty touches the essential. Beauty is silent; it becomes manifest as a language expressed by the body, the senses and the spirit. When an object achieves excellence, it resembles no known thing; it is justified by its very existence, beautiful on account of its intelligence, for the fact that it is an expression of the evident; it leaves no-one indifferent regardless of his culture. It is something that goes beyond words and cultural boundaries. A truly great work contains an infinite number of intentional and virtual traits and is simply extraordinary.

This then must be the secret of Xavier Lust's creations that enthralls manufacturers and general public alike.

Parlez-moi de ce destin de designer.
Le choix de ce métier s'est imposé dès mes 19 ans et c'est ainsi que j'ai entrepris des études supérieures d'architecture intérieure. Mon père travaillait dans les supports de communication originaux, souvent en papier imprimé, plié, collé (pop-up, origami…), j'étais apte à comprendre des problèmes techniques et à les résoudre facilement. J'aimais bricoler, expérimenter et je ressentais un grand bonheur quand j'étais satisfait du résultat. Au fil du temps, il est apparu que ce métier est un projet de vie, un don du ciel ; il n'y a pas de temps 'mort' ou d'horaires fixes, c'est un travail sensible de chaque instant. Je pense notamment à certains *maestri* italiens que j'admire comme Vico Magistretti, Achille Castiglioni… qui, à plus de 80 ans, créaient toujours avec autant de fraîcheur. Je pense aussi aux pionniers du design comme Maddalena De Padova, avec laquelle j'ai eu la chance d'établir une relation de travail mais aussi une réelle amitié. Dans ces relations, comme dans la création, on retrouve des aspects intelligents, indicibles, non révélés.

UNE BEAUTÉ SILENCIEUSE
Qu'en pensez-vous ?
La beauté touche à l'essentiel, elle est silencieuse et se révèle comme un langage qui s'exprime par le corps, les sens et l'esprit. Lorsqu'un objet atteint l'excellence, il ne ressemble à rien de connu, il se justifie par son existence propre, il est beau à travers son intelligence, il atteint par-là le concept d'évidence, il ne laisse personne indifférent, quelle que soit sa culture. Nous sommes à ce moment au-delà des mots et des frontières culturelles. Une œuvre qui atteint la grandeur contient une infinité d'intentions et de virtualités et c'est extraordinaire.

Ce serait donc ce mystère dans les créations de Xavier Lust qui séduit les éditeurs et le grand public.

Bibliography

Asensio, Oscar. *D! DES!GNDES!GN meubles et lampes.* Atrium, 2006.

Gnocchi, Didi. *De Padova / 50 years of design.* Milan, Fréderico Motta, 2006.

Hudson, Jennifer. *1000 new designs and where to find them.* London, Laurence King, 2006.

Lambert, Stéphane. Brussels, identités plurielles. In: *Collection Villes en mouvement.* Paris, Autrement, October 2006.

Stafford, Cliff. *Home.* London, Quadrille Publishing Limited, November 2006.

Coirier, Lise (ed.). *Label-Design. Design in Belgium after 2000.* Oostkamp, Stichting Kunstboek, 2005.

I.Dot points of view / What's moving in Italian design today. Milan, Italian Design Agency, 2005.

175 D. Brussels, DELVAUX créateurs s.a., 2004.

XXth ADI Compasso D'Oro Award Catalogue. Milan, Fondazione ADI per il Design Italiano, 2004.

Coirier, Lise & Laurent, Denis. *Design en Belgique 1945-2000.* Bruxelles, Racine, 2004.

Conran, Terence & Fraser, Max. *Designers on design.* London, Conran/Octopus, 2004.

Coirier, Lise (ed.). A to Z, Made in Belgium. Brussels, MMAP/HKRA, 2001.

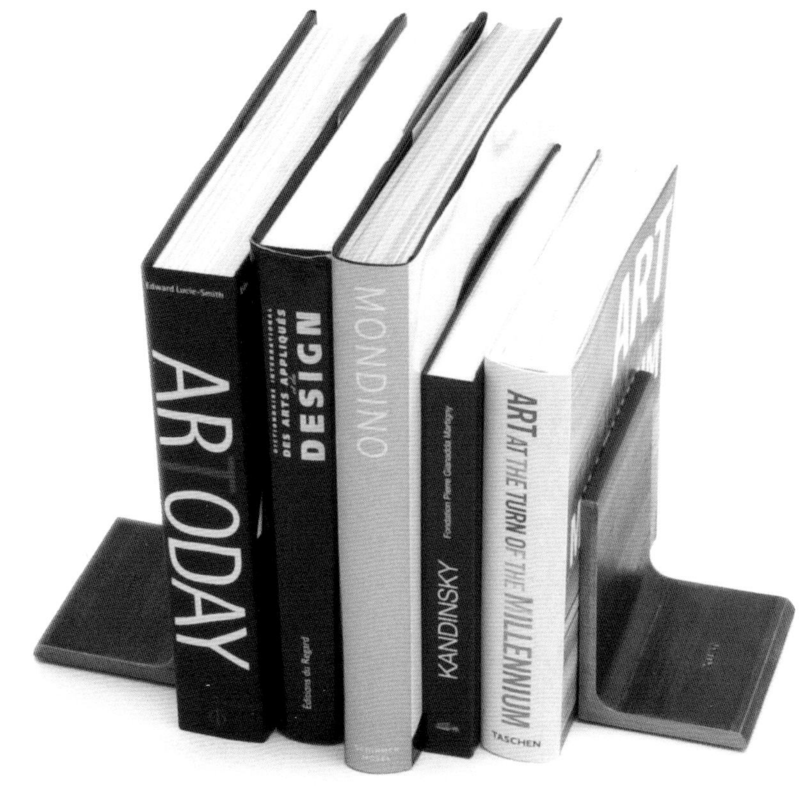

Awards

Sept. 2004 Milan (IT)
Special Mention for 'La Grande Table' at the XXth Compasso d'Oro Awards

7 Jan. 2004 Chicago (US)
GOOD DESIGN award 2003, from The Chicago Athenaeum (Museum of Architecture and Design)
'PicNik' is awarded the famous Good Design award, the oldest international design competition

2004 Milan (IT)
'Crédence', designed for De Padova in 2003, is selected by the 'Osservatorio Permanente per il Design' for the
XXth Compasso d'Oro Awards

Dec. 2003 Hannover (DE)
'PicNik' wins the iF Award 2004

Sept. 2003 Brussels (BE)
Prizewinner of the Henry van de Velde Award 2003 for Young Talent

Sept. 2003
'PicNik' is nominated in the FX awards (UK) & the Henry van de Velde awards – best product (BE)

Jul. 2003 Milan (IT)
'La Grande Table', designed for MDF Italia in 2002, is selected by the 'Osservatorio Permanente per il Design' for the
XXth Compasso d'Oro Awards

Jan. 2003 Köln (DE)
'PicNik' is awarded the first prize for 'Best Item' (Interior Innovation Award 2003) at the IMM – Internationale Möbelmesse

Jan. 2003 Paris (FR)
'PicNik' wins 'Les best of NOW!' first prize by a panel of purchasers (*Maison & Objet* – Now! Design à vivre)

Mar. 2002 London (UK)
'Le Banc' is winner of the 13th Design week 'Awards for the World's Best Furniture Design' at the Grosvenor House Hotel in Mayfair

May 2001 (BE)
'Le Banc' obtains the first prize for the seat: 'All Around Favorite' prize awarded by *Le Vif/l'Express* (BE)

Museum acquisitions

Sept. 2006 Musée des Arts Décoratifs, Paris (FR)
1 piece of 'Credence' for the contemporary design museum collection

Feb. 2006 Stedelijk Museum CS, Amsterdam (NL)
1 piece of 'Le Banc' and 1 piece of 'Crédence' for the contemporary design museum collection

Since 2006 Tate Modern, London (UK)
17 'PicNik' are displayed to be used by the visitors

Since 2005 Musée d'Art Japonais, Brussels (BE)
5 pieces of 'Le Banc' are displayed to admire the Japanese art

2001 – 2004 SFMOMA San Francisco Museum of Modern Art, San Francisco (US)
Series of 'T-chair' for the Museum store

A list of exhibitions

June – Oct 2007	'Xavier Lust (de)formations', Grand-Hornu Images, Hornu (BE)
June – Oct 2007	'Sur un fil tendu', Mac's, Museum of Contemporary Art, Hornu (BE)
May – June 2007	Belgische Vormgeving 1, Museum Waterland, Purmerend (NL)
May – Aug 2007	'Collections/Connections', Grand-Hornu Images, Hornu (BE)
April 2007	Salone Internazionale del Mobile, Milano (IT)
	– Rho Fiera Milano:
	MDF Italia, Modular, FEG, Zeritalia,
	'Avverati, a dream come true' the 10th anniversary of Salone Satellite
	– Milano City: Urban furniture presentation
	Bus stop & bike shelter in Corso Como + different bike shelters in Fortis Center
Sept – Dec 2006	'Il Cosmo Driade: Immagine del Design Italiano', Museum Die Neue Sammlung, Munich (DE)
Oct 2006	'USXL' at INTERIEUR, Kortrijk (BE)
July – Aug 2006	'2460 Design Momenten Mortsel', Mortsel (BE)
April 2006	Salone Internazionale del Mobile, Rho Fiera, Milano (IT)
Febr 2006 – May 2006	'Spotting' Stedelijk Museum CS, Amsterdam (NL)
Oct 2005 – Feb 2006	'Label-design.be, Design in Belgium after 2000', Grand-Hornu Images / ProMateria / Design Vlaanderen, Hornu (BE)
Sept – Nov 2005	Super!, Triënnale voor Beeldende Kunst, Mode en Design, Hasselt (BE)
May 2005	Guest of Honor at the SIDIM, Montreal (CA)
Jan – Feb 2005	'EDIFICE présente Xavier Lust', 27 bis, Bld Raspail, Paris (FR)
Dec 2004 – Feb 2005	[Im]perfect by Design, 4th Triennale of Design, Design Vlaanderen / Royal Museums of Art And History, Brussels (BE)
2004 – 2005	I.dot – Italian Design on tour
	17-26 May 04, Chelsea Art Museum, New-York (US)
	14-16 June 04, Neocon, Chicago (US)
	15-24 Oct 04, 'Back To School', Kortrijk (BE)
	1-10 Dec 04, Fad-foment de les arts decoratives, Barcelona (ES)
	12-20 Feb 05, Bulthaup Center, St Petersburg (RU)
	4-16 May 05, Designmay Forum, Berlin (DE)
	8-13 Sept 05, China Design Alliance, Beijing (CN)
	27 Sep-4 Oct 05, Science & Technology Museum, Shangaï (CN)
Sept 2004	'Œverture' / Pro Materia, MIAT, Gent (BE)
Sept 2004	XXth Compasso d'Oro ADI, Triennale da Milano, Milan (IT)
April 2004	Salone Internazionale del Mobile Milano (Driade showroom), Milan (IT)
Dec 2003	'World Best Design Exchange 2003', Oullim, Seoul (KR)
Nov 2003 – Jan 2004	'Henry Van De Velde Awards 2003', VIZO Gallery, Brussels (BE)
Oct 2003 – April 2004	'Iconen van Design in Vlaanderen', Vlaams Parlement, Brussels (BE)
Sept – Oct 2003	'San't in Buitenland', VIZO Gallery, Brussels (BE)

Sept 2003	'Privé 03', Médiatine, Brussels (BE)
June – Sept 2003	'De Nieuwe Oogst', VIZO Gallery, Brussels (BE)
April 2003	Salone Internazionale del Mobile, Milano (IT)
March – April 2003	'Hermes', La Verrière, Brussels (BE)
Dec 2002 – Jan 2003	Centre Wallonie – Brussels (BE), Paris (FR)
Nov '2002	Biennale Internationale Design, Saint-Etienne (FR)
Oct 2002	Interieur, Kortrijk (BE)
June 2002	Galerie Isy Brachot, Brussels (BE)
May 2002	Galerie Usage Externe, Brussels (BE)
May 2002	SAD, Paris (FR)
April 2002	Salone Internazionale del Mobile, Milan (IT)
March 2002	'Une nouvelle Belgique, des idées et des materiaux', VIZO-CIVA Brussels (BE)
Oct 2001	'Origines et originalités', Espace Morphosis, Brussels (BE)
	Transit, Brussels (BE)
	Classic, Kortrijk (BE)
June – Sept 2001	La Chataigneraie, Flémalle-Liège (BE)
May 2001	Le Vif/l'Express, Jodoigne (BE)
April 2001	Salone Internazionale del Mobile, Milan (IT)
March 2001	Detrois, 3 rue Macau, Brussels (BE)
Dec 2000 – Jan 2001	Musée des Techniques, Prague (CZ)
Nov 2000	Cocoon, Brussels (BE)
April 2000	Salone Internazionale del Mobile, Milan (IT)
Jan 2000	F3 expo, Cologne (DE)
1999	Galerie A-Ronne, Brussels (BE)
Oct 1998	Interieur, Kortrijk (BE)
April 1998	Galerie 6a Montenapoleone, Milan (IT)
June – Sept 1997	Centre Wallonie - Brussels (BE), Paris (FR)
May 1997	Galerie Théorèmes, Brussels (BE)
March – April 1997	Centre d'art contemporain, Brussels (BE)
Jan – Feb 1997	Das Belgische Haus, Cologne (DE)
1992 – 1996	12 exhibitions in Belgium

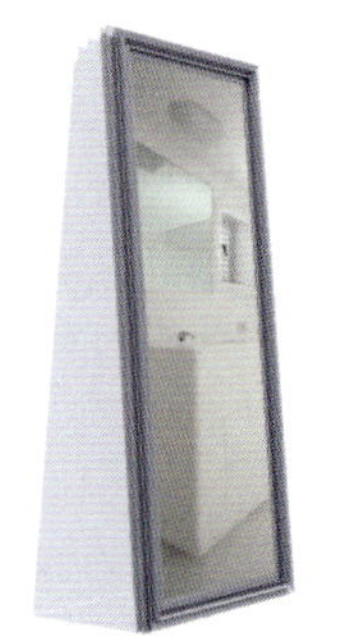

	year of creation	year of production
StarSystem	2005	2007

Mirror
Anodized aluminum
130 x 130 x 10 cm
240 x 90 x 10 cm
Driade, Caorso, Italy

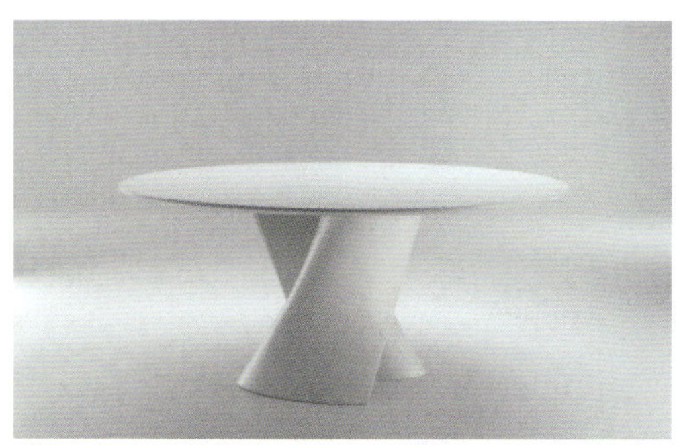

	year of creation	year of production
Archiduchaise	2004	2007

Chair
Mirror-polished aluminum
77 x Ø 100 cm
Limited edition

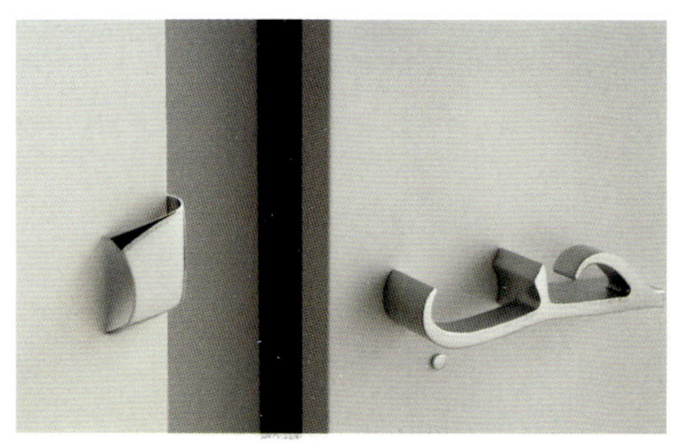

	year of creation	year of production
S-table	2004	2007

Table
Baydur®
73 x Ø 156 cm
MDF Italia, Milano, Italy

	year of creation	year of production
Jeu de Paume - HOB	2006	2007

Handles
6 x 6 x 3,6 cm
3,5 x 13,5 x 3 cm
Gruppo Feg, Milano, Italy

		year of production
Stove casing & tools		2007

Lacquered steel
Various dimensions
Bodart & Gonnay, Herzée, Belgium

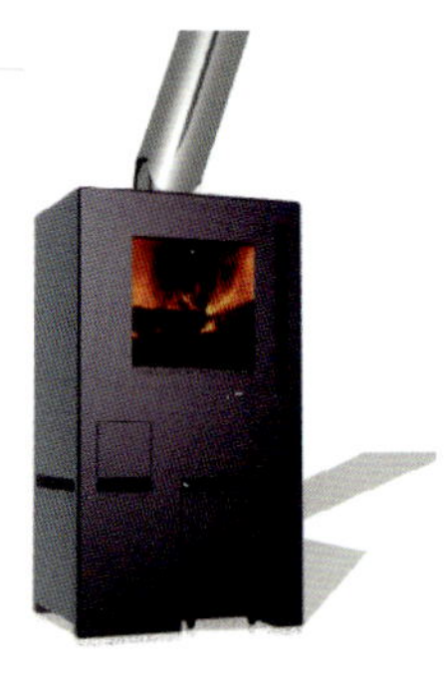

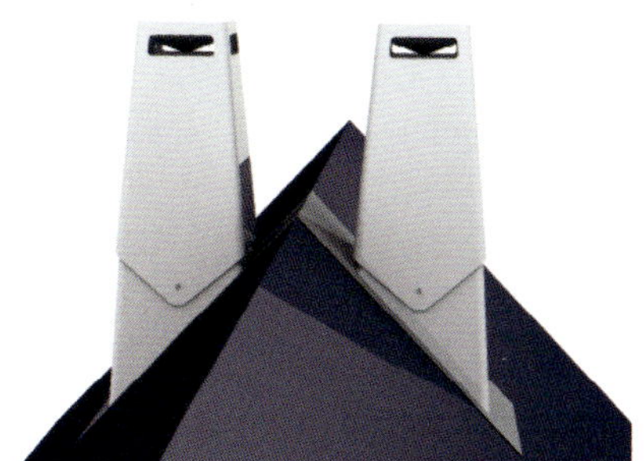

Cheminées Poujoulat	2006	2007

Lacquered or mirror-polished steel
Various dimensions
Poujoulat, Niort, France

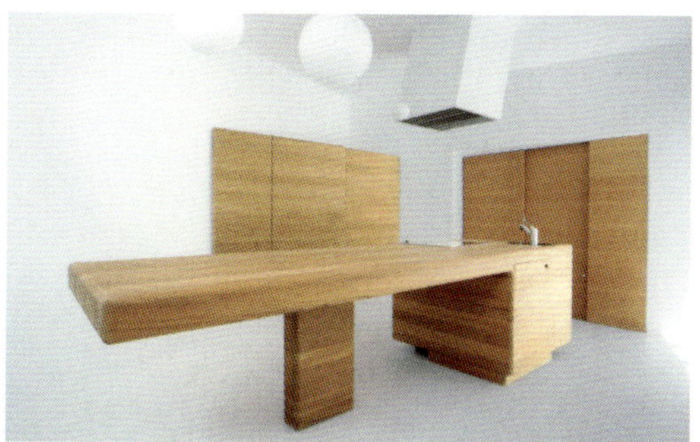

House in Ibiza, Spain	2005	2007

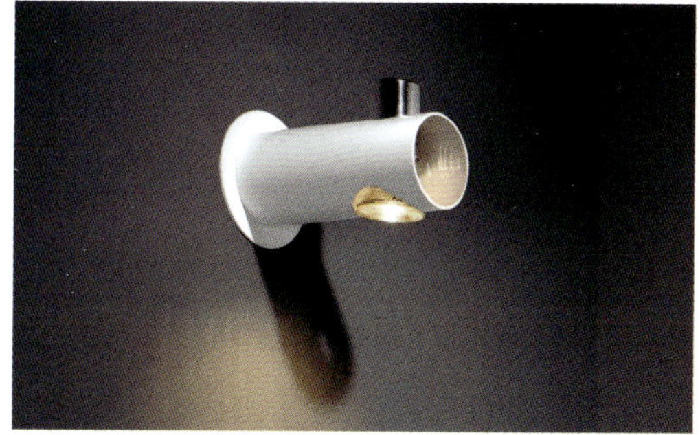

Pipelite	1996	2007

Lamp
Lacquered aluminum
14 x 12 x 13 cm
14 x 20 x 13 cm
14 x 30 x 13 cm
Modular Lighting Instruments, Kortrijk, Belgium

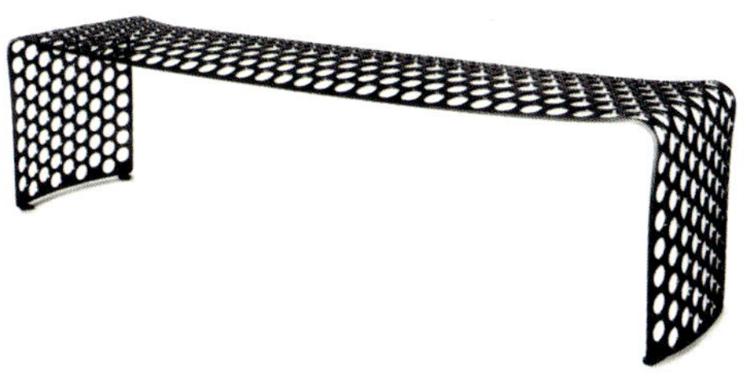

Gun Metal Bench	2006

Bench
Black steel
44 x 170 x 40 cm
Limited edition

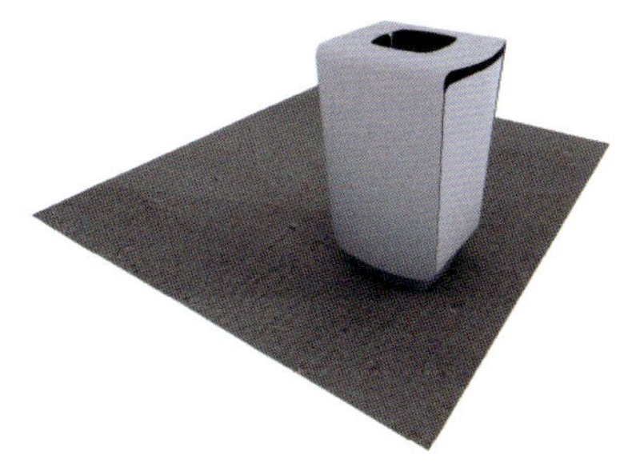

Corbeille urbaine	2006

Lacquered steel
89,5 x 52 x 46 cm

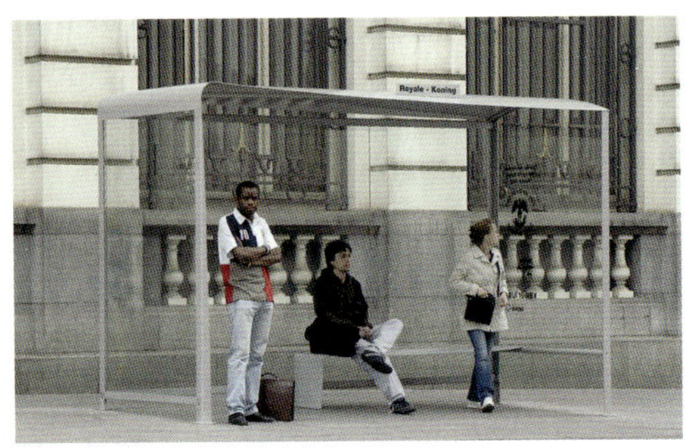

| Mont des Arts – Kunstberg | 2006 |

Street furniture installation
Ville de Bruxelles – Stad Brussel, Belgium

p. 67, 126-127

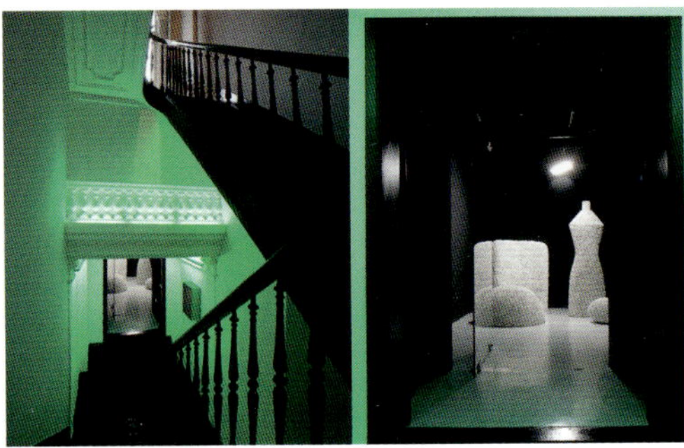

| Art gallery Isy Gabriel Brachot | 2006 |

Brussels, Belgium

p. 55

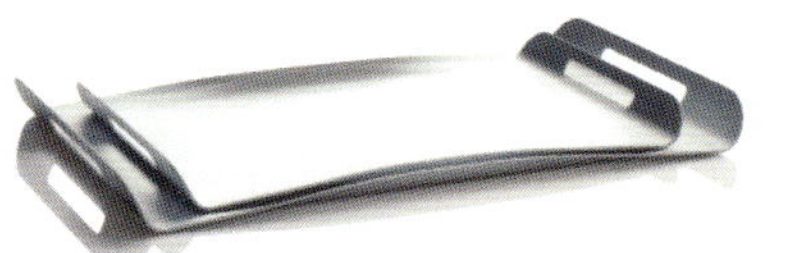

| **T42 & T43** | 2005 | 2006 |

Trays
Anodized aluminum
T42: 4,2 x 48,5 x 28 cm
T43: 4,8 x 58,2 x 39,6 cm
Driade Kosmo, Caorso, Italy

p. 32-33

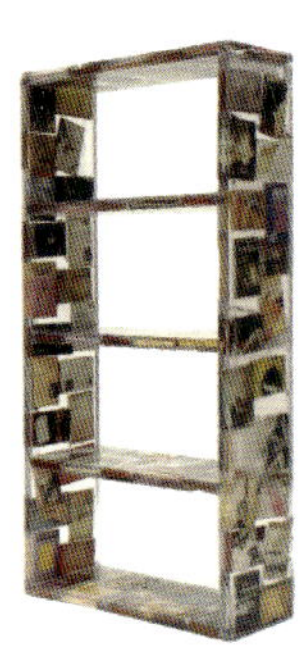

| **Bookshelf** | 2005 | 2006 |

Paperbacks, polyester resin
168 x 82 x 32 cm
Pièce unique
Les petits riens, Brussels, Belgium

p. 62, 63

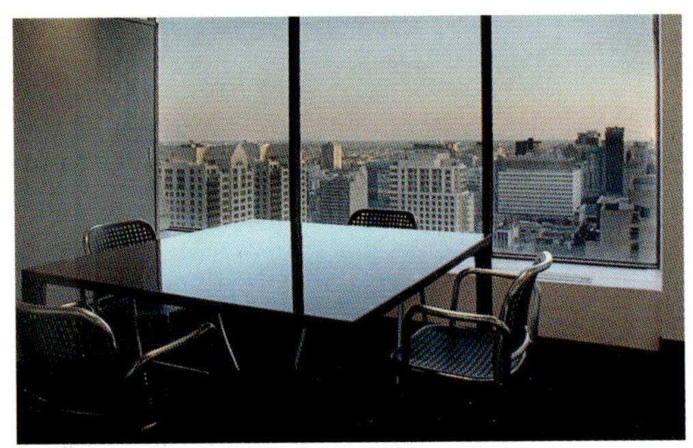

| General Consulate of Belgium | 2005 |

Montreal, Canada

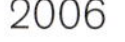

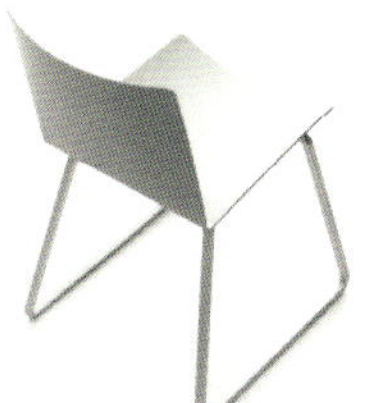
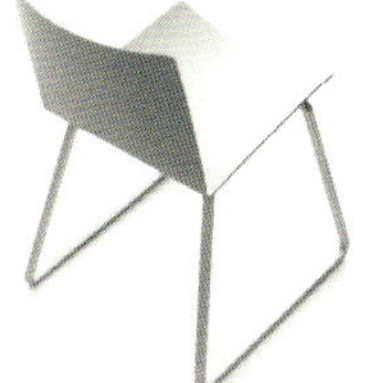

Bwb Chair | 2003 | 2006

Chair
Anodized aluminum
77 x 45 x 50 cm
Zeritalia, Italy

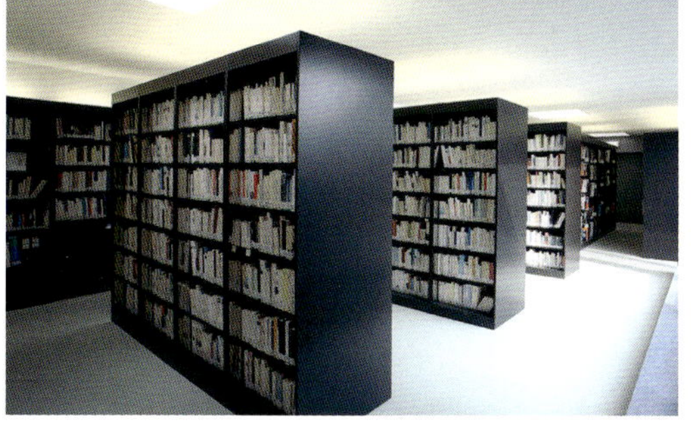

Public library | 2001 | 2006

Watermael-Boitsfort, Brussels, Belgium

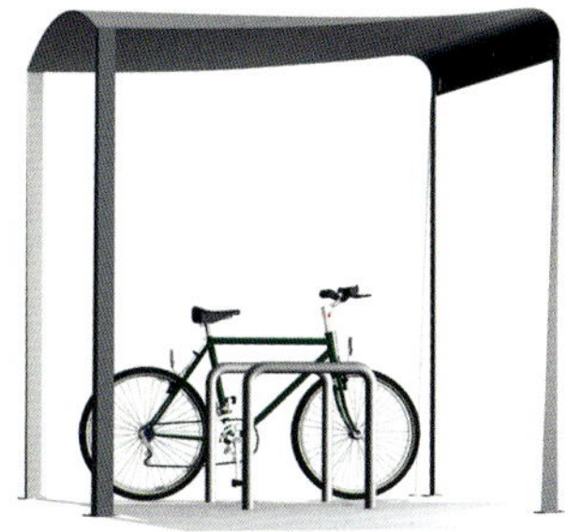

Abri-Vélo | 2005

Lacquered steel
235 x 200 cm > 500 x 200 cm

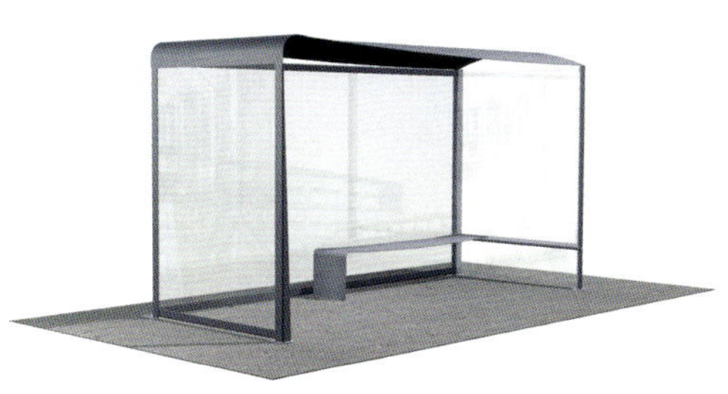

Abri-Voyageurs | 2002 | 2006

Lacquered steel
235 x 380 x 150 cm

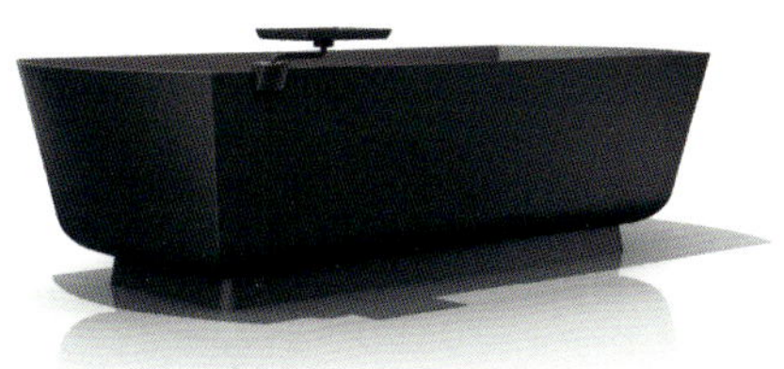

Navale | 2004

Bathtub
Anodized aluminum
52 x 180 x 75 cm
Aquamass, Brussels, Belgium

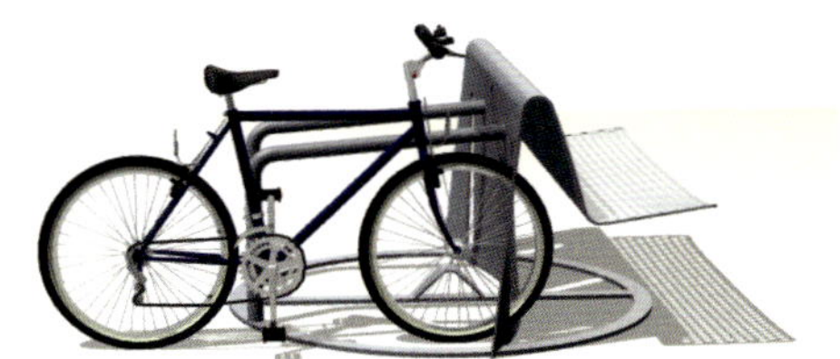

Banc-Vélo	2004

Lacquered steel
81 x 148 x 149 cm

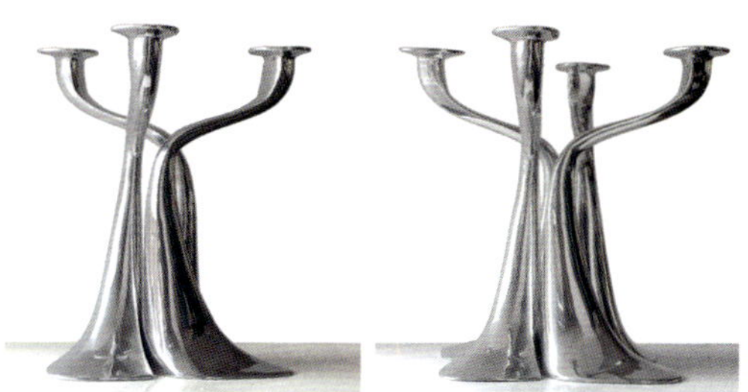

Turner	2003	2004

Candleholder
Mirror-polished aluminum
32,5 x 20,2 x 12 cm
Driade Kosmo, Caorso, Italy

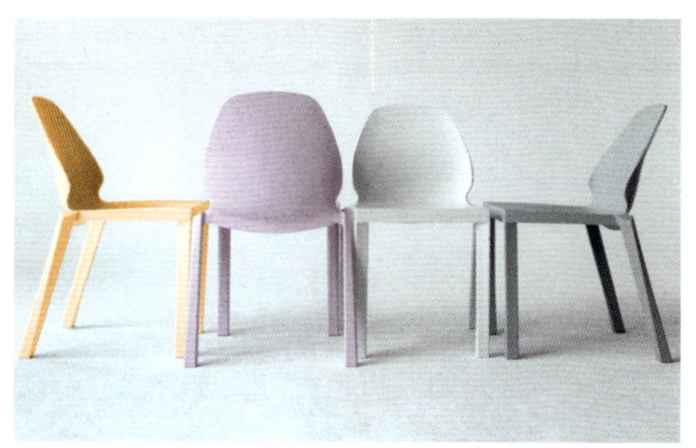

Extra Chair	2003	2004

Chair
Polypropylene
80 x 51 x 53 cm
Driade Store, Caorso, Italy

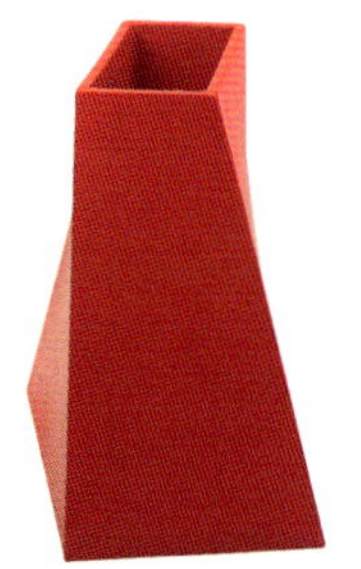

Paso Doble	2003	2004

Umbrella stand
Polypropylene
44,4 x 47 x 26 cm
Driade Kosmo, Caorso, Italy

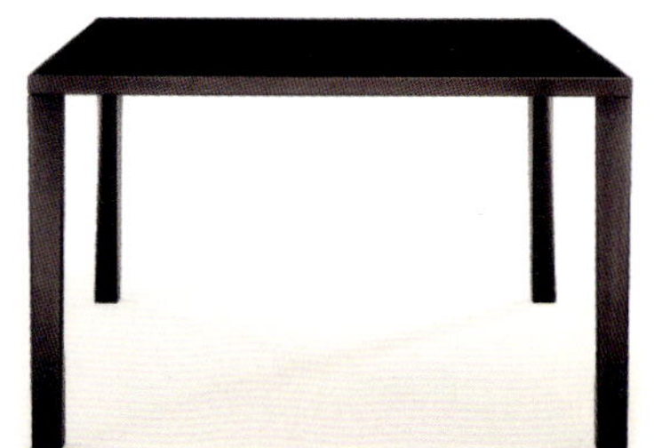

Tetra	2001	2004

Table
Lacquered steel, glass
72 x 130 x 130 cm
72 x 210 x 90 cm
Driade Aleph, Caorso, Italy

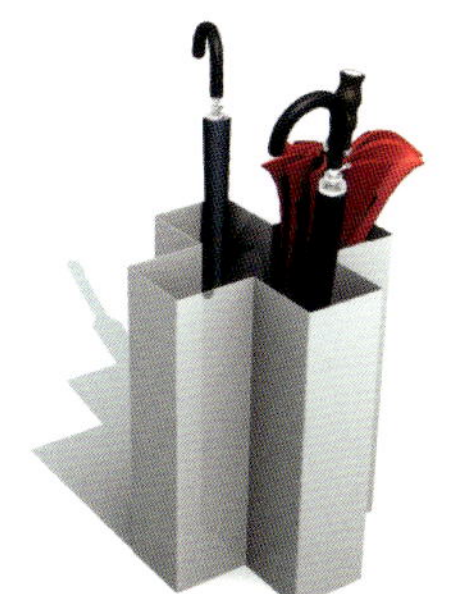

Rainy Day in Switzerland	2002	2003

Umbrella stand
Lacquered steel
48 x 36 x 36 cm
DePadova / Zoltan, Milano, Italy

p. 87

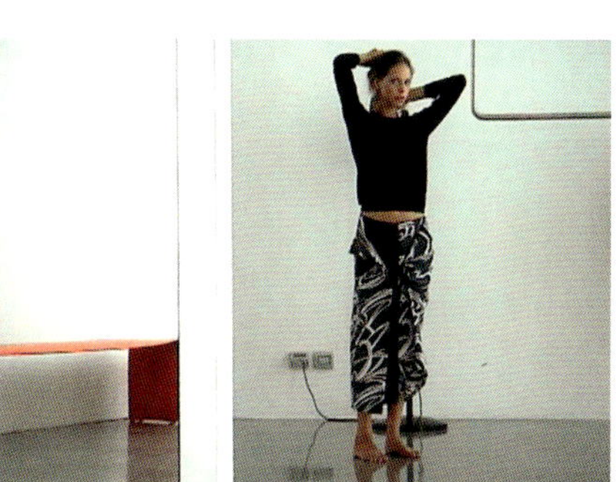
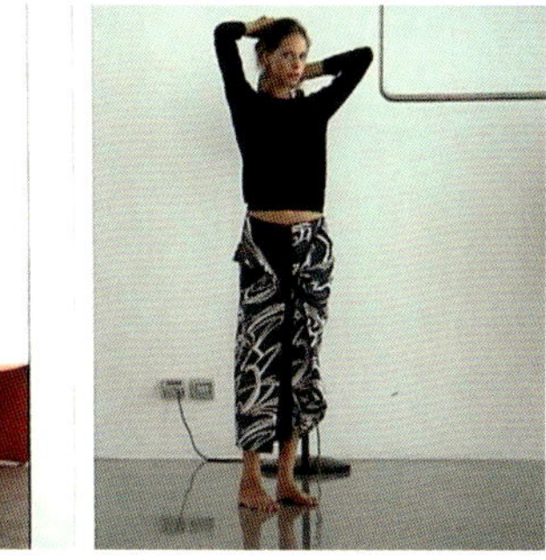

NEWS fashion show room	2003

Milano, Italy

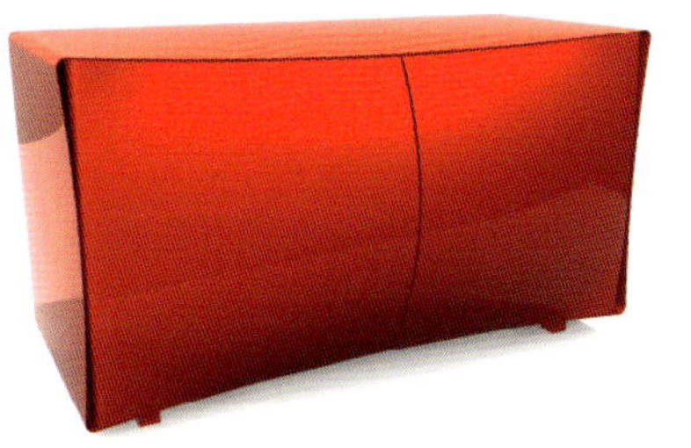

Crédence	2002	2003

Cupboard
Lacquered aluminum
79 x 140 x 70 cm
De Padova, Milano, Italy

p. 22-23, 24, 25, 27

Abri-4-Vélos	2002

Lacquered steel
221 x 135 x 150 cm

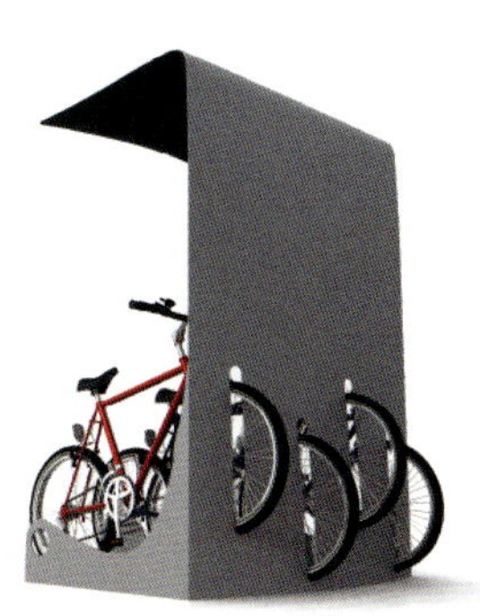

p. 124, 125

TANDEM, Press communication office	2001	2004

Brussels, Belgium

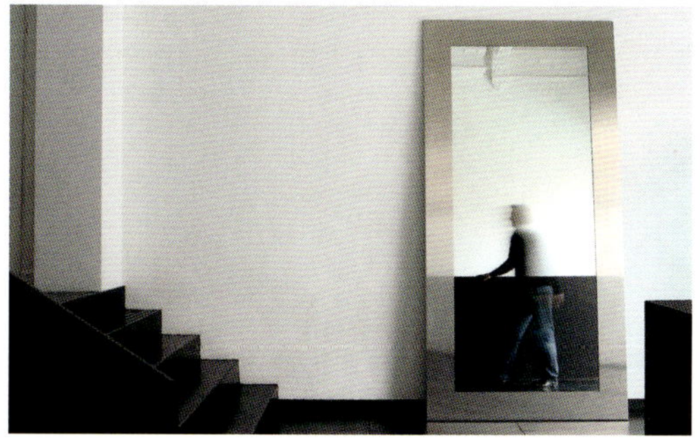

p. 25, 43, 77

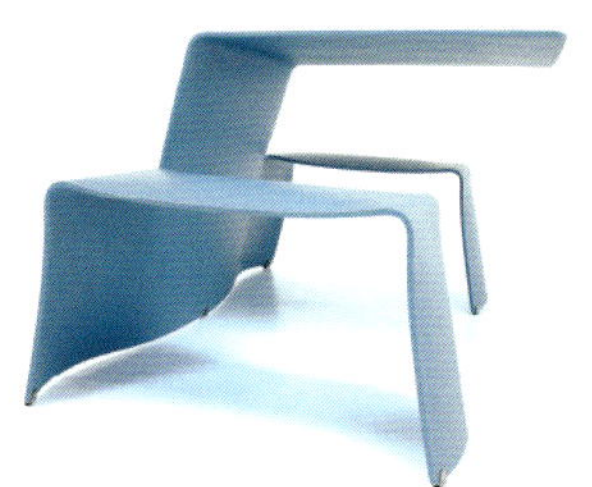

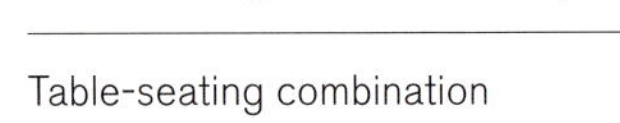

PicNik (design X. Lust & D. Wynants) | 2002

Table-seating combination
Lacquered or anodized aluminum
73 x 146 x 84 cm
Extremis, Gijverinkhove, Belgium

p. 64, 65, 67, 68, 69

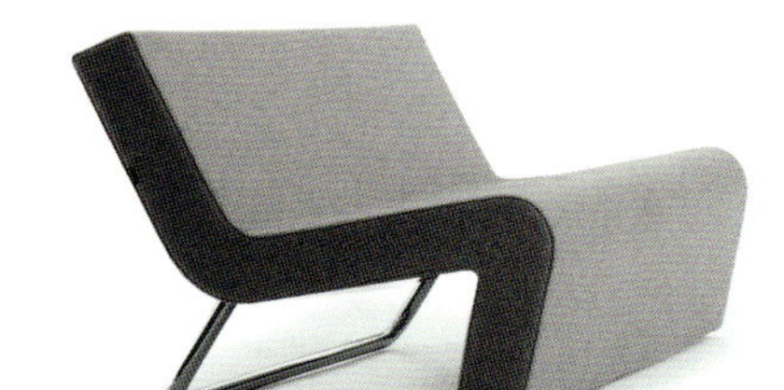

Lounge Sofa | 2000 | 2002

Sofa
Cold-foamed steel frame, removable upholstery
61 x 200 x 80 cm
MDF Italia, Milano, Italy

p. 17

La Chaise | 2001 | 2002

Chair
Anodized aluminum, satin or shiny
75 x 56 x 51 cm
MDF Italia, Milano, Italy

p. 15

La Grande Table | 2001 | 2002

Table
Anodized aluminum
73 x 200 x 80 cm | 73 x 220 x 80 cm
73 x 240 x 80 cm | 73 x 280 x 90 cm
73 x 320 x 90 cm | 73 x 360 x 90 cm
73 x 400 x 90 cm | 73 x 440 x 90 cm
MDF Italia, Milano, Italy

p. 12-13, 19

La Table Basse | 2001 | 2002

Coffee table
Anodized aluminum
27 x 94 x 90 cm
27 x 90 x 125 cm
MDF Italia, Milano, Italy

p. 7, 14

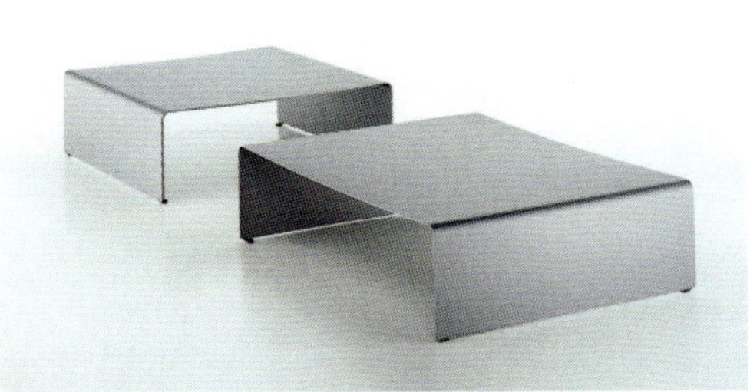

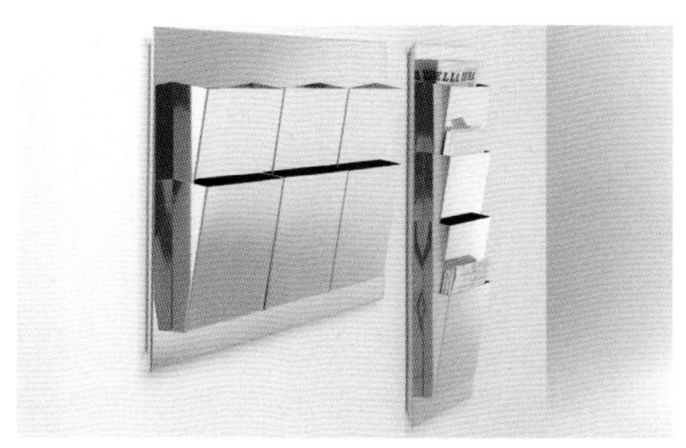

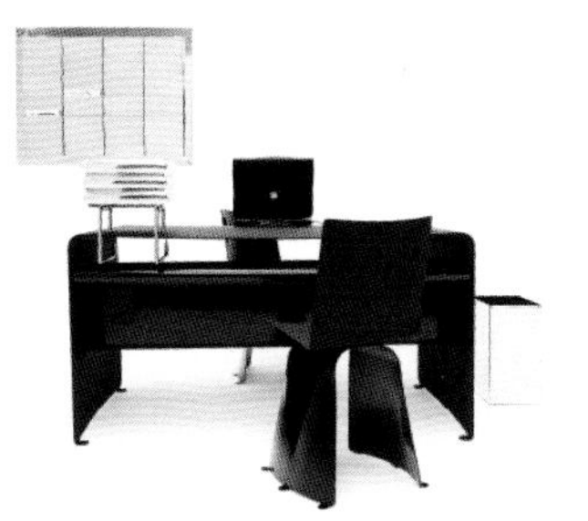

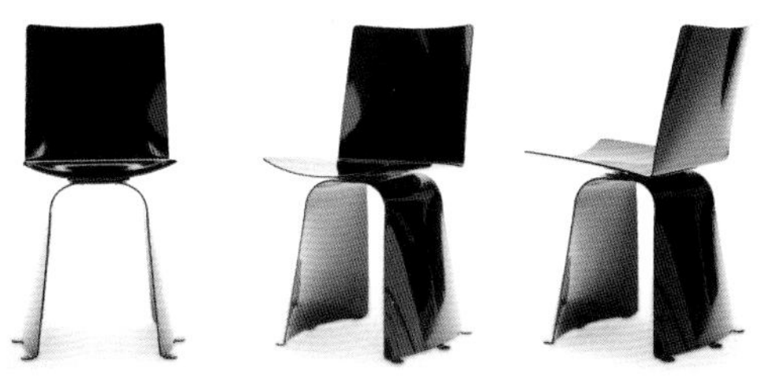

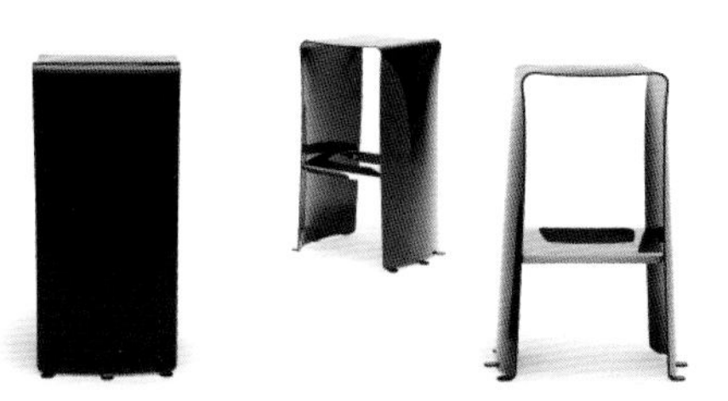

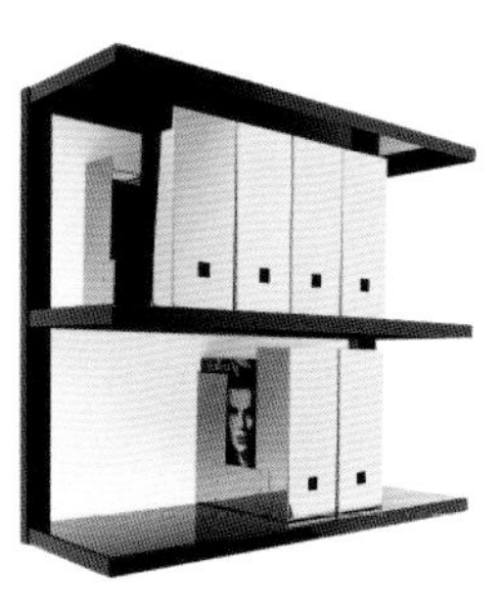

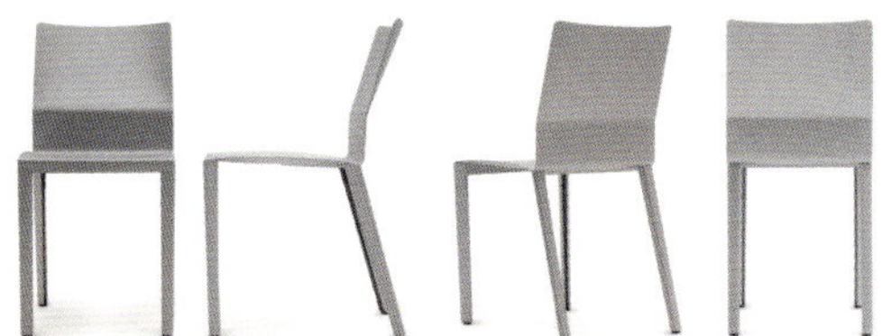

4U		2001

Chair
Anodized aluminum
78 x 38 x 48 cm
Prototype

p. 89

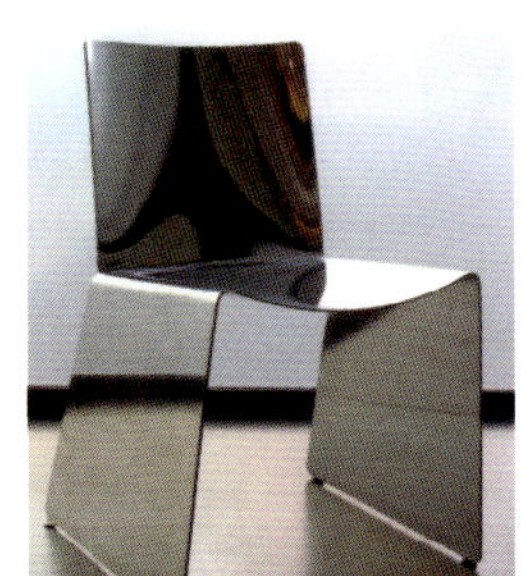

Le Miroir	2000	2001

Revolving mirror with coat-hanger
Anodized aluminum
200 x 70 x 5 cm
MDF Italia, Milano, Italy

p. 79

Le Banc	2000	2001

Bench
Anodized or lacquered aluminum
44 x 120 x 40 cm
44 x 170 x 40 cm
44 x 220 x 40 cm
MDF Italia, Milano, Italy

p. 7, 8-9, 10-11, 12-13, 126-127

T-chair		1999

Chair
Mirror-polished aluminum
78 x 52 x 52 cm
Elixir, Brussels, Belgium

p. 48, 49, 50, 51

Meteorite		1999

Black steel
Ø 70 cm
Pièce unique

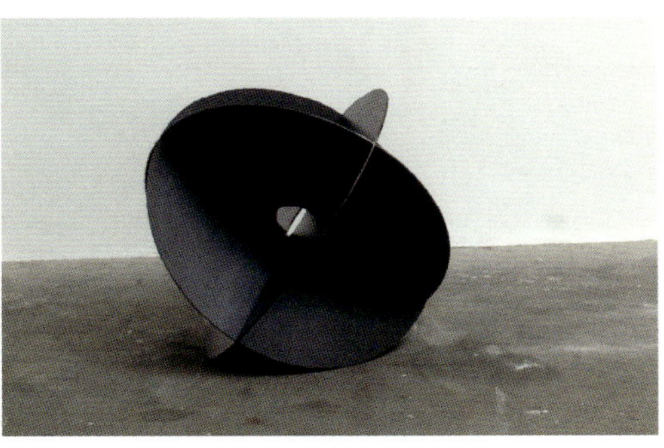

p. 110-111

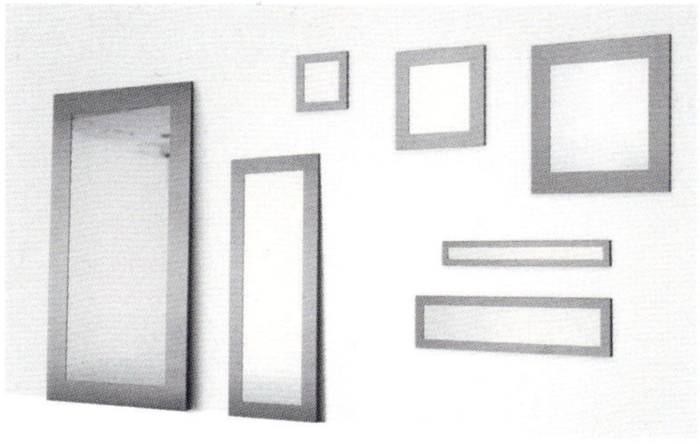

4P		1999

Chair
Anodized aluminum
80 x 40 x 40 cm
Prototype

Giga & Gigogne	1998	1999

Mirror
Brushed stainless steel, glass
173,5 x 23,5 x 2,8 cm | 52 x 52 x 2,8 cm
201,5 x 51,5 x 2,8 cm | 90 x 90 x 2,8 cm
239,5 x 89,5 x 3 cm | 288,5 x 138,5 x 3 cm
288,5 x 138,5 x 3 cm
A-Ronne / Elixir, Brussels, Belgium

p. 76, 77, 128

L&L		1997

Book ends (2 pieces)
Black steel
15 x 9 x 12 cm
Limited edition

p. 137

Tablet		1997

Coffee table / Fractionated magazine rack
Black steel, solid oak
21 x 35 x 45 cm

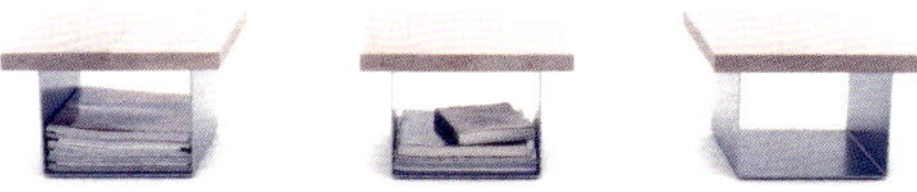

4 pattes		1996

Table
Anodized aluminum
74 x 90 x 90 cm
74 x 190 x 90 cm
74 x 290 x 90 cm
Elixir, Brussels, Belgium

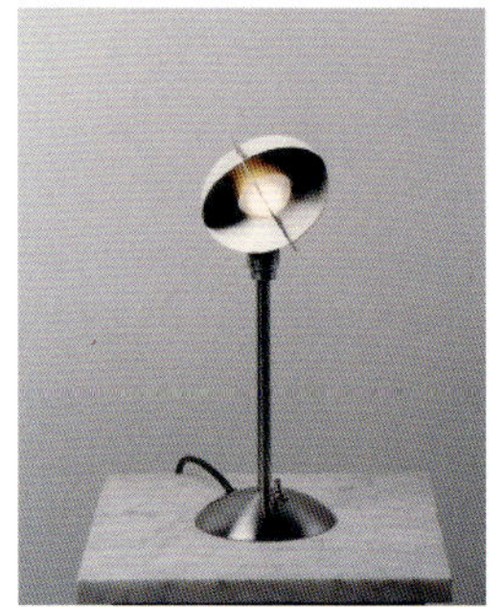

Meteor | 1996

Lamp
Brushed stainless steel
15 x Ø 12,2 cm
28 x Ø 12,2 cm
65 x Ø 12,2 cm
Elixir, Brussels, Belgium

p. 83

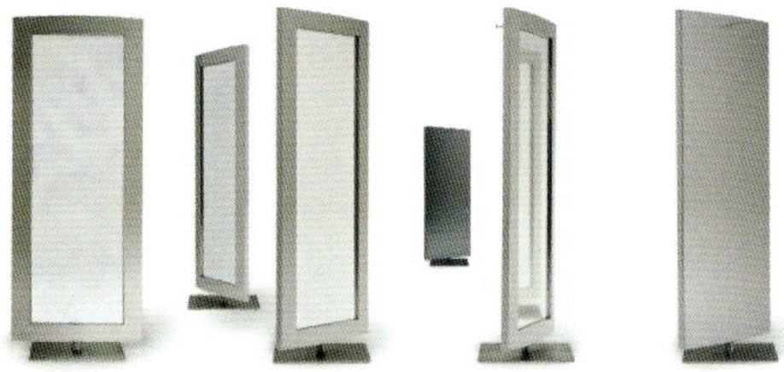

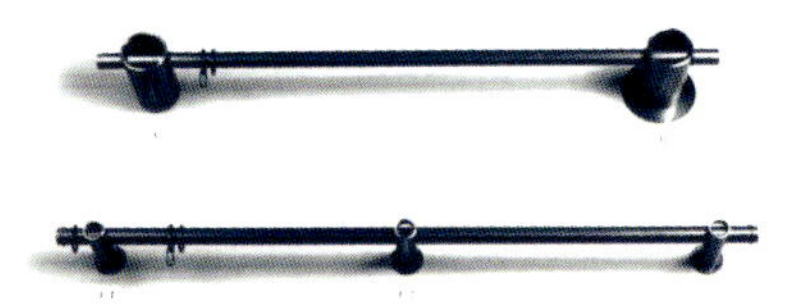

Vice Versa | 1995

Revolving mirror with coat-hanger
Brushed stainless steel, glass
200 x 70 x 50 cm
Elixir, Brussels, Belgium

p. 74-75

Barfix | 1995

Curtain rail
Brushed stainless steel or black steel
Various dimensions
Elixir, Brussels, Belgium

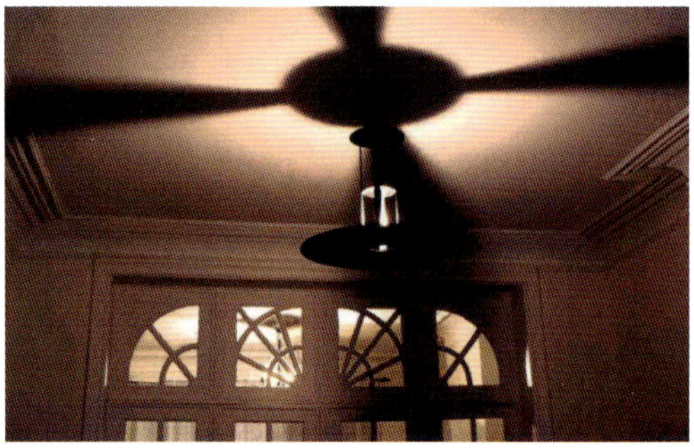

Eclipse | 1995

Lamp
Brushed stainless steel or black steel
10 x Ø 28 cm
50 x Ø 70 cm
Elixir, Brussels, Belgium

p. 43

Virgo | 1993

Shelves
Black steel
80 x 50 x 16 cm
130 x 81 x 20 cm
200 x 123 x 31 cm
Elixir, Brussels, Belgium

p. 154-155

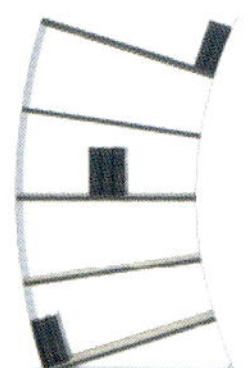
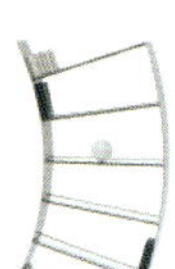
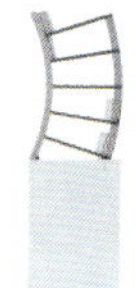

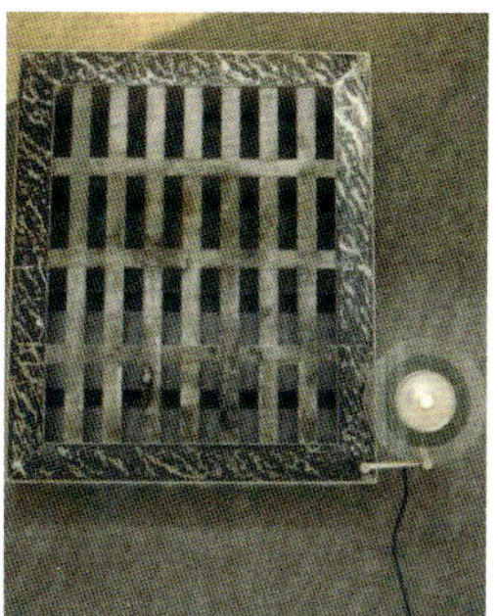

Magno | 1993

Bed
Black steel
85 x 185 x 225 cm
Prototype

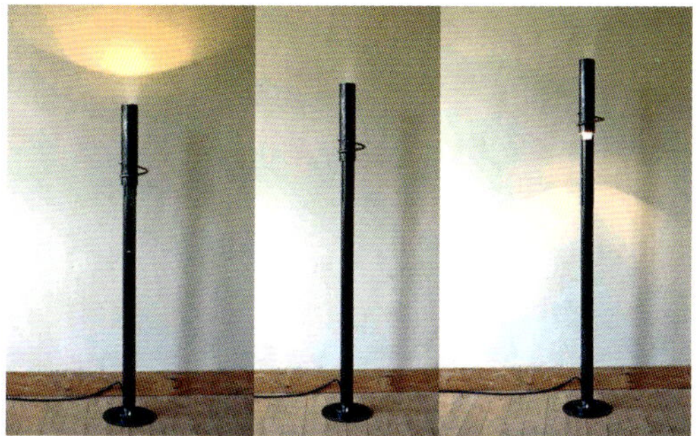

Mecavaria | 1993

Lamp
Black steel
136 > 170 x Ø 24
Limited edition of 9 pieces

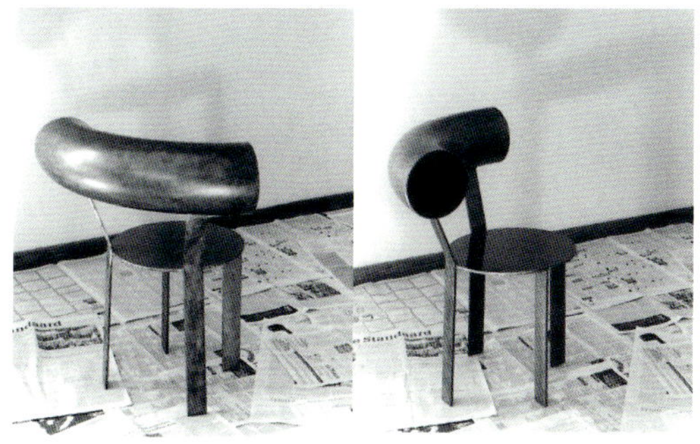

Circulaire | 1993

Chair
Steel
74 x 66 x 48 cm

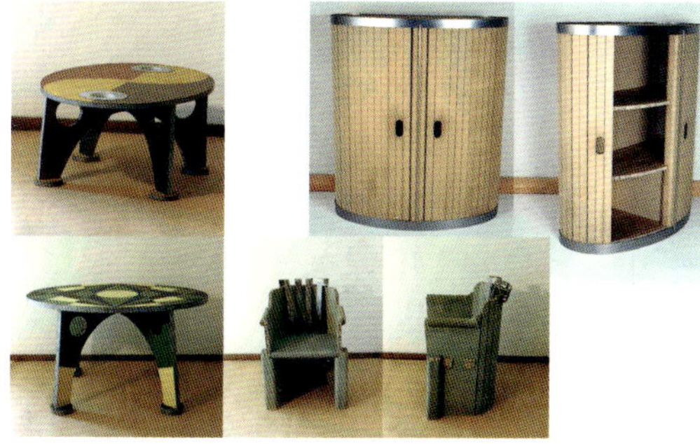

Cartomania collection | 1991 | 1994

Collection of cardboard furniture
Soaked and tinted recycled cardboard with geometrical graphics
Zioop, cupboard, 126 x 104 x 52 cm
Apero, coffee table, 40 x 96 x 64 cm
Table, 78 x 132 x 96 cm
Siège, armchair, 80 x 57 x 46 cm

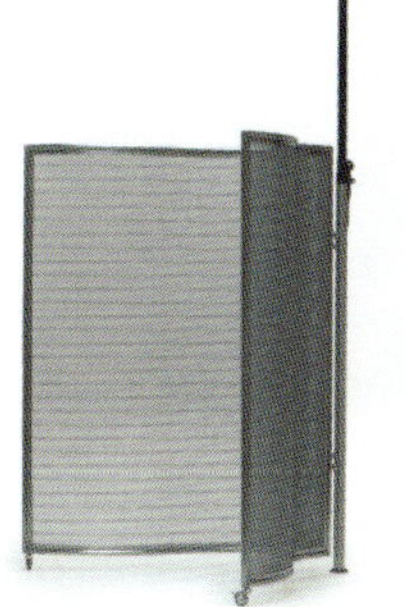

Paradoxe Mobile | 1990

Room-divider
Brushed stainless steel, galvanized steel
192 x 146 x Ø 286 cm
Limited edition

p. 95

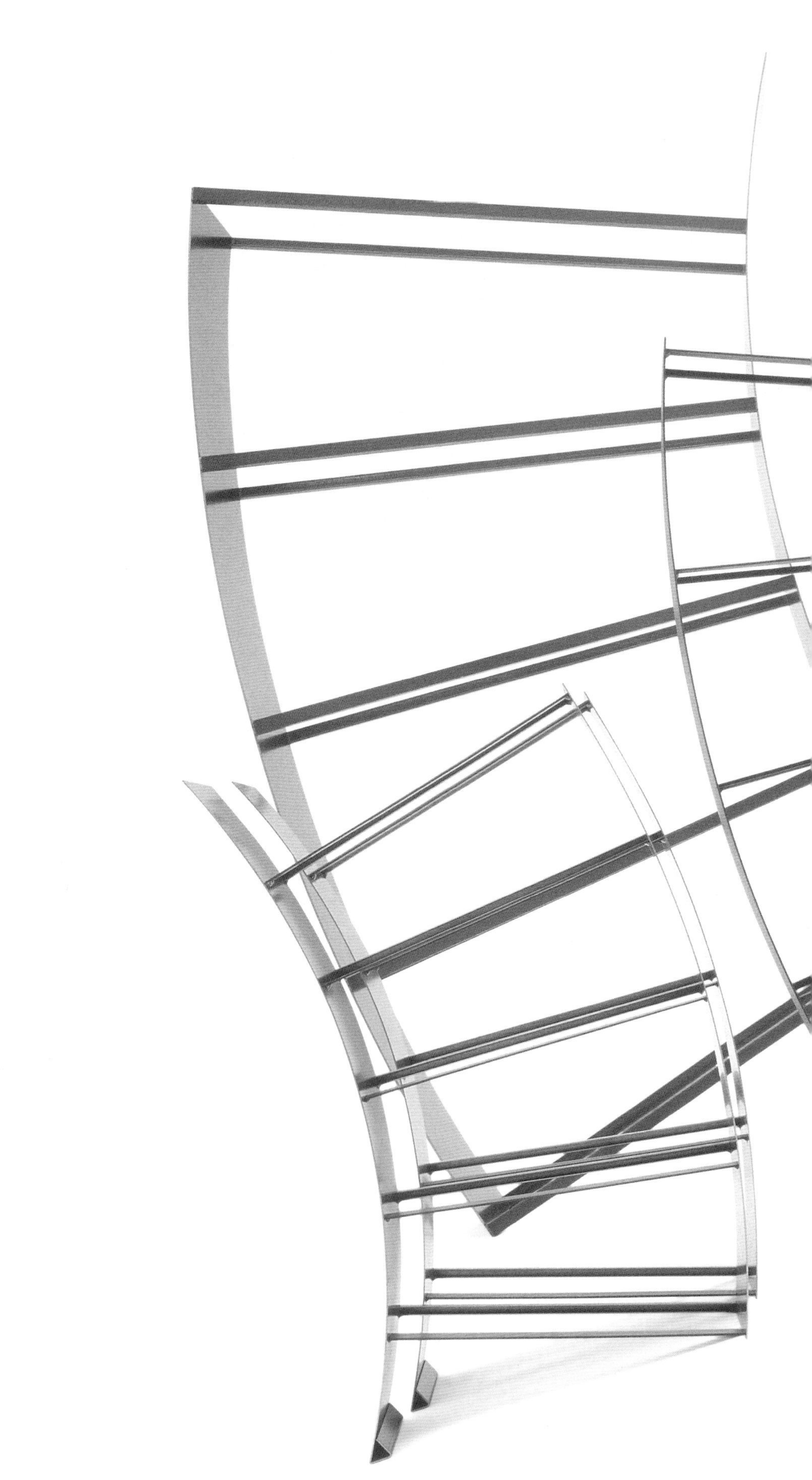

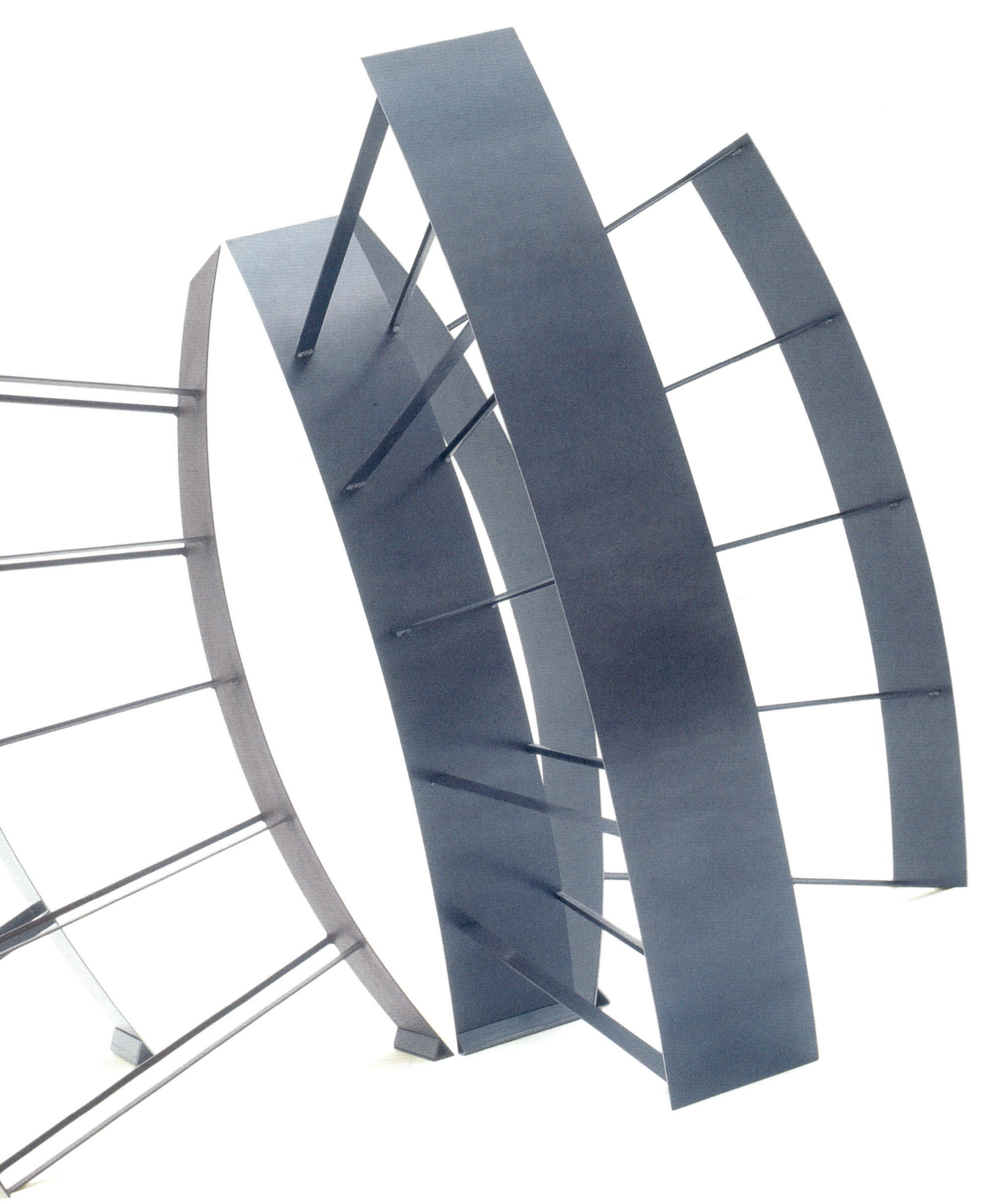

Commercial contacts

De Padova srl
Tel: +39 2 777 201
info@depadova.it
www.depadova.it

Driade spa
Tel: +39 523 822 360
export@driade.com
www.driade.com

Extremis nv
Tel: +32 58 299 725
info@extremis.be
www.extremis.be

Gruppo FEG
Tel: +39 362 8 691
info@gruppofeg.it
www.gruppofeg.it

MDF Italia srl
Tel: +39 281 804 100
infomdf@mdfitalia.it
www.mdfitalia.it

Modular Lighting Instruments
Tel: +32 51 26 56 56
www.supermodular.com
welcome@supermodular.com

Aquamass sa
Tel: +32 2 332 07 32
www.aquamass.com
info@aquamass.com

Bodart & Gonnay sa
Tel: +32 4 239 93 93
info@b-g.be
www.b-g.be

Zeritalia
Tel: +39 721 878 511
sales@zeritalia.it
www.zeritalia.it

Zoltan
Tel: +39 2 7600 9712
info@zoltan.it
www.zoltan.it

Xavier Lust
Elixir sprl
Bd du souverain, 151
1160 Brussels - Belgium
Tel: +32 2 673 60 51
Fax: +32 2 673 44 67
info@xavierlust.com
www.xavierlust.com

Photo credits

Erik Anthierens
p. 40-41

Anthierens & Hajji
p. 44-45, 74-75, 76, 84-85, 88, 89

Serge Anton
p. 8-9, 25, 30, 31, 43, 55, 64, 77, 81, 83, 97, 98-99, 100, 101, 102, 103, 105, 107

Adelaïde Astori
p. 39, 44

Renaud Callebaut
p. 128

Alain Charlot
p. 7, 10-11, 135, 154-155, back cover

Benoit Deneufbourg
p. 87, 125

Mathieu Ferrier
p. 52-53, 54

Maurizio Marcato
p. 19

Paolo Riolzi
p. 95

Lode Saïdane
Endpaper, 32-33, 34-35, 36-37, 62, 63, 67, 70-71, 108-109, 110-111, 118-119, 121, 124, 126-127

Studio Controluce
Front cover, p. 2-3, 4-5

Miro Zagnoli
p. 28, 29.

Acknowledgments

Thanks to the authors and the photographers published in this book.

Thanks to Nathalie, Kathy, Coralie, Claudine, Michel, Axel, Jean-Marc, Erwan and Martin who have contributed to the realization of this book.

Thanks to all the producers who have trusted me.

Special thanks to Roger Georis and Mimoun Amrous, faithful partners in production since 2000.

Book concept

Xavier Lust

Texts

Elisa Astori

Olga Bozhko

Lise Coirier

Luca De Padova

Bruno Fattorini

Cristina Morozzi

Nick Vinson

Dirk Wynants

Translation

Sally-Ann Hopwood (French to English)

Stevie Johnson (Italian to English)

Ilze Raath (Dutch to English)

Final editing

Femke De Lameillieure

Eva Joos

Co-ordination

Lise Coirier

Karel Puype

Layout & print

Graphic Group Van Damme, Oostkamp (BE)

Published by

Stichting Kunstboek bvba

Legeweg 165

B-8020 Oostkamp

T +32 50 46 19 10

F +32 50 46 19 18

www.stichtingkunstboek.com

This book was published with the support of

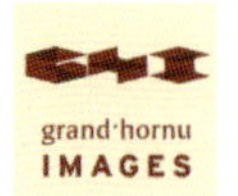
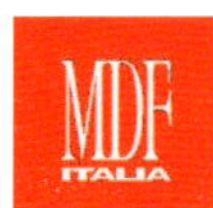
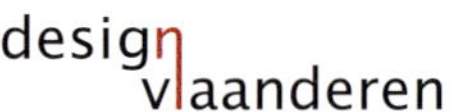

NUR 656

D/2007/6407/15

ISBN 978-90-5856-211-1

Front cover, p. 2: **S-table** MDF Italia 2007

Back cover: **Le Banc** 170 cm, MDF Italia 2001

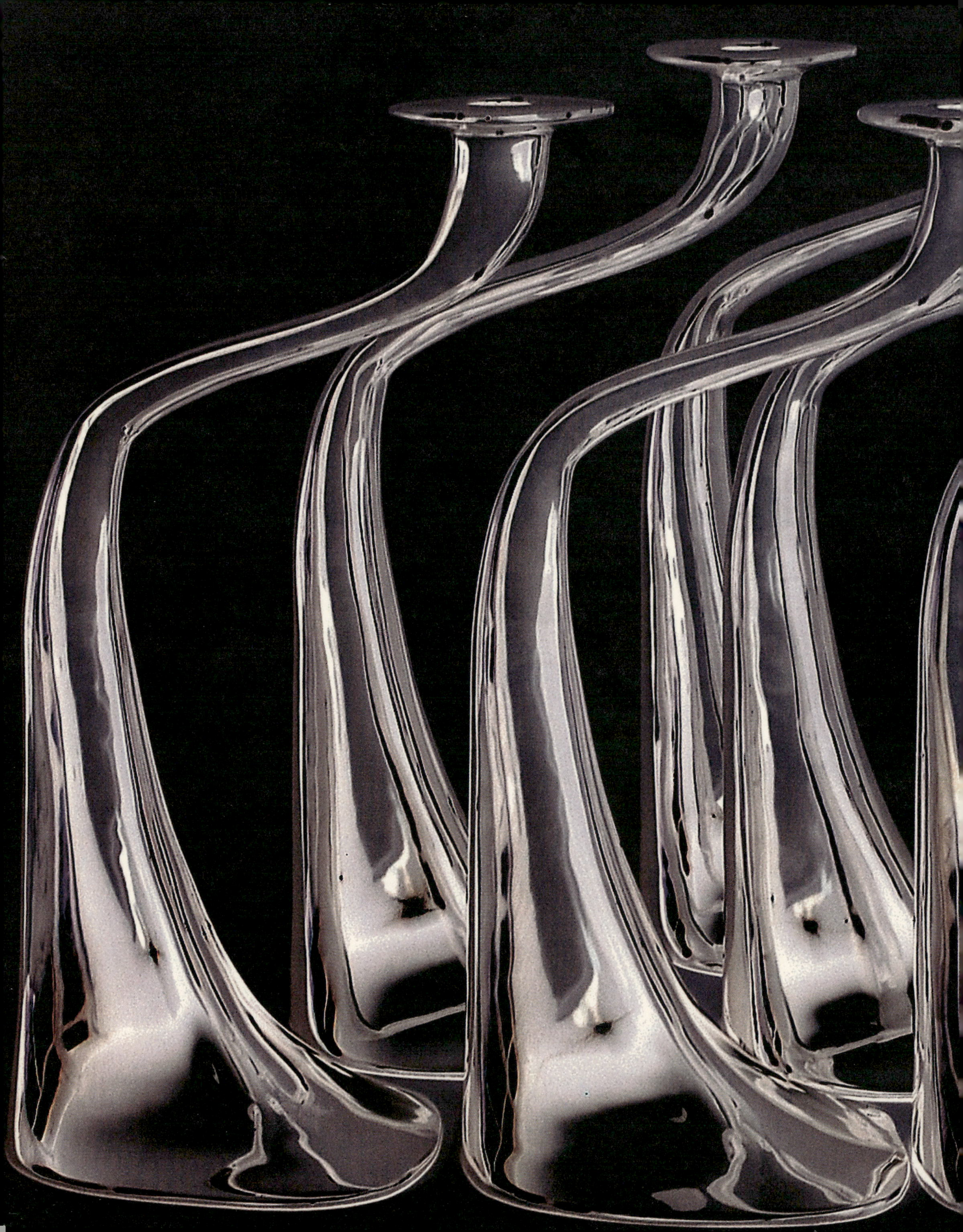